A Musical Legacy of 100 Years

A History of the
National Federation of Music Clubs

Lucile Parrish Ward

edited by
Past National Presidents
Mrs. C. Arthur Bullock and Mrs. Glenn L. Brown

Library of Congress Catalog Card Number 95-67308

ISBN 1-884416-11-X

Published by

A-Press

P.O. Box 8796
Greenville, South Carolina 29604

Printed in the United States of America

In the beginning God created the world—
that was Sculpture;
He painted it with the blue of the sky, the
green of the grass, and the myriad tints
of sunset's glow—that was Art;
He peopled it with human beings, and
that was the Eternal Drama;
Then he breathed through every living
thing something of God, inspiring us
and all who listened understood—that
was Music.

—Agnes Bishop Jardine
NFMC President, 1933-1937

4

TABLE OF CONTENTS

ACKNOWLEDGMENTS 11

FOREWORD 13

DEDICATION 15

PROLOGUE 17

PART ONE   *In the beginning...*
THE SETTING 22
THE TORCH IS LIGHTED 26
INTERLUDE 38
HIGH MUSICAL CONFUSION 44

PART TWO   *The Seed Takes Root*
THE RETURN TO CHICAGO 56
STORMY WITHOUT – STORMY WITHIN 63
RING UP THE CURTAIN 70

PART THREE   *Footnotes to History*
FROM THE GRASSROOTS 76
MILESTONES 78
AN ERA OF BEAUTY AND GRANDEUR
    Stan Hywet Hall 87
BACKSTAGE 90

PART FOUR   *Extending Our Horizons*
GREAT INVESTMENTS
    Junior Division 96
SPOTLIGHT ON YOUTH
    Student Division 108

PART FIVE   *Gems of a Musical Heritage*
FEDERATION INSIGNIA 114
FEDERATION COLLECT 116
OFFICIAL INVOCATION 120
FEDERATION BANNER 122
FEDERATION HYMN 123
OFFICIAL BENEDICTION 125
OFFICIAL MAGAZINES 126

6

PART SIX   *The Cornerstone: American Music*
THE JEWEL OF THE FEDERATION TIARA
   American Music 132
KEEPERS OF THE PAST
   Folk Music 139
MUSICAL ACCENTS
   Oratorio and Opera 143
I HEAR AMERICA SINGING
   Choral Music 152
FROM SONG TO SYMPHONY
   Crusade for Strings 155
THEY FOLLOW THE BATON
   Bands and Orchestras 158
MUSIC HATH CHARMS
   Music in Prisons 161
ONE COMMON TIE – MUSIC
   American Society of Composers, Authors and Publishers 163

PART SEVEN   *A Musical Showcase*
AN ONGOING LEGACY
   Scholarships and Awards 166
ON WINGS OF SONG
   Young Artists 174
DUO PIANO COMPETITION 181
WE SALUTE... 182
THERE'S MUSIC IN THE HILLS
   Summer Scholarships 186
MUSIC IN MOTION
   The Dance 223

PART EIGHT   *Service that is Song*
MUSIC OF THE FAITHS
   Sacred Music 226
MUSIC – AN INSTRUMENT OF MORALE
   War Service 230
NO EAST, NO WEST – NO NORTH, NO SOUTH
   Music in Hospitals 237
"... LIKE WATER ON PARCHED TONGUES"
   International Music Relations 240
"BRIGHTEN THE CORNER..."
   Music in Industry 245
PEOPLES TO PEOPLES
   Philanthropic Music 247
TOGETHER IN MUSIC
   Audio-Visual 249

ONE GREAT FELLOWSHIP OF LOVE
Music for the Blind 256

PART NINE   *Business A'Tempo*
BUSINESS A'TEMPO
Finance 260
ROSE FAY THOMAS FELLOWS 266
PAST PRESIDENT'S ASSEMBLY 267

PART TEN   *Overview*
A DREAM FULFILLED
Little Red House 272
SERANAK
Berkshire Music Center 276
A SYMBOL OF A CENTURY
National Federation of Music Clubs Headquarters 278

PART ELEVEN   *A Rich Heritage Shared*
"...FOOD FOR THE SOUL"
National Music Week 310
ONE VOICE ON MUSIC
National Music Council 314
HANDS ACROSS THE SEAS
United Nations 317
A FITTING TRIBUTE
Citations 322
"– IN THE GLOW OF FREEDOM'S LIGHT"
Bicentennial Parade of American Music 324
MAKING MUSIC – MAKING HISTORY
Congressional Charter 327
DIAMOND JUBILEE 332
MUSICAL POTPOURRI 334

AFTERGLOW 339

EPILOGUE 345

APPENDICES 347

BIBLIOGRAPHY 357

INDEX 359

8

THE PUBLISHERS ACKNOWLEDGMENT

Who shall tell the next generation?

Who shall record the glories of this first century?

The uniquely able and highly qualified historian is Lucile Parrish Ward, daughter of the late William Albrittan Parrish, M.D. and Emma Hughes Parrish; and wife of Jack Christopher Ward, attorney, now retired from thirty years service with the Federal Bureau of Investigation, living on beautiful Paris Mountain in "Woodwind," high above Greenville, South Carolina.

In a friendship which has spanned almost a half century, this publisher has known and marvelled at the tireless and effective work of this lovely and gifted lady in behalf of the National Federation of Music Clubs. She has promulgated its great goals faithfully and devotedly.

A B.A. degree in Piano, English and History from [now] the University of Montevallo equipped her for a lifetime of service; and in 1981, she became only the third graduate in the 100 year history of her alma mater ever to be named recipient of the coveted "President's Award for Outstanding Achievement in the Performing Arts."

On the local level, she has served as President of the Music Club of Greenville, the Guild of the Greenville Symphony, Eta Province, Delta Omicron International Music Fraternity, Zeta Omega Chapter, Delta Omicron, and has served on the Board of the Greenville Symphony Association and on the County Foundation Music and Arts Committee. Her local music club honored her by establishing the annual college student "Lucile Parrish Ward Scholarship."

On the state level, Mrs. Ward held numerous offices in the South Carolina Federation of Music Clubs, succeeding to the presidency, 1959-1963. During this time, through her leadership the legislation created the Office of Public School Music Supervisor, passed by the South Carolina General Assembly. She was named by then Governor Robert McNair to serve on South Carolina's First Arts Commission, an office to which she brought distinction. The South Carolina Federation of Music Clubs honored her with the endowment of the $10,000 "Lucile Parrish Ward Chair in Opera" at the Brevard Music Center.

On the national level, Mrs. Ward served as twenty-fourth President, and a Life Member of NFMC. The national headquarters building, purchased, restored and furnished in Indianapolis during her presidency is the repository for many of the historical records which have gone into this book. During her presidency, also, a twenty-five year project was brought to fruition when President Reagan signed into law the legislation granting a Congressional Charter for the National Federation of Music Clubs.

To attempt to name all the honors which have come to Mrs. Ward would take many pages. It is sufficient to say that her appreciation for history and her undying love for the Federation have combined to produce this important and interesting record of the first one hundred years of the National Federation of Music Clubs. May it inspire and challenge all members and friends to continue your high musical standards and may facts and events spring to life as real, living people whose visions have become your achievements.

... and the music goes on.

ACKNOWLEDGMENTS

"Oh, for a pen dipped in magic" to thank adequately everyone who contributed in helping to make this one hundred year history of the National Federation of Music Clubs possible. It could not have been completed without the help of many wonderful friends – first and foremost Shirley and the late Ligon Duncan of A Press: Lig who "lit the fire" to "get this book going" – and when the end was so near warned me not to "let up"; Shirley's intelligence, sensitivity, and style have made working with her a real joy.

To Lori J. King and Mel Duncan of A Press, I express my deepest appreciation for their patience and cooperation – to Lori, who so patiently shaped and reshaped the manuscript, and to Mel, for his helpfulness and thoughtful encouragement throughout.

I owe a debt of gratitude to Mary Prudie Brown, promotional editor, for her never failing encouragement and enthusiasm. With her constant research assistance and advice, she has been a mainstay throughout the writing and researching for these pages.

To contributing editors, Gretchen Van Roy and Cornelia Freeman I express sincere appreciation: to Gretchen for traveling with me and assisting me with research at the Library of Congress and the Federation's archives in Indianapolis, Indiana – and most especially for her researching and writing the biographies of the twenty-seven presidents of the National Federation; and to Cornelia for her exhaustive research of the histories of the Federation's scholarships and awards.

A special thank you goes to Mr. Arnold Broido, president, Theodore Presser Publishing Company for his graciousness in permitting this writer to quote from *Etude Magazine* articles dating back to 1897, all pertaining to the history of the National Federation of Music Clubs.

To Martha Ann Blackwell I owe a debt of gratitude for the endless hours she spent helping with the typing and proofing of this history.

I am grateful to Gwen Johnson of the Greenville County Public Library, who has been most helpful in countless ways in securing copies of clippings and old newspapers from Chicago and New York, all containing articles pertinent to the organization of the National Federation of Music Clubs in 1898; to the office staff in the Indianapolis headquarters – Pat Midgley, Paul Hall, and Ruth Shannon for their help while researching the archives at the headquarters; to Stillman Kelly for his many contributions, including the *Memoirs* of his grandmother, Mrs. Edgar Stillman Kelley, past president of the National Federation; to Loretta and Bill Ezell for the old copies of *Music Clubs Magazine* which have proven an invaluable contribution in this research; to Eva Johnston for her contribution on the Past Presidents' Assembly of the Federation; to Julie Dawn Andelin, Executive Secretary, Musicians Club of Women, Chicago, for historical material pertaining to the club and Rose Fay Thomas; to Dicksie and Kenneth Cribb, Jr., for the trip to Pennsylvania which proved invaluable in obtaining material for this history.

For the original and artistic design of the promotional flyer, I gratefully acknowledge and thank Suzanna Brown. The countless hours given to this, truly was a gift of love, for which I am deeply grateful.

To one very special person, the late Desta Gibby, president, the Music Club of Burley, Idaho, whom I knew for only one fleeting moment, I express my deep and sincere gratitude, for it was her contribution of historical material in 1979, that inspired this writer to write a much needed history of the National Federation of Music Clubs.

A very special thank you goes to James Hudson for his kindness in accepting the responsibility of the sales of this 100 year history.

To Mary and Billy Harris, Carol Giesick, Myrt Mehan, Dr. Charles Treas, Virginia Darracott, Mae Ruth Abbott, Marjorie Gloyd, Dr. Alpha Corinne Mayfield, Jeanne C. Giese, Mildred E. Kern, Miss Ann Ready, Gerri Greenspan of National Music Camp, and the many others who have contributed historical material of value and interest, all of which has enriched these pages, I express my profound gratitude. Only with the help of dear friends as these, has it been possible to write a history of this magnitude covering a span in time of one century.

To my family I express deep appreciation: to my brother, Emmett Parrish and Mignonette Williams Parrish for their untiring research for pictures and material relating to the founding of the Federation; to Pamela Parrish Prideaux, my niece, for traveling with me as driver, photographer, and companion – to the gravesites of Rose Fay and Theodore Thomas in Mt. Auburn Cemetery in Cambridge, Massachusetts; and to my nephews Britt Parrish and Gary Prideaux for their special help and thoughtfulness along the way.

To one other person I owe an everlasting debt of gratitude – my husband, Jack, for his patience, understanding, and wise counseling – one who took part every step of the way, to the benefit of the book and the author.

And – lastly, my thanks to Ginger, Tiger, Little Bits and James – my best friends and constant companions through these twelve years of working on these pages.

—Lucile Parrish Ward

FOREWORD

The Federation has proven over all the years of its existence that it is a great National Institution for the promotion of the "musical experience" in the lives of young and old.

Its tireless members have given so unstintingly in the realm of the Junior members to insure the musical heritage of these wonderful United States of ours.

The opportunities that the National Federation of Music Clubs gives for its major and minor awards year after year are a permanent insurance policy against the outmoded story of the unknown, starving, unrecognized young genius in the garret. Of course music in all of the shapes through which it is promoted is a much better peace plan than the atomic bomb.

Today we live in a world of many mixed emotions – fear, struggle, beauty, power, gigantic enterprises, financial uncertainty, high taxes as well as the age old problem of death, heartbreak and the very unglamorous everyday problems.

Through it all music is certainly a "balm of Gilead" that soothes the soul. When music is entered into with this purpose and with this very realistic attitude, the real rewards are intangible, and far removed from the world.

—Van Cliburn

Note: *Van Cliburn is the only person to have received from the National Federation of Music Clubs, the Federation's Citation (1959) and a Presidential Citation (1983). Van's mother, Rildia Bee O'Bryan Cliburn, an ardent supporter of the National Federation, was a Life Member, and in 1989 received a Presidential Citation at the Fort Worth Biennial Convention.*

DEDICATION

Dedicated on the one-hundredth anniversary of the National Convention of the Women's Amateur Musical Clubs, to the memory of Rose Fay Thomas who ignited the torch, lighting the way for the birth of the National Federation of Music Clubs – a torch which has been passed from president to president, and from generation to generation.

At the first convention of the Women's Amateur Musical Clubs at the World's Columbian Exposition in Chicago in 1893, which had been planned and called by Rose Fay Thomas, the president of the Ladies Matinee Musicale of La Fayette, Indiana, Lulu Emerson Davis, expressed the feeling of everyone present:

> *"I cannot close without one word to the chairman of this convention, to whom we owe so much. Whatever of inspiration may be received here – and it should be so much – we owe to her, not only because of its conception, but because of the long months of untiring labor which she has devoted to it. We desire to return to her our most sincere thanks; and if in 100 years our glorious country should again celebrate its discovery, and someone with her wisdom and forethought should again call upon the women's musical clubs to show the world what they are doing toward the elevation of their fellows, many will say:*
>
> > *'We read in the history of our club that its inspiration was received at the World's Fair held in Chicago in 1893, at a convention called together by one Mrs. Theodore Thomas, to whose memory we would today do grateful homage,'*
>
> *and we the listening choirs, shall chant, Amen and Amen."*

PROLOGUE

It was Cicero who said, "History is the witness that testifies to the passing of time, it illuminates reality, vitalizes memory, provides guidance in daily life, and brings us tidings of antiquity."

Today – one hundred years since thirty-five clubs met at the World's Columbian Exposition in Chicago in 1893, at the call of Mrs. Theodore Thomas, we stand at the portal, offering our most precious possession, the history that we have received from our ancestors – the history that our own generation has increased with its deeds and accomplishments, and a history into which each coming year will add more remarkable chapters.

It is with great humility that this writer has undertaken to write a one-hundred year history. It has not been easy, for there are those who served before us who have given so much of themselves. There was talent for organization, and there has been foresighted vision in charting the course the organization would take.

Records have been checked: old letters, yellowed with age; minutes of long ago meetings, newspaper clippings, magazine articles – all have been studied carefully in an effort to capture a real life picture. Yet, we wonder if a writer is ever completely satisfied with the research that has been done and sometimes cannot help wondering if there is still something "out there" that could have been found. In the words of Francis Parkman, "Faithfulness to the truth of history involves more than research... the narrator must seek to imbue himself with the life and spirit of the time. He must study the events in their bearings... in the character, habits, and manners of those who took part in them. He must himself be, as if he were, a sharer or a spectator of the action he describes." This writer has tried to do just that. Throughout these one hundred years there was never a page that was void of interest, never one we felt we could leave unread without a loss, never one that we wished to skip.

We have made every effort to attain a minimum of errors in the history in the succeeding pages. It is too much to expect that all inconsistencies have been removed, for in so vast an array of facts some errors are bound to be. This is due to many causes – chief of which is disagreement among the very highest authorities and the lack of uniformity of many of the statistical records. Many times the information in the records has been conflicting, in which instances we have tried to piece together the available facts and draw our own conclusions as best we could.

In the hopes of making the history interesting and more than a book of mere facts and statistics, this writer has tried to include events of interest which both directly and indirectly have contributed to the history of the Federation.

This writer learned early that the first law for the history is that one should never dare utter an untruth. The second is that he shall suppress nothing that is true. That, we also have tried to follow from the material available to us.

We regret that the Federation's historical material dating from about 1900 until about 1910 is not available in either the Federation's historical files or in the Library of Congress's Federation Archives – a fact which was lamented by Harold Spivacke and Benjamin Hill, Music Archivists, Library of Congress.

We of the National Federation of Music Clubs are a proud people – proud of our founders, proud of our history. It is our responsibility to preserve the history we cherish, for the links that bind us to our ancestors are fragile. True is the old adage, "He who cares not for the past, will love little his future."

Writing this history has not been easy – recounting the days of our one hundred years, and trying to condense them into a few thousand words on a few printed pages. We sometimes felt as did the Editor of the March issue, 1922, of the *Etude Magazine*, James Francis Cooke. The issue was dedicated to the National Federation of Music Clubs and in paying tribute to those who had helped in the preparation of the issue he spoke of how overwhelmed he was with the enormity of the work, and the impossibility of including in only one issue more than a fraction of the recognition the Federation should have been given. He said, "We have done our best with this issue and hope that at some time in the future we may have an opportunity to do better. The whole subject of clubdom is so big that we continually felt in the position of Rastus who was asked to tell how he hunted the bear. 'T'warn't no use for me to cotch dat bar, for before I know it, it dun gone cotched me.'"

Chicago – 1898

PART ONE

In the beginning...

The beginning is the most important part of the past.—Plato

THE SETTING

1

In these diamond anniversary years since the first convention to assemble music clubs from throughout the United States, a need is felt to communicate with Clio, goddess of history, by calling on Mnemosyne, goddess of memory, and mother of all the muses for a glance backward – 100 years – to the birthplace and beginning of our beloved National Federation of Music Clubs.

The year was 1893 – the place: Chicago. Only twenty-two years had passed since Mother O'Leary's cow had kicked over the lighted lantern in a little frame barn on DeKoven Street, causing the greatest calamity in Chicago's short history. The city, however, had recovered rapidly. The business district rebuilt largely within a year, and within three years there were few scars remaining from the disastrous fire of 1871, which had damaged and destroyed property amounting to almost $200,000,000.

Chicagoans were a proud people – taking pride in their fast recovery, and they wished to show the world – the United States and those foreign countries who had contributed almost $5,000,000 toward rebuilding their city just what had been accomplished.

Now in 1893 the occasion presented itself – a gala celebration of the four-hundredth anniversary of Christopher Columbus's discovery of the New World and America. Chicago, a city ambitious to win world approval and applause, met every requisite of a World's Fair – unlimited territory, Jackson Park with two miles of shoreline washed by the waters of Lake Michigan, a population of over one million, in the center of a vast railroad system "stretching gigantic arms" to the confines of the continent, and with a "disregard for money where pride was concerned... truly the ideal place in which the Exposition should have birth."

Chosen to convert this 666 acres of swampland into a fairyland for all the world to see was landscape architect, Frederick L. Olmstead. Selected to engineer the construction of approximately one hundred-fifty buildings was architect Daniel H. Burnham.

To head the Bureau of Music for the Exposition, Theodore Thomas, "eminent conductor, educator, and stimulator of musical tastes in America", was chosen as Musical Director, an endeavor in which he had the full cooperation of his innovative wife, Rose Fay Thomas. Assisting him were the distinguished Choral Conductor of London, William L. Tomlins, and George W. Wilson, Secretary.

As musical director, Mr. Thomas designed a vast plan of events to demonstrate American musical achievements to the world. The schedule brought symphony orchestras from New York and Boston, and bands and soloists from afar. There were thousands of singers trained by Tomlins with their inspired interpretation of the oratorio choruses; a children's chorus of 1500; and a daily organ recital by Clarence Eddy – all of which helped set the scene for the birthplace of the National Federation of Music Clubs.

2

Shepps' World's Fair Photographed recorded the setting at the opening:

"Jackson Park... the setting of the magnificent architectural jewels, shining in splendor before the astonished sight of mankind... Today it is the Venice of the Western World, and when myriads of electric lights shed their opalescent rays upon the sapphire waters of the lagoons, it presents a fairy scene of inexpressible splendor... Thirteen glorious structures of the beautiful tint of time-kissed ivory are mirrored in the deep waters and represent the contribution of the most generous government in the world to the grandest Exposition this planet has ever witnessed."

There, on October 22, 1892, before 150,000 spectators, the World's Columbian Exposition was dedicated. When the mighty multitude joined in singing *America*, "tears glistened in thousands of eyes, and myriad hearts were full to bursting with the great strain of sustained enthusiasm."

On the opening day of the Exposition, May 1, 1893, a vast multitude assembled. President Grover Cleveland, attended by his Cabinet, appeared on the grandstand, and in a clear resonant voice, made a short address, pertinent of which was:

"Let us hold fast to the meaning that underlies this ceremony, and let us not lose the impressiveness of this moment. As by a touch the machinery that gives life to this vast Exhibition is now set in motion, so at the same instant, let our hopes and aspirations awaken forces which in all time to come shall influence the welfare, the dignity, and the freedom of mankind."

"Never since the Nomads were transformed into city builders, and capitols of empires became sights of international exhibitions, has there been such universal interest displayed in any project conceived by man. The greatest of exhibitions which has passed into history will compare but feebly with the grandeur of this stupendous undertaking. No spot in all the world could have been selected susceptible to so many advantages as is the site of the Columbian Exposition on the shores of beautiful Lake Michigan."

> *From ice-bound lands where weary stars*
> *Look down on nights a half year long:*
> *From lands by old historic wars*
> *Made rich in legend and in song:*
> *From every country, every clime*
> *Will come the peoples of the earth*
> *To join the pageantry sublime*
> *In honor of Thy birth,*
> *COLUMBIA!*

3

The Peristyle connecting the Music Hall and the Casino was "one of the crowning beauties of the Exposition." Located in the vicinity of the main lagoon entrance, and about one thousand feet from the shores of Lake Michigan, it spanned the lagoon entrance by a grand arch, forming a "sight never to be forgotten... so harmonious the setting, that it seems as though the Exposition was made for it, and not that it was made for the Exposition... The blue of sky and water sets off its marble whiteness... The clouds that drift above it cast soft shadows on its noble front"... making even more pronounced its beautiful outline and proportions. The Peristyle had forty eight pillars representing the states and territories, and atop the triumphal arch spanning the lagoon, stood above the promenade the crowning glory – the Columbus Quadriga. In the chariot "Columbus stands looking out to the far distance. His face bears traces of anxiety curbed by indomitable will... a certain dreaminess in the face, well befitting the man who had pondered so long in solitude the great project he afterwards developed." The four horses, flanking Columbus, "are led by beautiful female grooms who look as spirited as the animals they restrain... an air of nobility about the whole group."

To the north, and joined to the Triumphal Arch by the Peristyle, was the Music Hall, from which one looked to the East to "the flashing waters of Lake Michigan spread out like a diamond sea." It was in this magnificent setting that representatives from thirty-five clubs came together, June 21-24, 1893, at the invitation of Rose Fay Thomas, to participate in the "World's Fair Congress of Musicians". "From this idea and its triumphant success, the National Federation of Music Clubs came into being." It was Mrs. Thomas's "idea, and the enthusiasm of those participating in the 1893 Festival that were responsible for establishing a permanent national musical organization."

The Music Hall, measuring one hundred forty by two hundred feet, had an auditorium which seated two thousand people. There also, was a rehearsal hall seating six hundred. The Music Hall was designed to be used by the musical talent and connoisseurs of the art.*

* On the evening of January 8, 1894, just a little more than six months after the Women's Amateur Musical Clubs met in the Music Hall, a blaze broke out in the Casino, at the south end of the Peristyle, spread along the Peristyle and gutted the Music Hall at the opposite end of the colonnade.

CHAPTER TWO

THE TORCH IS LIGHTED

1

The wise old Confucius said, "If one would know aught of anything – one must seek the roots." For these "roots" of the National Federation of Music Clubs one must look back across the years to 1893 – to that magnificent setting in Jackson Park in Chicago. There, silhouetted against a backdrop of history, a seed was planted – a seed that would take "root", sprout, and grow into the world's largest and most powerful philanthropic musical organization, working for music in America and the world.

Mrs. Theodore Thomas, a fine musician, and at the time president of the Amateur Musical Club of Chicago, had become very much interested in the possibility of a national organization rendering a music service to America. She envisioned an "all together" plan which might be realized through the cooperation of groups of musical women.

Mrs. Thomas, working closely with her husband, Theodore Thomas, realized this World's Columbian Exposition was the opportune time to call together the music clubs of the country. Forty-two clubs responded to her invitation, and thirty-five – scattered from Maine to California – sent delegates. Until Mrs. Thomas assembled this national convention of the women's amateur musical clubs of the country, on June 21-24, 1893, no general attention had been accorded to the woman's musical club movement.

On the first day of the session Mrs. Thomas welcomed the clubs' representatives:

"Ladies: It is with feelings of the greatest pride and pleasure that I stand here today to welcome you in the name of the Exposition, the Bureau of Music, and our own committee, to the World's Fair and to Chicago. The branch of woman's work, which many of you have come such great distances to exhibit this week, is one which has an important bearing on the intellectual culture of America... Of course it would be too much to say that these amateur clubs are the absolute foundation of the music of America, but it is not too much to say that in them, musical art has its most powerful ally, and its most beneficent friend. The fundamental value of amateur music does not lie in the facility with which the fingers can manipulate the keys or the voice can trill a song, but in the deeper and broader culture it gives to the mind and heart – the power to think and feel with the mighty creator and their noble interpreters, and to follow them into those supernal realms of art whose portals only fully open to those who hold the mystic keys...."

The ladies were in session for four days. Each club was allotted one "short hour", during which the president, or her representative, read a paper descriptive of her club – its objects and achievements – after which her associates gave a musical program. This first convention of music clubs was a great success as an exhibition of the standard of musical culture among the best class of American women, and the character and quality of the educational work the clubs were accomplishing in the field of music.

The honor of being the pioneer club in attendance was claimed by the Rossini Club of Portland, Maine – a claim which never was disputed. It was on December 14, 1869 that the Rossini Club held its "first meeting of a business character at a private house." The president, Mrs. Emily K. Rand closed her report to the assemblage by saying:

> "The inevitable changes come year by year. Loved faces are missed, and others take the places; still the interesting work goes on, as planned by thoughtful women of twenty-four years ago, that the music born in one may be given an impetus toward as great development as possible. In the words of our own Longfellow:

> > *But the great Master said, "I see*
> > *No best in kind, but in degree;*
> > *I gave a various gift to each,*
> > *To charm, to strengthen and to teach.*
> > *These are the three great chords of might,*
> > *And he whose ear is tuned aright*
> > *Will hear no discord in the three,*
> > *But the most perfect harmony."*

Mrs. Edwin F. Uhl, president of the St. Cecilia Society of Grand Rapids, Michigan, and who was to become the first president of the National Federation of Music Clubs, said in closing: "This convention of amateur clubs, so thoroughly planned and successfully carried out, must prove an inspiration to us all, and this thought has been uppermost in my mind and must find expression, that the great wonder is that such a gathering had not been planned before, and to express the hope that the Women's Amateur Musical Clubs may, in the near future, hold many more successful conventions."

The eight sessions of the assembly were held in the auditorium of the Music Hall. As each member gave her report, there was a feeling of gratitude to Mrs. Thomas for having assembled the clubs in this first convention, as was evidenced by some of the concluding remarks of the thirty-four clubs reporting:

"May she (Mrs. Thomas) receive such deserved recognition and appreciation of her efforts that she will be persuaded to make this congress the initial of a series of annual congresses which may serve to advance the work so ably begun."
—Beethoven Club, Moline, Illinois

"We cannot refrain from expressing our admiration for the genius and executive ability of Mrs. Thomas... in carrying to so brilliant conclusion this first national convention of women's amateur musical clubs...."
—Amateur Musical Club, Ottawa, Illinois

"I cannot help wishing that the outcome of this most happy occasion may be a grand federation of clubs with national officers and annual conventions in the years to come."
—Ladies Musical Society, Independence, Iowa

At the close of the four day convention, Mrs. Uhl proposed to Mr. and Mrs. Thomas appreciative resolutions of thanks. The convention rose to its feet to vote unanimous approval of the resolutions providing for future gatherings of a like nature and possibly a permanent national organization.

Mr. and Mrs. Thomas expressed their gratification at the cordial sympathy with which all the clubs had worked with them in promoting the success of the convention, and their "sincere hope that a permanent organization may grow out of this vigorous and healthy beginning, which shall be the best friend of the musical art throughout America."

Mrs. Thomas presented her well thought out ideas. There were formulated plans of national scope for working cooperatively. Soon it was realized that this plan was much too big to be completed in this one session, and according to Dr. Frances Elliott Clark, who was in attendance, "A motion was made and carried for forming a national organization. Committees were appointed and arrangements made for a meeting in 1894." However, due to the great panic of 1893 and other unforeseen obstacles, it was not until 1897 in New York City that the organizational work was completed, and not until 1898 "that the Federation came back home to Illinois for its charter." Approximately fifteen years later Mrs. Thomas in a letter to Mrs. Kelsey, national president, described the meeting of 1893:

"My dear Mrs. Kelsey – I learn with pleasure that the next biennial of the National Federation of Musical Clubs is to be held in your home city, as it recalls to my mind very pleasant recollection of my first meeting with the St. Cecilia Society of Grand Rapids at the national convention of Women's Amateur Musical clubs held at the World's Columbian Exposition in June 1893. This convention was the source from which the present federation sprang, and its stated objects were:

"'First – To show the actual standard of musical culture among the best class of women in all parts of the country, and the character and quality of the educational work in music being done by Women's Amateur Musical clubs.

"'Second – To stimulate the formation of such clubs in places where they do not now exist....

"'Third – To give a national recognition to this department of women's education work which has hitherto been overlooked.'

"It was an extraordinary meeting, thirty-five clubs from Maine to California being represented, and in nearly every case the president of the club was in attendance, as well as a large delegation of members. The convention lasted four days, with sessions from 9 o'clock in the morning to 3 o'clock in the afternoon....

"Of the clubs participating in that initial movement I believe that a majority are now active members of the National Federation, which is doing such a noble work to raise the musical education among American women.

"Feeling that this organization has before it a still greater career of success and usefulness, I am,

Sincerely yours,
Rose Fay Thomas"

To Rose Fay Thomas all the honor is due for originating the idea of this Woman's Musical Congress. The musical women throughout the United States hailed this convention as an event which marked an era in music in this country, and one which gave a strong impulse to the organization of clubs, Mrs. Thomas, already famous in the musical world gained an added renown for this valuable work.

According to the February 1898 issue of *Etude Magazine*, it was Mrs. Theodore Thomas who "set in motion at the Columbian Exposition, a great wave of musical activity in the line of women's musical clubs." Mr. Thomas felt so strongly the great influence these clubs would have on the musical culture of the country, that he gave great help to the movement which his wife, Rose Fay Thomas, carried out.

2

Attending the first convention of Women's Amateur Musical Clubs at the World's Columbian Exposition in 1893 was one who later was to become an outstanding leader and educator, Frances Elliott Clark.

Mrs. Marie Morrisey Keith, sixteenth president of the National Federation of Music Clubs, wrote for the *Music Educators' Journal* a Memorial to Dr. Clark:

> "Frances Elliott Clark passed through many places and many lands during her long distinguished lifetime. And she made abiding impressions not only on the people she met but on the events of her time as well.
>
> "She first passed through Chicago as a child of 11 (on October 8, 1871) just two hours before Mother O'Leary's cow upset the lantern. Twenty years later she passed through again on her way to become music supervisor in Monmouth, Illinois....
>
> "In Monmouth Mrs. Clark joined the Tuesday Musicale Club. She was chosen... as a club delegate to a meeting called by Mrs. Theodore Thomas, wife of the first conductor of the Chicago Symphony. This was the time of the Columbian Exposition in Chicago, and Mrs. Thomas brought together members from all over America to formulate plans on a national scale to open new opportunities for gifted young artists....
>
> "Mrs. Clark later reported that Mrs. Thomas presided well and that her plans for the cooperative work were well received. The meeting was noteworthy for still another important reason: The idea of a National Federation of Music Clubs was born...."

"Mrs. Clark became the first life member of the Federation. She gave her time and talents generously to promote its goals, and retained active interest all of the remaining years of her life."

It was at the convention in Salt Lake City in 1951 that Mrs. Clark was awarded a coveted citation from the National Federation of Music Clubs. The Federation is proud that this magnetic woman was a charter member, and very influential after its inception in Chicago in 1893.

3

It is Mrs. Frank P. Whitmore, Chicago District President of the Illinois Federation of Music Clubs, 1938, to whom we owe a debt of gratitude, for it was she who secured the memoirs of the life of Rose Fay Thomas.

These she obtained through a chain of events beginning with the publishing of a letter which she wrote to the *Chicago Tribune*. The letter was published in December 1938, and it referred to Mrs. Theodore Thomas as the "founder of the National Federation of Music Clubs, and as a power in fostering American music."

Mrs. Thomas's cousin, the Reverend John Henry Hopkins of Hyde Park, read the letter in the *Tribune* and wrote to thank her. Soon afterwards Mrs. Whitmore, realizing the Federation had no authoritative sketch of its founder's career, wrote asking the Reverend Mr. Hopkins to supply one. He in turn referred her to Mrs. Thomas's only surviving brother and sister, Charles Norman Fay of Cambridge, Massachusetts, and Mrs. Charles Wilmerding of New York, "both either in their late eighties or nineties."

Mr. Fay responded most graciously and in December, 1939, he wrote for the Federation the *Memoirs of Rose Fay Thomas*. Mr. Fay had been the leading spirit in organizing the association which brought Theodore Thomas's orchestra permanently to Chicago. He was one of the orchestra's most generous backers, from which he lost heavily in helping it through those first difficult years.

Rose Emily Fay was born on September 4, 1852, in St. Albans, New York, "next to the youngest of nine children of Dr. Charles Fay, an Episcopal Clergyman and his wife, Emily Hopkins Fay." Like her younger sister, Lily, she was named for one of the two favorite flowers of her mother, who was a famous gardener.

Rose's mother, Charlotte Emily Hopkins Fay was the eldest child of the Rt. Reverend John Henry Hopkins – the first Bishop of Vermont, and the Presiding Bishop of the Episcopal Church in the United States. Rose's father – the Reverend Dr. Charles Fay, an Episcopal clergyman – was a son of Judge S. P. P. Fay, of "Fay House", Cambridge. That house is now the Executive Building of Radcliffe College; and the song *Fair Harvard* was written there in 1836 by Dr. Gilman, who was visiting his brother-in-law, Judge Fay, for the two hundredth anniversary of that college.

Her brother said that Rose Fay never took any interest in genealogy and probably never knew of her illustrious forbears. "But," he continued, "it is a pleasure, and not difficult, to associate Rose Thomas with high birth and breeding; she certainly was a born lady."

Rose's mother, an invalid when she was born, died of consumption when Rose was only four. It was then her father "loaned" her to his childless friends, Judge and Mrs. Selden of Rochester, New York – only to be taken from them four years later on the death of Mrs. Selden. In 1867, she went to live with her married and childless sister, Mrs. Charles S. Peirce of Cambridge, Massachusetts, until 1873. (The Peirce's were of the Harvard University aristocracy.) Rose was at once welcomed by the children of that group and found there her life-long and dearest friend, Edith Longfellow. The governess of the Longfellow girls was allowed to teach Rose also, and she enjoyed "that charming privilege".

"From sixteen to seventeen, Rose went to Miss Harris's notable girls school in Hancock Street in Cambridge. 'College' was then practically unknown for girls, and Rose never went to finishing school anywhere."

In 1879 Rose and her sisters – Mrs. Peirce, Amy and Lily Fay – joined their brother in Chicago. There she met Theodore Thomas, who with his orchestra gave Summer Night Concerts in the old Exposition Building until 1891, when the organization came to Chicago for good. In the meantime he had become an intimate family friend, and the year after the death of his first wife, Rose and he were married in 1890. Rose took her place as head of his house at New York and Fairhaven, Massachusetts. Mrs. Peirce and Amy Fay went to New York to live, leaving the house on Bellevue Place in Chicago to Rose and Mr. Thomas. It was here that Theodore Thomas died in 1905. Their summers were spent first in "Fairhaven," and a year later at "Felsengarten" – a lovely retreat which Thomas had built, overlooking the "Gale River" Valley, on the mountain of Bethlehem, New Hampshire, which the town then named "Mount Theodore Thomas". After the death of her husband she lived only one year on Bellevue Place, after which she took an apartment in Chicago and later on Fifth Avenue in New York – always going to

"Felsengarten" for the summers. In 1915, she rented a small house belonging to her friend, Edith Longfellow Dana in Willard Court, Cambridge, where with summers at "Felsengarten" she lived until she passed away on April 19, 1929.

"Such a brief outline of her journey through life and her abiding place on the way. As to her personality, to use the words of Miss Elizabeth Bond, daughter of the famous Harvard astronomer, 'Rose Fay was a dear!'"

Miss Bond voiced the tender feeling for Rose's radiant and gracious charm, that heartened her throughout her busy life. In the words of her brother, Charles Norman Fay, "Her family, the Sheldens, her distinguished friends of all sorts, in Cambridge, New York and Chicago, loved her for sweetness and vivacity; and respected her for sincerity and ability."

Rose was a perfect dancer, and pretty enough to have had many boyfriends, but the family never suspected her of special interest in them until at the age of thirty-eight she fell in love with a widower with five almost grown children – Theodore Thomas. Rose married him in 1890.

At her father's death in 1883, Rose had inherited a small income, but for the ten years before, she had in part supported herself by doing interior decorating, which at that time had not become a profession. She was interested mainly in flower and foliage painting – directly on the walls.

In the words of Mr. Fay, Rose "probably had an active part in forming... as well as the founding, from the World's Fair of 1893,... the National Federation of Music Clubs... Her energies broke loose again around 1916 over the World War... she went to work at the 'Army & Navy' – later called 'Soldiers and Sailors' Club... a free club house for enlisted men from ships and camps near Boston when off duty in town... She was hostess, companion and friend to those lonesome young fellows, for several hours, several days a week – from then until she died."

Rose Thomas was a woman of extraordinary talent and versatility. If a thought came to her active mind, her busy hand put it into prompt and effortless execution, without preliminary blunder.

"But ladies of the Music Clubs will probably recall best her lovable personality. One of the happiest and certainly most flattering events of her life, was the tribute paid to her as the Original Founder, by the National Federation of Music Clubs, at Los Angeles Rose Bowl in 1922. The youthful zest, on that occasion was equally in evidence in 1924, when she accepted an invitation from the French Commandant, or Governor General Azan – the writer has not his exact title – of Morocco, to visit him at his headquarters, at Tlemcen, North Africa... She gaily took the Mediterranean cruise – was escorted by a guard of honor from Oran on the seacoast, through the wild Riff Country – and had one of the 'times of her life', among Arabs and Moors! "Late in 1928 she went to visit a niece in New York; came down with grippe... was brought back to her bed in Cambridge by a special car where she lingered until April 19th, and passed away in unconsciousness... so closed a lovely and useful life."

4

It might be interesting to know something of the husband of Rose Fay Thomas – Theodore Thomas, who supported his wife in all of her musical endeavors. It was because of his help and encouragement, that the meeting of the Women's Amateur Musical Clubs in Chicago in 1893 was the tremendous success it proved to be.

Theodore Thomas was born in Esens, Germany on October 11, 1835. His father was a musician and the young Theodore studied violin from early childhood – making his first public appearance as a violinist at the age of five. In 1845 he came to America with his family. In 1850 he toured the South alone on horseback as a boy violinist, and one year later, at the age of fifteen, he played first violin in the orchestra that accompanied Jenny Lind. His first visit to Chicago as a violinist was in 1854.

In 1862 Thomas began organizing his first concert orchestra, and to him is due largely the popularization of the works of Richard Wagner, Saint-Saens, Richard Strauss, Brahms and Tchaikovsky. It was in 1869 that he came to Chicago for the third time – this time to conduct his own orchestra. They gave Summer Night concerts to two to four thousand people for six weeks each summer in the old Exposition Building on the lake front.

It was during this time that Rose Fay joined her brother, Charles Norman Fay, in Chicago in 1879, and met Theodore Thomas who had become an intimate family friend. According to Mr. Fay, "it was with serious hesitation on both sides that they were married, for he had five nearly full grown children at home... Rose won their respect and affection as she did that of everyone else."

It was Rose's brother, who encouraged Mr. Thomas to bring his orchestra to Chicago, and in his words they "were brought bodily" in 1891. He said those first years were "troublesome" years – so many vicissitudes: the money-pinch of the panic of 1893 caught those who had guaranteed financial support, making them slow to pay, and some never paid at all. It became evident that the association would run out of cash, making it impossible for Mr. Fay (then acting executive) to carry on an increasing deficit. In the words of Theodore Thomas, "It looked as though the Chicago Symphony Orchestra must go out like a smoked cigar, leaving a fragrant but evanescent memory."

During the years 1893-1904 the orchestra managed to hold together, and according to Mr. Fay, "its work grew better and better... and its audiences more devoted and larger; its deficit, smaller and smaller." Mr. Thomas lived to see his dream to have an Orchestra Hall come true. Arthur Orr, hearing of Thomas's wish, became enthusiastic, "Make it a Hall, and I'll start the subscription with $25,000." Other civic leaders in Chicago followed, and the "campaign that enlisted some 60,000 Chicagoans even down to a group of scrub-women in skyscrapers, built Orchestra Hall."

"Thomas conducted a Dedicatory Concert on the opening of the Hall on December 16, 1904; (on the program of which strangely enough was Richard Strauss's Tone Poem, 'Death and Transfiguration') and although ill he lasted through the regular concerts of the next week. But, winter rehearsals, in a hall yet damp with fresh plaster... gave him a heavy cold, developing pneumonia, and ten days later," on January 4, 1905, the light of Theodore Thomas's life went out. His passing was mourned by millions everywhere.

The orchestra which was founded in 1891 – at the time of his death, was considered by notables throughout the world as the world's greatest orchestra. And – today it continues to be one of the foremost orchestras. In 1905, after Thomas's death, the orchestra was renamed the Theodore Thomas Orchestra, a name it kept until 1913, when it became the Chicago Symphony Orchestra.

Theodore Thomas was "the first and most important pioneer in the popularization of orchestral music in the United States. He traveled across the American continent stimulating interest in the symphonic literature and the formation of other orchestras in several cities as Boston and Philadelphia. He was appointed conductor of the Philharmonic Society of New York in 1876."

The eminent John Tasker Howard, said of him,

"Theodore Thomas is an epic figure in American history – one of our great heroes. Compare the state of musical culture at the time of the Civil War with conditions today and then thank

Theodore Thomas for the difference. It is through his efforts that this country is the home of the best in orchestral music, that almost all major cities have symphony orchestras of the first rank, and what is more important, that in each of these cities there is a public that will listen to the finest symphonic works."

At the meeting of the Federation's Board of Management in St. Louis, October, 1898, Theodore Thomas was made an Honorary Member of the National Federation of Music Clubs. It was at this same meeting that his wife, Rose Fay Thomas, was accorded the honor of being named Honorary President – the only person ever to hold this honor.

Mr. Thomas frequently praised the National Federation of Music Clubs to both its members and others in saying, "No other one influence in America had been so potent and far reaching for good results as had women's musical clubs," modestly forgetting his own tremendous influence and years as an inspired standard bearer. Would that music clubs of America could themselves build for him a fitting monument!

The Board of Directors of the National Federation of Music Clubs in session in Milwaukee, November 17-21, 1929, endorsed the name of Theodore Thomas for nomination and election to The Hall of Fame, of New York University. Mrs. Elmer James Ottaway, president of the Federation joined with other distinguished men and women in making the nomination.

A collection of press clippings noting his passing included more than two thousand editorials lauding his career, while unreserved tributes poured in from abroad.

The *New York Times*: "It is hard to estimate the debt that the country owes to Theodore Thomas." *New York and Chicago American*: "Theodore Thomas was undoubtedly the greatest interpreter of orchestral music who has lived upon this earth." Richard Strauss, famous composer, Berlin: "What he signified for musical development in America is well known. What we Germans owe him will be held in everlasting remembrance." Ignace J. Paderewski, famous pianist, and world-war Premier of Poland – engraved on a magnificent silver drinking-horn which was presented publicly on the concert stage in New York in 1896: "To Theodore Thomas, the great conductor, the true man, and the cherished friend, in admiration and love."

5

No history including Rose Fay and Theodore Thomas would be com-

plete without some mention of their beloved "Felsengarten."
Tucked away in the White Mountains of northern New Hampshire, near Bethlehem, "on the eastern slope of what is now called 'Mount Theodore Thomas', on a rough wooded tract of land containing outcropping crests of foundation rock, stands 'Felsengarten', the former home of Theodore Thomas... and his wife Rose Fay, the founder of the National Federation of Music Clubs. Felsengarten, meaning 'Rock Garden', was so named because of the rock formations and boulders, and the brilliant blossoms of many wild flowers, which flourished on the mountain-side."

Thomas's first summer home had been purchased in 1887 in the seaside village of Fairhaven, Massachusetts, before he and Rose Fay were married. The climate of Fairhaven was very damp, and was not the place for one with chronic catarrh. In 1890 he purchased thirteen acres of wooded land in the White Mountains with the intent of building a cottage on it. He hoped that the pure, clean air of the outdoors would rid him of the catarrh. In 1896 Rose went to Bethlehem and supervised the construction.

First, built as a shack, the Thomases loved it so much that in 1900 they decided to upgrade the "shack" and make it a home. Again Mrs. Thomas went to Bethlehem and supervised. To Mr. Thomas it was a "paradise on earth, and he never spent an unhappy moment there."

The house, three floors in height, gave one a feeling of peace, tranquility and spaciousness – the ideal retreat for a composer or conductor.

After Mr. Thomas died in 1905, Mrs. Thomas spent the first summer at Fairhaven, and thereafter, until she died in 1929, all of her summers were spent at "Felsengarten" overlooking the beautiful "Gale River" valley.

Charles Norman Fay wrote, "besides her memories, there survive two evidences of her unusual talent as a writer – one, a little book, *Our Mountain Garden*... whose freshness, charm and style have captured the reviewers, as well as the garden-lovers. It is the story of 'Felsengarten.'"

The second and larger work was *Memoirs of Theodore Thomas* – lavishly praised by reviewers as a perfect biography. Felsengarten was declared a historic landmark in 1973.

Note: *During the administration of Dr. Merle Montgomery, president, National Federation of Music Clubs, (1971-1975) the possibility of the National Federation of Music Clubs buying "Felsengarten", which was for sale, was presented to the Board of Directors. No action was taken. It was afterward learned that the house contained original furniture and artifacts – consisting of important letters, photos, historical relics, scores and mementos.*

INTERLUDE

1

The enthusiasm of the Chicago Convention in 1893 was great, and each expressed a wish that this meeting of the clubs would "grow" into a permanent organization of the National Federation of Women's Amateur Musical Clubs.

After this enthusiastic meeting, however there possibly was good reason that the seed planted there lay dormant for the next four years. Almost immediately after the Exposition opened in 1893, America was thrown into one of the worst depressions in its history. The stock market crashed; the branch bank in the Fair's Administration Building, where several foreign visitors had deposits, failed, all of which had to be made good; unemployment soared; and there were riots and strikes, for which President Cleveland had to call out federal troops. The winter of 1894 – immediately following the closing of the Fair on October 31, was one of great hardship for many people.

2

The story of the founding of the National Federation of Music Clubs is legend. It began as a dream in which hope for a more musical America was the driving force. It was the momentum created by the 1893 meeting that was to carry forward the idea of organizing the country's music clubs into a federation. This was the opportune time.

Mrs. Edwin F. Uhl, who had attended and reported at the World's Columbian Exposition, had at that time expressed the wish that a permanent organization might grow from that first convention. In 1894, Mrs. Uhl, then living in Washington, hired a secretary, and at her own expense corresponded with music clubs throughout the country. According to Mrs. Uhl's daughter, Lucy Uhl Wood, Mrs. Uhl's idea was not to create a Bureau for obtaining professional artists, but a Bureau of Reciprocity inside the Federation, whereby small clubs could obtain amateurs or semi-professional artists from the different clubs' members at reduced rates. She urged the value of federating and asked for suggestions. The replies "were few and led nowhere." Soon Mrs. Uhl was to leave for Germany where her husband had been appointed ambassador. Another attempt for organization was made in 1895 when the Tuesday Musicale of St. Louis, Missouri asked the secretary, Miss F. Marion Ralston, to contact clubs in adjoining states stressing "the great necessity of forming a circle of clubs for the purpose of engaging artists jointly." The original idea was "to find ten clubs to cooperate in some plan enabling an artist to deal with them directly, thus making lower rates possible." In the summer Miss Ralston mailed copies of a plan to "form such a circle, and it was to be called the Federation of Women's Musical Clubs."

The circular was mailed:

"DEAR MADAM PRESIDENT:
    The Tuesday Musicale of Saint Louis has decided to form a Federation of Musical Clubs, and I have been requested by our board of directors to invite you to join.
    Enclosed you will find the details of the plan.
    We feel that no step has ever been taken in this country which will be as generally beneficial to the growth of music as this Federation.
    You are therefore urged to carefully consider the matter, and we hope soon to add your name to our list of clubs.
    The plan of Federation will be open to revision and criticism by the board of Federation, as soon as that board will have been appointed.

                  Fraternally yours,
                  F. MARION RALSTON,
                  Chairman of Artists' Committee
                  St. Louis Tuesday Musicale Club"

Again the attempt was unsuccessful and the responses few. Miss Ralston felt the only thing accomplished in this effort was that it "brought the clubs into line for the step which followed in New York City in June 1897 at the meeting of the Music Teachers National Association."

Although these attempts were not successful, the idea of a National Federation – the seed which had been planted four years earlier – became vital to the thinking of a number of women who had faith and were determined to do something about it.

3

It was not until June 28, 1897 at a rather unique meeting of the Music Teachers National Association at the Grand Central Palace Hotel in New York City that the dream of four years earlier began to take shape. Mrs. Russell R. Dorr, of St. Paul, Minnesota wrote, "As the result of correspondence, Miss Marion Ralston, of St. Louis, Missouri, Mrs. Chandler Starr of Rockford, Illinois, – president of its leading musical club, and I decided to be present at the next meeting of the MTNA in New York and sound federation sentiment. We had all three been present at the World's Fair convention in Chicago in 1893 and had kept in touch... Many of the ablest of the club women who had been at the Chicago Music Festival, and who were also successful teachers were present and exchanged enthusiastic reminiscences. Mrs. Theodore Sutro, Chairman, Woman's Department, Music Teachers National Association, was not at the Chicago Festival, nor was she at that time, nor in 1897 well-known to many of us."

The bottom of the front page of the program of the Woman's Department, MTNA, carried: "Note, All members of musical clubs and friends interested in the work are cordially invited to attend a meeting in the Woman's Salon, Monday afternoon, 5 o'clock, for the purpose of forming a National Federation of Musical Clubs."

Of interest, on the program of the Monday afternoon session of the Woman's Department was a "Reading, Music Study Abroad" by Miss Amy Fay, sister of Mrs. Theodore Thomas. (Miss Fay had studied with Franz Liszt.) Mrs. Chandler Starr gave a paper, "Review of World's Fair Congress of Music Clubs."

Mrs. Charles Virgil, Chairman of Committee on Musical Clubs, "read a short paper on what is being accomplished and attempted" by musical clubs. "There is hardly a city in the country that has not one or more of them, and some of them are almost a quarter of a century old... There can be no doubt that these clubs have done much to elevate the musical taste of the country, and that in the smaller cities which are distant from the musical centers, they are a mighty power for good."

At 5:00 o'clock, on Monday afternoon, June 28, 1897, immediately following the close of the program, representatives of "approximately fifty clubs" met in the Woman's Salon of the Grand Central Palace Hotel in New York City. It was decided unanimously, to form a temporary committee, which should call the clubs together at some suitable place six months later for formal organization of a federation. Mrs. Dorr was selected to preside at this first meeting.

In addition to Miss Amy Fay, also in attendance was Mrs. Charles S. Peirce, another sister of Mrs. Thomas. It was through these two, according to Mrs. Dorr, "by wire we endeavored to persuade Mrs. Thomas to be our temporary president or chairman, but she declined." Temporary officers elected were:

Mrs. Theodore Sutro, New York City – Chairman
Mrs. Chandler Starr, Rockford, Illinois – Vice Chairman
Miss Marion Ralston, St. Louis, Missouri – Secretary and
    Treasurer
Mrs. James Pedersen, New York City – Assistant Recording
    Secretary
Mrs. Charles Virgil, Elmhurst, Long Island – Auditor
Mrs. Russell R. Dorr, St. Paul, Minnesota – Chairman, Artists
    Committee
Mrs. Dorr, also was named Chairman of the Nominating
    Committee.

Mr. Henry E. Krehbiel, dean of New York music critics and musical director of the *New York Tribune*, was in attendance, and was asked to address the meeting. When he pleaded that he had no right to do so, they removed his excuse, making him an Honorary Member of the group. It is noted that after the formal organization in Chicago, the Federation followed up on this and named Mr. Krehbiel the first Honorary Member of the National Federation of Musical Clubs at the October 1898 board meeting in St. Louis. It was at this same meeting that Theodore Thomas was named the second Honorary Member, and Edward MacDowell the third.

The christening name originally selected for the organization was "The National Federation of Women's Amateur Musical Clubs."

In attendance at that meeting on June 28, 1897 were:

Miss Amy Fay, Sister of Mrs. Theodore Thomas
Mrs. Charles S. Peirce, Sister of Mrs. Theodore Thomas
Mrs. Chandler Starr
Miss Frances Marion Ralston
Miss Rosalie B. Smith
Mrs. Theodore Sutro
Mrs. Charles Virgil
Mrs. James Pedersen
Dr. Waldo S. Pratt
Mrs. F. S. Wardwell

Mr. H. Krehbiel
Mrs. Russell R. Dorr
Mr. Lawerence Erb

Miss Ralston, forty-four years later – at the age of sixty-six in writing about this meeting in 1897, wrote that she and Mrs. Chandler Starr "now well along in her 80's were the only two of that first group of seven who met in New York who are still living."
She said also,

"My efforts over the number of years to have a history of the founding of the federation truly stated has been impersonal I can assure you. I have felt that it is very essential that the history of this great organization be correctly recorded. There was an unselfish spirit in this first little group. They were quite unanimous in working for the cause. Pioneer work... I am sure that no one who attended the recent biennial in Los Angeles felt so sure of the future of this organization, as I.
"To realize that it was the outgrowth of that little pioneer committee of 1897, left me rather breathless and very humble. It renewed my faith in the triumph of a good cause, no matter what obstacles may endeavor to stand in the way. My prayers are for the onward and upward progress of the National Federation of Music Clubs."

4

The *New York Tribune* of Tuesday, June 29, 1897 carried an account of the last day's proceedings of the Music Teachers National Association convention at the Grand Central Palace in New York City, written by Mr. Henry E. Krehbiel. This article followed, carrying pictures of Mrs. Russell R. Dorr and Mrs. Chandler Starr:

"Next, a meeting was held in the Woman's Salon for the consideration of the project of forming a National Federation of Musical Clubs. Mrs. Russell R. Dorr presided and about fifty clubs from all parts of the country were represented. It was voted that such a federation should be formed. Mrs. Theodore Sutro was made temporary chairman and Miss Ralston of St. Louis, secretary. A circular setting forth the objects of the proposed organization, asking for suggestions on the subject, and signed by all those who took part in yesterday's proceedings, will be sent to all the musical clubs of women in the country, and it is hoped that the first convention may be held next Spring. "Among those present at the meeting was Henry E. Krehbiel. The women insisted on his addressing them, and when he pleaded that he had no right to do so, they removed his excuse by making him an honorary member of their body."

"Words of Encouragement"
"Mr. Krehbiel said that for the last 30 years no influence for the furtherance of musical culture had been so powerful as that of the Women's Musical Clubs. "The IDEA of a federation of women's musical clubs had its origin in the convention under Mrs. Theodore Thomas at the World's Fair, Chicago in 1893, but until now there has been no opportune time for carrying it into execution. Mrs. Edwin F. Uhl is much interested in the matter, and with her colleagues, had almost completed arrangements for a decisive step, when the plan was frustrated by her husband's appointment as Ambassador to Germany. Mrs. Dorr and Mrs. Chandler Starr, who are both members of the Committee on Musical Clubs, have taken an active part in the movement from the beginning."

HIGH MUSICAL CONFUSION

1

The first executive session of the newly organized National Federation of Musical Clubs met on the day following the temporary organization – June 29, in New York. The second session of the executive committee followed three months later, September 1, 1897, in New York City, at the home of Mrs. James Pedersen. It was at this latter meeting that the decision was reached to accept the invitation of the Amateur Musical Club of Chicago to hold the convention for the election of permanent officers in Chicago, Illinois, January 25, 1898.

"A great moment in the life of the amateur musicians in America had arrived!... No crystal ball could reveal the future – only the leaders could ferret it out. Would they meet the challenge or be found wanting in courage?"

The Pianist and Organist, October 1897, carried an account of the September 1st Executive Committee meeting:

"The National Federation"
"By order of the president (chairman), Mrs. Sutro, a meeting of the Temporary Board of the National Federation of Women's Musical Clubs was called at the home of Mrs. James Pedersen, in New York, recently. Though the members of the board are drawn from various cities, six out of the fourteen were present and the circular to be sent to the clubs regarding the federation was discussed and formulated. The main object of the circular is to gain the opinion of clubs generally on the four following questions:
1. Does your club approve of a National Federation of Women's Musical Clubs?
2. Will your club send a delegate to the first annual meeting?
3. Which place do you prefer for the first meeting: New York, Chicago, St. Louis or Omaha?

4. What date do you prefer between October 15th and December 1st?

The secretaries of the Federation are anxious that circulars should reach every Woman's Musical Club in the country. All clubs not in receipt of the same by October 1st, will confer a great favor by sending name and address to the editor of this department."

2

Following the meeting of the Board at the home of Mrs. Pedersen in New York, the following circular was sent by Mrs. Sutro "to all Women's Musical Clubs in the U.S., 1897":

"At the recent Convention of the MTNA held in New York City from June 24th to June 28th, inclusive, an attempt was made for the first time in the history of the organization to show what women have done as individuals or as organized bodies for the cause of music. Unfortunately the effort was begun too late – scarcely a month before the convention – to make an adequate showing but so surprising were the results even in that short space of time that all of the many hundred women who were present felt proud of the exhibit. Especially gratifying to the many club women in attendance was the record of the work done by Women's Clubs during the last quarter of century.

"It chanced that representation from over fifty clubs were present at the convention and after several informal conferences among those most interested – it was decided to call a meeting on Monday afternoon, June 28, at 5 p.m. in the Woman's Salon – to consider and discuss the advisability of a National Federation of Women's Musical Clubs. Such a meeting was held and the attendance was so enthusiastic the expression of belief in the value and importance of a National Federation that a temporary board of officers was at once elected to serve until such time as an expression of opinion could be obtained from the Women's Musical Clubs of the United States.

"The undersigned club women who were present agreed to use their influence with their respective clubs to bring about such a Federation, and to become personally responsible for the slight expense incurred in sending these preliminary notices. We enclose a copy of a Constitution and By-Laws which has been prepared for the consideration of all Clubs. Does it meet your approval and are you willing to become a member of such a Federation? What changes can you suggest? Are you willing that the present Board of Officers shall serve until May 1898 when it is hoped that the first Convention of Women's Musical Clubs can be held? What woman-member of the Woman's Musical Club can you suggest as regent for your state? Kindly reply at the earliest possible moment to the Secretary, Miss Marion Ralston.

"We do not enclose stamp for reply because we believe that your interest in Women's work is sufficient to induce you to advise and help us in the important step we are about to take whether you care to join the Federation or not.

(Signed)
Mrs. Theodore Sutro,
Temporary Chairman
Mrs. Chandler Starr
Mrs. Russell R. Dorr
Miss Marion F. Ralston"

3

During the seven months following the temporary organization and preceding the formal organization in Chicago in January, 1898, according to Mrs. Dorr, "all of the officers elected in New York performed almost herculean tasks, working entirely at their own expense and with complete unselfishness," but misunderstandings arose.

At the meeting in New York, the group voted unanimously to ask Mrs. Theodore Thomas to serve as chairman of the Executive Committee. Present and voting were Mrs. Thomas's two sisters, Miss Amy Fay and Mrs. Charles S. Peirce, both of New York. Miss Fay also accepted a position on the Board.

Miss Ralston, the secretary, wrote to Mrs. Thomas telling her of her election. Mrs. Thomas was traveling at the time and failed to receive the letter until after the "circulars" carrying her name had been printed. In a letter declining the honor Mrs. Thomas gave as her reason that she "had not the time to attend to the necessary duties." Mrs. Thomas wrote later in a letter to Mrs. Helen Harrison Mills, that she "declined because she

(Mrs. Sutro) had not worked with us in the convention, or even attended it, and was entirely unknown to all the clubs who had, and I did not feel that I could endorse her project when she was a total stranger to me, and I did not know anything about the lines upon which she was planning to organize the Federation, as she had not consulted me."

Mrs. Thomas's letter to Mrs. Mills continued, "For some reason or other she chose to disregard my refusal and had my name announced officially on circulars, etc., as the Chairman of her Committee. I protested in vain repeatedly against this unauthorized use of my name, and finally sent a statement to all the clubs of the Convention, disclaiming all official connection with Mrs. Sutro's committee."

After that mistake was made, a second "circular" was issued by Mrs. Sutro, the temporary chairman, calling the delegates together in Chicago, in which she again used the name of Mrs. Thomas as chairman of the Executive Board, without the knowledge or consent of Mrs. Thomas.

Mrs. Thomas put notices in several publications to the effect that her name had been used fraudulently. The notice which appeared in the February, 1898 issue of *Etude Magazine* read:

"A Card From Mrs. Theodore Thomas"

"Mrs. Theodore Thomas desires to inform the press, the public, and the amateur musical clubs of America, that her name has been a second time fraudulently used in the circulars of the National Federation of Women's Musical Clubs, as the chairman of its Board, in spite of her published statement to the contrary and her indignant protest against its unauthorized use in the same connection last fall. Mrs. Thomas wishes to state emphatically that she is not, and never has been, connected with the Federation in any capacity whatsoever, and that the circulars issued by that Association signed with her name as president of its Board, are, so far as she is concerned, fraudulent."

In a letter to Mrs. Dorr, chairman of the Nominating Committee, in January, 1898, before the official organization, Mrs. Thomas wrote,

"My musical work in connection with our own Orchestra Association entirely takes all the time I ought to spare from my home duties. But I want the Federation to be put into hands who will carry it out in the right way, and if this is done I will gladly work with them in every way I can without any office and help it to succeed. You know I really care nothing at all for the glory of being a prominent officer and I perfectly hate to have my name in the papers. I want to see the work done right, and under the right leaders I am just as ready to work amongst the rank and file as if I were on the Board. But under the wrong leaders I won't work in any capacity or come near the Federation at all."

Miss Ralston was to write Mrs. Dorr later, "There was only one misunderstanding if you could call it that, – when Mrs. Sutro got out that circular with a list of officers, including Mrs. Thomas as honorary president – after she had declined the honor. She signed my name to the circulars, though I didn't know they were being printed until I received one from New York in the same mail as everybody else."

Mrs. Charles Allen Cale, who as Rosalie Balmer Smith of St. Louis, was one of those in attendance at the meeting in New York in 1897. According to Mrs. Cale, she had been elected recording secretary, pro tem, at the meeting of the Executive Committee at the home of Mrs. Pedersen in New York on September 1, 1897. It was there, that Mrs. Cale, in her words, "recorded what took place." Mrs. Sutro requested that the minutes be sent to her, "as she would like to look them over." She sent them to Mrs. Sutro, "and was surprised to find when she returned them that she had altered them in a way to be complimentary to herself, when such was not the case at the meeting." Mrs. Cale told this to Marion Ralston, the recording secretary, when she turned the minutes over to her, but she said, "I fixed them back again the way they were when I first sent them to her, (guess this is what the trouble was about with Mrs. Sutro)."

The Federation's historical files contain the following letter which Mrs. Thomas wrote to Miss Ralston in 1922, regarding the "fraudulent" use of Mrs. Thomas's name by Mrs. Sutro:

Ap- 29th 1922

My dear Miss Ralston

I did not hold you in
any way responsible for the
unauthorized use of my name
in Mrs. Fulto's circulars, as I
supposed you were only acting
under her instructions as
secretaries ordinarily do. But
I was very angry with her
for she tried to make it
appear to the Clubs which
I had brought together at
the Convention, that I was
officially connected with the
Federation she was interested
in promoting, whereas I was
not connected with it, and
did not know anything about
her personally, or about the
kind of Association she had
in mind, and I was not
willing to endorse it blindly
in any such way.

When the Clubs finally
came together in Chicago
I did not attend any of

the meetings because I did
not wish to come into any
conflict with Mrs. Sutro. But
as soon as I was informed that
Mrs. Uhl had been elected
I gave my hearty support
and my name, very gladly
to the Federation, because I
knew Mrs. Uhl very well and
knew exactly what her plans
and ideals were in regard
to it. She more than justified
my faith in her and
organized it on such broad
and judicious lines that it
was afterwards able to build up,
on her foundation, to the present
magnificent organization. I
realize that I could never have
done what she and her
successors have accomplished,
and have always been glad
that I remained in the
background as a mere honorary
officer and left the field open
to them in their able
efficient management.

Thanks for your very courteous
letter which interested me
very much — Sincerely yours,
Rose F. Thomas

4

As the time drew near for the meeting to be held in Chicago on January 25, 1898, at which time permanent officers would be elected, there was a growing concern as to who would be nominated by Mrs. Dorr and her committee. The success of the new Federation rested solely in the hands of those nominated and elected to lead. Mrs. Sutro was not known to those in the musical world, and neither was she known to Mrs. Dorr. A culturally prominent New York matron who had been in attendance at the meeting in Chicago in 1893, and again at the meeting of the temporary committee in New York in 1897, was prompted to write Mrs. Dorr, a letter dated September 15, 1897, which read in part:

> "I was shocked to find from Mrs. Sutro's and Miss Ralston's letters equally, how the whole enterprise is already playing into the hand, and is committed to this presidency of Mrs. Sutro – recognized in this city as a woman of undoubted ability and at first acquaintance, of charm – but also of a vanity which is insatiable as her ambition is colossal and unscrupulous.
>
> "If you make her the head of the Federation... you give a woman without a shadow of a claim upon it, musically, professionally, or socially, one of the four to five preeminent national positions of women in the country. I ask, my dear madam – what do you and Miss Ralston know about Mrs. Sutro that you so absolutely trust and confide in her for this important national position?"

She continued by saying she had contacted President Greene of the Music Teachers National Association asking why he gave Mrs. Sutro "the responsible position he did, at the same convention of the MTNA."

> "He said that Mrs. Sutro's department was a source of heavy expense to the MTNA – that her claim made in newspapers to have paid her own stenographers for their work was false... and rather than have Mrs. Sutro again as president of the Woman's Department of MTNA he would not have any woman's department, that his fellow officers were indignant at her management and 'used very highly colored language' regarding her."

President Greene said he had been influenced to appoint her to that position because of her newspaper notoriety. The writer continued by

52

asking Mrs. Dorr that:

> "We not commit the infant Federation to a mother who will
> nourish it only for her own glorification and who – when you
> count up cost and expenses after her regime – may find your
> treasury empty, flaccid and drained...
> "Why do these rumors of financial management and of per-
> sistent self exaltation, and all with the one result of trumpeting
> 'Mrs. Sutro' – why do these features invariably pursue every
> enterprise with which she is identified?
> "She is immensely able, brilliant and aesthetic as an orga-
> nizer. She is a little Napoleon... and her vanity, egotism and
> despotism are parallel with Napoleon's... for she uses human
> nature with master skill to exalt herself... Every action of her
> life is published in the newspapers but who she is originally or
> where is her native home I know no more than you... She has
> no social recognition in New York 'society' whatsoever...
> "A dreadful thing she did I know of personally. She went to
> a very gifted... little English portrait painter – Miss Marie
> Brooks... and wanted her to make a large three quarter oil por-
> trait of her in antique costume – with which curling wig and
> picture hat – to be called 'An American Duchess'. She told the
> artist she could not buy the $1,000 portrait, but her friends were
> such people as Miss Helen Gould and Mrs. George Gould and
> this would bring her important orders."

The portrait was painted and displayed in the store picture windows
in the leading stores of New York. Miss Brooks never got one commission from it. The writer felt the title "A Gypsy" would have suited the
part better.

She begged Mrs. Dorr for the nominating committee not to let her
statement stand in the way, but asked her to contact others.

> "But my own personal judgement of Mrs. Sutro is – that she
> does not love the art, she does not love culture, she doesn't love
> womanhood – but only for what they can do for Mrs. Sutro!
> Sooner or later all women who work with her become indig-
> nant and disaffected because they find her like the Vampire, she
> has drawn their force and their talent, and their money into her
> own insatiable ambition and vanity."

She continued that she would make similar statements to Mrs. Thomas and "let her act with light and knowledge as to involving herself before the nation with an absolute self-seeker like Mrs. Sutro and one who in her own city is a social cipher."

5

On January 19, 1898 – only six days before the scheduled organizational meeting to be held in Chicago on January 25th, the following article appeared in the *New York Tribune*:

AN AMATEUR MUSICAL FEDERATION

DELEGATES TO MEET IN CHICAGO NEXT WEEK TO ORGANIZE IT

Chicago, Jan 18. – At Steinway Hall next Tuesday and Wednesday there will be a convention of delegates representing the amateur clubs of the country for the purpose of effecting a permanent federation. The object is to stimulate musical culture and to enable cities and organizations unable to pay grand opera prices to secure by cooperation the services of eminent musical artists. The movement originated at the Musical Congress of the World's Fair, and was endorsed last year by the Music Teachers National Association. One hundred delegates are expected. Many Eastern delegates are understood to favor Mrs. Theodore Sutro, of New York, for president, while those from the Central and Western States would prefer Mrs. Uhl of Grand Rapids, Mich., wife of the former Ambassador to Germany. Mrs. Chandler Starr, of Rockford, Ill., is another favorite. Mrs. Russell Dorr of St. Paul, Minn., and Mrs. J. H. Webster, of Cleveland, Ohio are also supported.

The permanent federation will be governed by a National Executive Board, and its chief business officer will be a National secretary who will supply artists at their own rates on club terms to the clubs of the federation. The convention will be under the hospitality of the Chicago Amateur Musical Club, which consists of five hundred women representing the intellectual and artistic life of the city. Among the active and associate members are Mrs. Theodore Thomas, Mrs. Genevra Johnstone Bishop, Mrs. F. S. Coolidge, Mrs. George H. Carpenter, Mrs. Alexander Sullivan, Mrs. Clarence Eddy, Mrs. Clarence Peck, Mrs. Regin-Watson, Mrs. Fanny Bloomfield-Zeisler and Mrs. John M. Clark.

When the clubs met in Chicago to organize the Federation, a delegation went to see Mrs. Thomas in hopes that she would allow her name to be put in nomination for the first president. Again she declined, "because I felt that to Mrs. Uhl justly belonged the honor... She had worked with us, heart and soul... She knew us all, was in sympathy with our ideals and possessed our confidence." The day prior to the opening of the meeting Mrs. Thomas met with some of the ladies who had arrived in Chicago, and outlined a carefully thought out plan she would like to see incorporated into the permanent organization.

PART TWO

The Seed Takes Root

THE RETURN TO CHICAGO

1

Chicagoans awoke on January 25, 1898 to one of the worst snow-storms and blizzards in the city's history. It was hard to remember when traffic had suffered as much in one day as it did during the snowstorm. According to the January 27, 1898 *Chicago Record Herald*:

"... Almost everywhere in the usually congested thoroughfare, business was at a standstill. The high heaps of snow made it difficult and at many places next to impossible for the wagons to be handled systematically. Dealers and clerks could do no more than hug the stoves, stand at the doors and windows and watch the fury of the elements, or 'straighten' up the books and treat the stores to a cleaning up from cellar to garret. The few buyers that braved the storm to go into the street were in a reminiscent mood and recalled the heavy snowfalls of former years."

2

But alas! – on that bleak and memorable day of January 25, 1898, some one hundred brave women representing Women's Amateur Musical Clubs from eleven states arrived in Chicago to organize formally a federation of all the "musical" clubs in the United States, the seeds which had been planted four and one-half years before – in 1893, at the World's Columbian Exposition in this same city of Chicago. They were not to be daunted by the worst snowstorm in years.

They had responded to a call from the temporary committee to meet in Steinway Hall, January 25-28 for the purpose of adopting a constitution and bylaws, electing permanent officers, and applying for a charter and articles of incorporation.

Courageous women were they – many of whom had attended and received their inspiration for a federation from the World's Columbian Exposition – Mrs. Russell R. Dorr, St. Paul, Minnesota; Miss Marion

Ralston, St. Louis, Missouri; Mrs. Chandler Starr, Rockford, Illinois; Mrs. William S. Warren, Chicago; Mrs. Charles Virgil, Elmhurst, Long Island. The enthusiasm of these ladies to organize a Federation of Music Clubs had not diminished.

Even though Mrs. Thomas preferred to remain in the background, and was not present at the organizational meeting in Steinway Hall, January 25, 1898, she was a "guiding light" and her presence was felt in many of the decisions that were made that day. Mrs. Dorr wrote, "I have in her own handwriting under the date, January 17th a long letter in which (Mrs. Thomas) outlined a carefully thought-out plan for permanent organization... She adds: 'You are at liberty to make any use of this letter you like unofficially', and requests that I meet her and other members of the committee at a private conference on Monday, January 24th (the day before the officially called meeting)."

3

Hosting the January 25-28, 1898 meeting of a National Federation of Women's Amateur Musical Clubs was one of America's oldest clubs, the Amateur Musical Club of Chicago – a club of several hundred members.

The Amateur Musical Club was founded and chartered in 1875, when four "music loving women, living in Chicago agreed to set apart one morning each week for the purpose of reading piano quartets together." Serving in those early years as secretary and treasurer was Miss Rose Fay, who served also as librarian. It was in 1891, as Mrs. Theodore Thomas, that she was elected the club's second president – an office she held until 1893. It was as president of the club that Mrs. Thomas called the clubs of the United States together to meet at the World's Columbian Exposition, and it was she who gave the report of the Amateur Musical Club to those ladies assembled.

The club's minutes record that the members "voted to give a wedding gift of not less than $100.00 to Rose Fay and Theodore Thomas." A "piece of silver was given" with the engraving, "Presented by the Amateur Musical Club to Rose Fay and Theodore Thomas." The minutes continued, "A letter of acknowledgment has been received from Mrs. Thomas, which is presumed will interest all present."

"In 1898-1899 the club opened its doors on January 25, to the National Federation of Musical Clubs. During this day and the one following, representatives from all over the country as-

58

sembled in Steinway Hall for the purpose of adopting a constitution and bylaws, and electing permanent officers....
"The Amateur Musical Club was represented ably by its fifth
president, Mrs. William S. Warren," who welcomed and brought
greetings to the group of approximately 100 ladies assembled."

The Club's history continued:

"A graceful compliment on the part of the executive committee of the Amateur Musical Club was the Concert given on
the evening of Tuesday, January 25th in honor of the Federation. The program was furnished entirely by members of the
club with one exception – Miss Marion Ralston, representing
the Federation, was given the place of honor and played several
of her own compositions. One of the early features in the life of
our club was our assistance in the organization of the National
Federation of Music Clubs. It has grown to be one of the most
dominant and powerful forces in the cultural life of every city
of importance in America, and the Amateur Musical Club en-
joys the distinction of having been among the founders of this
great and growing organization... We are proud to be among
those organizations known as the 'parent clubs.'"

Note: *In September 1916 the name of the Amateur Musical Club was changed
to The Musicians Club of Women of Chicago.*

4

The meeting was called to order by the temporary chairman, Mrs.
Theodore Sutro, on January 25, 1898 in Steinway Hall, Chicago.
Members were welcomed by Mrs. William S. Warren, president of
the Amateur Musical Club of Chicago. The response was given by the
temporary chairman. Miss Marion Ralston, corresponding secretary, gave
a brief summary of the growth of the movement for a National Federation from the meeting at the Music Teachers National Association in
New York in June, 1897.
Mrs. Sutro reported and named the following committees:

Nominating Committee:
Mrs. Russell R. Dorr, St. Paul, Chairman
Mrs. Clara A. Korn, New York

Mrs. Frederick Ullman, Chicago
Mrs. James L. Blair, St. Louis
Mrs. Jirah Cole, Los Angeles
Artist Committee:
   Mrs. J. H. Webster, Cleveland, Chairman
   Mrs. Philip N. Moore, St. Louis
   Mrs. Eliot West, Rockford, Illinois

A letter from Mrs. H. H. A. Beach was read after which a musical "programme" was heard: Miss Schade of Copenhagen played three Scarlatti sonatas, and a nocturne and ballad of Chopin; Mrs. Clara Korn of New York gave two of her original compositions; and Miss Mary Angell of the Amateur Musical Club of Chicago played Gottschalk's *Tremolo.*

Reports from eighteen clubs representing eleven states were read and the Federation received a cordial invitation from Mrs. Warren to attend a musicale and reception to be given by the Amateur Musical Club that evening. The club had hosted previously a luncheon at the Congress Hotel for the delegates.

The report of the first meeting of the Board of Management held the previous day, January 24, was read by Mrs. Nelson Burritt, secretary pro tem.

The report of the committee on Constitution and Bylaws was presented by the chairman, Mrs. James Pedersen. This report was considered section by section, and with the consent of the Federation, the corresponding sections of the unofficial suggestions of the Amateur Musical Club were considered at the same time.

5

Those women assembled had the imagination to realize that the time had come to encourage and advance American music and to promote the American composer and artist. Filled with hope and optimism, to them fell the task of gaining support and making ready for formal birth. The *New York Tribune* on January 26, 1898 carried the following article:

THE UNIVERSAL LANGUAGE

MEMBERS OF THE N. F. W. M. C.
MEET IN CHICAGO AND DISCUSS MUSIC

Much Interest Shown
in the Election of a President
for the National Federation of Music Clubs

"At the opening of the National Federation of Women's Musical Clubs in Chicago yesterday, the address of welcome was made by Mrs. William S. Warren, and Mrs. Theodore Sutro, of this city, president pro tem, responded. She spoke in part as follows:

'This gathering represents women who are not only interested in music but in literary pursuits, for not only are many musical clubs represented here, but others who include among their departments, one of music. There is after all, a close connection between music and literature, as the underlying basis of all music must be thoughts, which have found expression in many an immortal song of dramatic adaptation.

'The benefits of a federation such as is here proposed are apparent to all. The beneficent influence of music, as a civilizer I need not dwell on. If through unity of action and interchange of thought we raise its standard, we are in the same proportion at the same time helping to advance the civilization of our entire population. Music is the universal language, which is broad as the world, and no doubt could therefore unite closely the representatives who are gathered here from every point of the compass in a movement like this. Selfishness and individual considerations must be absolutely banished if we desire success. Locality must not be considered, but the main object always kept in view, that the highest and best thing in the whole country must be our aim.

'The present gathering is only to perfect a permanent organization. I hope and believe that state federations of musical clubs will grow from this movement....

'I trust that self-abnegation will be the distinguishing characteristic of every delegate. I hope that every member will study to be an altruist. Egotism has been the death of hundreds of clubs... Let harmony prevail among us, not only musical but actual... There must be no salaried officers in this federation. Every member must feel honored to hold any official position and make her duties a labor of love....'

"In closing, Mrs. Sutro continued with a personal reference to herself:

'If I may be permitted to refer to myself a moment, I may say that in being honored today as temporary president of this, the first National Federation of Musical Clubs, I may attribute it to the trifling matter of responding to an invitation... in 1893 to deliver an essay on woman's work in music. I was asked to make... an address before the Clef Club of New York, composed of some of New York's best professional musicians and organists... Subsequently I was invited to form and take charge of the Woman's Department of the Music Teachers National Association, and again to this I may trace my presence in this great gathering....' "

6

In that same January 26, 1898 issue of the *New York Tribune* there was a letter to the Editor, entitled, "Mrs. Sutro's Work for the National Federation of Musical Clubs and Societies." The letter stated that Mrs. Sutro, "a young society woman of New York desired to correct the statements she often heard while attending teas and other social functions, that women were only fit to ornament and beautify the world."

The letter to the editor continued by saying that she "was prevailed upon to accept the honorary place as president and founder of a Woman's Department for the Music Teachers National Association, which she organized successfully. Of the fourteen departments that she organized, one was the committee of Women's Music Clubs and Societies from which the present National Federation of Women's Musical Clubs and Societies is an outgrowth." The letter continued, "In September last, Mrs. Sutro felt she could not continue working for the federation. She therefore called a meeting of all the officers and tendered her resignation," whereupon every other officer resigned also. She was "urged to reconsider" being reminded of how the federation "which was started by Mrs. Theodore Thomas of Chicago, had completely banished out of existence." She reconsidered, but according to the letter she again resigned. It was Miss Marion Ralston who wrote to her, "Allow me again to state emphatically that Mrs. Dorr, Mrs. Starr and myself urge you not to withdraw your name; all we need is a clear-sighted and decided woman at the helm, and I am sure as such, you can restore proper order, with your undisputed place in everything you have undertaken...."

The editor noted, "The result of today's meeting in Chicago will be watched with great interest, since the election of its president is one of the events, and the endeavor will be made to put in office a Western candidate (Mrs. Edwin F. Uhl) in the place of Mrs. Sutro... The Eastern and Central States seem united on Mrs. Sutro."

CHAPTER TWO

STORMY WITHOUT – STORMY WITHIN

1

On January 26, 1898 the second session of the National Federation of Women's Amateur Musical Clubs was called to order by the temporary chairman, Mrs. Theodore S. Sutro. Approximately one hundred voting delegates, representing thirty-eight clubs were in attendance. Noticeably absent were Mrs. Theodore Thomas and her sisters, Mrs. Charles Peirce and Miss Amy Fay – although the latter's name was listed on the program to deliver an address on "Women in Music" at the afternoon session.

At the morning session the main order of business was adopting a constitution and bylaws. Taking precedent was the changing of the name of the new infant federation – "dropping the 'Women's Amateur' from the official title, now to be called, 'The National Federation of Musical Clubs.'"

Membership in the Federation was to be limited "to those clubs officered by women only", and "musical sections of women's clubs were not eligible for membership." The only limit set upon the officers and directors was the fact that the organization was committed to the promotion of music – music in every form.

The afternoon session was called to order at 2:00 o'clock for the purpose of electing permanent officers for the new federation. Again Mrs. Sutro was in the chair. The meeting which lasted from 2:00 until 9:00 in the evening was referred to the following day by the *Chicago Tribune* with headlines which read, "Stormy Without, and Stormy Within Steinway Hall, as the Music Clubs Elect Officers."

Nominating the officers of the National Federation of Musical Clubs was the chairman of the Nominating Committee, Mrs. Russell R. Dorr, who nominated for president of the permanent organization, Mrs. Edwin F. Uhl of Grand Rapids, Michigan.

The temporary chairman called for nominations from the floor, at which time, Mrs. Clara Korn, of New York, nominated Mrs. Theodore Sutro of that same city. When the votes were counted Mrs. Uhl was elected with eighty-seven votes. Mrs. Sutro received twelve.

The *Chicago Record Herald* the next day carried the following:

MRS. SUTRO DEFEATED

FAILS TO REACH THE PRESIDENCY

"... Mrs. Theodore Sutro, after being given the credit of bringing to a successful realization the project to establish a national federation of women's amateur musical clubs, was humiliated by a sweeping defeat of her cherished ambition to be president of the new league at the convention in Steinway Hall yesterday.

"The young New York woman, fascinating in beauty, dazzling in diamonds and radiant in a superb gown of gray and white, was given no official recognition of her work on behalf of the musical clubs of the country. She said she had only one friend, Mrs. Clara A. Korn, also of New York city, who proposed her for the presidency.

Got Twelve Votes

"Twelve delegates to the convention voted for Mrs. Sutro however, and the remaining eighty-seven votes were cast for Mrs. Edwin F. Uhl, Grand Rapids, Michigan, but at present a resident of Berlin, where she went when her husband was appointed by President Cleveland ambassador to Germany. The friends of Mrs. Sutro say that Mrs. Uhl was the leader in the organization of a similar federation, which was a failure, during the World's Fair.

"... Mrs. Sutro said that Mrs. Thomas, was the moving power behind her opponents on the floor of the convention. She was smiling and plucky to the end, but when the announcement of the vote was made her voice had the tone of a bitterly disappointed woman.

"... A little later Mrs. William S. Warren of Chicago, the accredited representative of Mrs. Theodore Thomas, said; 'I think we all feel that the president is fatigued and we will excuse her if she would like to retire. I suggest that Mrs. Starr take her place.'

"Mrs. Sutro saw through the delicate hint to give way in face of defeat, but she rose and said in a firm voice, slightly sarcastic: 'I thank you, Mrs. Warren, but I feel that it would be cowardly not to meet my defeat with fortitude. I think I shall remain until the end.

"The decision was greeted with a ripple of applause, which was more than Mrs. Sutro received when she announced her retirement in the following brief speech: 'Your temporary president will now retire. I thank you for your kindness.'"

Other officers elected were:

First Vice President –
Mrs. Chandler Starr, Rockport, Illinois
Second Vice President –
Mrs. Philip N. Moore, St. Louis, Missouri
Vice Presidents –
Eastern Section: Mrs. Clara A. Korn, New York, New York
Northern Middle Section: Mrs. J. H. Webster, Cleveland, Ohio
Southern Middle Section: Mrs. Napoleon Hill, Memphis, Tennessee
Western Section: Mrs. Emily S. Trevitt, Portland, Oregon
Recording Secretary –
Mrs. T. E. Ellison, Ft. Wayne, Indiana
Corresponding Secretary –
Mrs. James Pedersen, New York, New York
Treasurer –
Miss Ada B. Douglas, Newark, New Jersey
Auditor –
Mrs. Russell R. Dorr, St. Paul, Minnesota
Directors –
Eastern Section:
Mrs. Linda B. Wardwell, Danbury, Connecticut
Mrs. Hadden Alexander, New York, New York
Northern Middle Section:
Mrs. A. M. Robertson, Indianapolis, Indiana
Miss Helen A. Storer, Akron, Ohio
Southern Middle Section:
Mrs. E. F. Verdery, Augusta, Georgia
Mrs. A. F. Perry, Jacksonville, Florida
Western Section:
Mrs. D. A. Campbell, Lincoln, Nebraska
Mrs. J. W. Hardt, Topeka, Kansas

Upon the election of permanent officers, the first Vice President, Mrs. Chandler Starr, took the chair as the presiding officer in the absence of the newly elected president, Mrs. Uhl.

Mrs. Starr was to write to Mrs. Dorr, twenty-five years later, in 1923: "You will remember well about that stormy meeting in Chicago – Stormy without (do you remember the blizzard?) and Stormy within, on account of that little Napoleon, Mrs. Sutro."

2

The January 27, 1898 *New York Tribune* was even less complimentary of the organizational meeting of the new National Federation of Musical Clubs – appearing under the heading, *NO SISTERLY FEELING THERE, DISCORD ALL THROUGH THE MEETINGS OF THE N. F. W. M. C.*, the article continued:

"Chicago, Jan 26 – Sisterly feeling does not hover over the meeting of the National Federation of Women's Musical Clubs and Societies. The first session of the Federation, in Steinway Hall, yesterday, had not progressed far before the delegates were saying unkind things about one another, and there was talk of secession and revolt.

"One faction is led by Mrs. Theodore Sutro, of New York, and another is composed of the friends of Mrs. Theodore Thomas, wife of the famous orchestra leader. As has already been stated, Mrs. Thomas declares that her name was used fraudulently, and it was an attempt of Mrs. Sutro to refute this which led to the unpleasantness.

"Ill feeling slumbered until the delegates listened to the report of the president regarding the work accomplished. In the report, the Thomas affair was referred to as a 'delicate and sorrowful subject,' and the president (Mrs. Sutro) said her honor was at stake, and that she therefore must touch upon the subject... The use of Mrs. Thomas's name in the circular was explained and the charge of fraud resented.

"'How much better and wiser it would have been,' concludes the report, 'if our secretary, Miss Ralston, instead of spending her time in sending out printed notices pronouncing my work ineffectual, had spent her time in working for the success of the meeting.'

"This reference to the matter raised a storm of protest, and the Chicago friends of Mrs. Thomas insisted that it be expunged from the report. Mrs. Sutro, assisted by Mrs. Clara Korn, the New York composer, insisted that in justice to the honor of the president, the clause be permitted to remain....

"Both sides profess to deplore the turn affairs have taken."

3

On this same day, January 27, 1898 the *Chicago Tribune* carried a 6 x 8 inch picture of "Mrs. Edwin F. Uhl, Wife of the Ex-Minister to Germany," which read:

MRS. EDWIN F. UHL WINS

PRESIDENT OF THE NATIONAL FEDERATION OF MUSICAL CLUBS

She defeats Mrs. Theodore Sutro, the New York Candidate, on the First Formal Ballot, with Votes to Spare – Final Meeting in Steinway Hall – New Constitution Adopted – Those Who May become Members of the Organization

"Mrs. Edwin F. Uhl of Grand Rapids, Mich., was elected President of the National Federation of Musical Clubs at its final meeting in Steinway Hall yesterday defeating Mrs. Theodore Sutro, the New York candidate.

"... The election of permanent officers for the new federation, and the adoption of the constitution and bylaws, totally eclipsed all other events on the program. The constitution was voted on at the morning session.

"By the new ruling all musical clubs which have women for their officers may be admitted to the federation. Musical sections of women's clubs are not eligible for membership.

"The election occupied the time of the afternoon session, which lasted until 9 o'clock. The battle was a long one, but at its close the participants declared it had not been stormy. The West had triumphed over the East, and the defeated candidate was graciousness itself. She left the hall accompanied by her friend, Miss Korn, carrying the great bunch of pink roses which had stood on the desk all day, and a telegram which her husband had sent:

Flash the greeting, O East to the West,
To the loveliest, the brightest, the best!
Whether President or not she be,
Three cheers for dear little wife,
Who will ever preside over me,
As queen of my heart and my life.

Her Object Accomplished

"'The object of which I have worked so hard has been accomplished,' she said. 'That is my first and dearest wish. I would have liked to have had my name go into the printed constitution as one of the promoters of the work, but the majority did not will it so; and I bow to its decree.

"'I have presided over this meeting to the best of my ability. I have tried to be fair and just, and I think the fact that today's meeting, though a trying one for all of us, has passed off without disagreeable squabbles and testifies that I have not failed.'

"A vote of thanks was extended by the Federation to Mrs. Sutro for her work during the year, also one to the Amateur Musical Club of Chicago 'for its kindness and hospitality, its artistic musicale and reception, and for the many courtesies extended to its guests....' The Federation adjourned sine die, believing that the organization had been laid on firm foundations and that its future success was assured."

4

Mrs. Dorr wrote that immediately after the permanent organizational meeting was held, an informal meeting of the newly elected officers and directors was held "at the residence of Mrs. William Warren, president of the Amateur Musical Club of Chicago. Mrs. Thomas was present and expressed her satisfaction at the outcome of the permanent organization" the previous day and her special pleasure that Mrs. Uhl was to be the first president.

Mrs. Thomas wrote of the meeting that she thought the Federation accomplished very good work, but "it had a horrid snarl to get itself out of. It seems to be in the main started right and it will go on all right if it keeps itself strictly in its own hands, and doesn't bring 'outsiders'... into its official ranks."

5

Mrs. James Pedersen was later to write Mrs. Dorr:

Nov. 10th, 1922.

260 WEST SEVENTY-SIXTH STREET

I was present at the M. T. A. convention which was held in the Grand Central Palace in June 1897, and was one of the group of women which met at the same time and place to talk over the formation of a national federation of musical clubs. I shall not give the details of this meeting, for Mrs. Dorr has so ably and correctly stated all these in her story of those preliminary meetings. I know that Mrs. Theodore Sutro was a stranger to us all except as we had met her there in her department for women composers in connection with the M. T. A. I think I am correct in saying that Mrs. Sutro had had no connection with the musical club work of the country prior to the time when she was asked to serve as the temporary chairman of the organization which was being planned. Mrs. Sutro dropped out of the Federation completely after the election of Mrs. Edwin F. Uhl in Chicago as the first President of the National Federation of Musical Clubs.

Anna S. (Mrs. James) Pedersen

CHAPTER THREE

RING UP THE CURTAIN

1

Immediately following the adjournment of the permanent organizational meeting on January 26, 1898, a post meeting of the Board of Management was held the next day, January 27th with the First Vice President, Mrs. Chandler Starr, presiding. Of the nineteen members elected to the Board eight members were present.

The constitution and bylaws adopted the day before, were edited and ordered printed. The first blueprint called for the selection of appropriate and necessary tools essential to forming the new organization. These were chiefly:

1. Extension – the securing of member clubs became the "chief means of implementing the infant Federation, assuring its growth." Under the plan, each of the four vice presidents in charge of "sections" had the responsibility of selecting state presidents and organizing states within their respective sections.

2. The promotion of Artists Concerts became one of the main projects. An Artists Committee, whose duties were to arrange artists concerts and recitals "which would be advantageous to both the clubs and the artists," was appointed. Letters were formulated and sent the clubs accompanied by a roster of available artists and their respective fees. (The furnishing of concert artists to clubs at reasonable rates continued for ten years and later grew into the NFMC Artist Presentation Department for the purpose of promoting the Federation's Young Artist winners.)

3. The promotion of the works of American Composers, through a national librarian, became one of the Federation's newly implemented projects.

Each of the three projects has been sustained and grown throughout the years.

Elected to the Artists Committee were: Mrs. Russell R. Dorr, chairman; Mrs. J. H. Webster; Mrs. David A. Campbell; Mrs. Napoleon Hill; and Mrs. James Pedersen.

"The very attractive and cordial invitation" of the musical clubs of

St. Louis, for the Federation to hold its next meeting in that city, October 17-18, 1898, was presented and accepted.

Immediate steps were taken to incorporate the newly organized National Federation of Musical Clubs. There were only nineteen signers of the document (charter) that was executed after the permanent organizational meeting; Miss Ralston, Mrs. Virgil, Mrs. Cale, Mrs. Pedersen and others who had worked valiantly under the temporary organization left immediately at the close of the permanent organization. Hence, the list of charter members was increased at the first Board meeting.

Formal application was made to the Secretary of State, James A. Rose, of the State of Illinois. Specified as the object of the new Federation stated:

"To bring into working relation with one another music clubs and other musical organizations and individuals directly or indirectly associated with musical activities, for the purpose of aiding and encouraging musical education, and developing and maintaining high musical standards throughout America."

2

Blanch Ellis Starr, Anna S. Pedersen, and Fannie P. Warren applied to James A. Rose, Secretary of State, State of Illinois, Cook County, for incorporation of the National Federation of Music Clubs.

On February 29, 1898, The National Federation of Musical Clubs was granted a Certificate of Incorporation by the State of Illinois at the State Capitol in Springfield, Illinois.

The original charter, which the State of Illinois granted to the National Federation of Musical Clubs in 1898, is in the Federation's Archives in the Library of Congress in Washington, D.C.

3

The February 1898 issue of *Etude Magazine* – less than one month following the organizational meeting in Chicago – carried an article, "Woman's Work in Music" in which Ada B. Douglas, one of the nineteen directors applying for the charter, wrote:

"Set in motion by Mrs. Theodore Thomas at the Columbian Exposition, a great wave of musical activity in the line of women's musical clubs has swept over the country. In a directory of women's musical clubs of the United States recently compiled... by Mrs. C. S. Virgil, there are over 225 clubs represented, and exactly one-half that number have been organized during or since the Columbian year. Mr. Thomas felt so strongly the great influence these clubs... would have on the musical culture of the country, that he gave great help to the movement which Mrs. Thomas so ably carried out."

In the same article, Mrs. George H. Carpenter wrote:

"There is no means of correctly estimating the value of the amateur clubs to the musical culture of a community. The incentive to study and the inspiration of competition are inestimable; and the opportunity for acquaintance with classical and modern compositions, as also hearing artists in the profession, are by no means so attainable. To my mind many benefits would accrue by federating... the amateur club... establishes a national, rather than a local plane, insuring more progressive and pretentious results."

But then there are always those who wish to throw "cold water" on any new innovation. Could it have been prompted by the fact that member clubs of the new federation were to be "officered by women only" that led W. S. B. Mathews to write in the same article:

"It is feared that... the work of women's musical clubs will expend itself without good results; that a sort of amiable faddism will be its characteristic note, and the ladies will hold their meetings and have a nice sweet time, and hear a lot of sweet talk about music, with all the necessary fluffiness, without leaving any more serious impression upon the community than a large soap bubble... which when it bursts, leaves behind it nothing."

It was against such odds as these that these devoted, dedicated and brave women triumphed – and triumph they did! From the original plan of organization to the present, the National Federation of Music Clubs has been a non-political and non-sectarian organization. It has been a philanthropic, educational and cultural corporation in which no officer, department or committee chairman has received any remuneration for services rendered.

4

On February 10, 1898, an informal meeting of some members of the Board was held at the home of the corresponding secretary, Mrs. James Pedersen in New York. Present were Mesdames Curran, Battin, Alexander, Wardwell, and Pedersen. The chief business of the day "was the getting acquainted for the members who had known each other thus far (only) by correspondence." Upon the return of Mrs. Uhl from Germany in May, an effort was made to hold a meeting of the Board of Management in New York, but serious illness in Mrs. Uhl's family hastened her departure from New York, and the meeting was cancelled.

5

"An auspicious day had arrived on October 17, 1898 when the National President, Mrs. Uhl, met the Board of Management for the first time." At the home of Mrs. A. Deane Cooper, 5713 Washington Avenue, St. Louis, Missouri, the president called to order the second meeting of the Board of the National Federation of Musical Clubs. Ten members responded to roll call.

New Committees created, included the Executive Committee of three members: Mrs. Uhl, president; Mrs. Philip N. Moore, second vice president; and Mrs. Frederick Ullman, director, Northern Middle Section. Also named were committees of the Press, Publicity, Circulating Library, and a Bureau of Registry.

Standing rules adopted included, "Only bills bearing the signature of the recording secretary and president (shall) be paid by the treasurer." The treasurer's report showed that thirty-nine clubs had paid dues in the amount of $203.05, and the expenditures of $128.30 left in the treasury a balance of $75.75.

The second day's session on October 18, 1898, was held at the home of the corresponding secretary, Mrs. James A. Pedersen, 4482 Lindell Avenue. Committees named by the president were Badge and Revisions.

Mrs. John Leverett of Alton, Illinois was appointed chairman of the Badge Committee, and was asked to present a design at the St. Louis Biennial in May, 1899.

Mrs. Theodore Thomas was made Honorary President of the National Federation of Musical Clubs. When informed by Mrs. Uhl, the president, Mrs. Thomas graciously accepted the honor.

At this same meeting the first Honorary Memberships were bestowed upon: Henry Krehbiel, eminent music critic of New York, "for service rendered at the preliminary meeting in June 1897"; Theodore Thomas of Chicago, well known orchestra conductor; and Edward MacDowell, dean of American composition.

Of significance were two future policies established for the Federation: (1) that of holding biennial conventions in the odd numbered years, and (2) emphasis on American music, with conventions to be gala musical festivals, and setting the pattern of participation on biennial programs of representative groups from federated clubs together with professional musicians. Time was to be provided for addresses by outstanding speakers, and there were to be papers and discussions in addition to the regular reports. Biennials would celebrate past achievements only as a "springboard" to future goals.

It was decided that there would be held Fall Meetings of the Board of Management.

Four subscriptions were sent from this meeting to the Brahms "Monument Association" of which Theodore Thomas was president.

Plans were adopted for a circulating library by means of which federated clubs may, by payment of a normal sum, have the use of music loaned by different clubs. Mrs. David A. Campbell was appointed librarian.

"The very attractive and cordial invitation of the musical clubs of St. Louis for the Federation to hold its next meeting in that city, May 3-7, 1899, was accepted." Mrs. James L. Blair of St. Louis was named chairman of the 1899 Biennial Committee. On the committee were: "Mrs. Warren of Chicago; Miss Hill of Denver; Mrs. Lyle; Mrs. Carpenter, Grand Rapids; Mrs. Fletcher, Little Rock; and Mrs. Meek, Knoxville."

6

At the third meeting of the Board of Management, May 2, 1899 in St. Louis, immediately preceding the first Biennial Convention of the National Federation of Musical Clubs, twelve members were in attendance. "A plan was adopted by which each Sectional Vice President with her two Directors, shall appoint one person who shall look up all clubs in her state and report to her Sectional Vice President; also that children's clubs shall be admitted to the Federation as Student Clubs, without power to vote or take part in discussions".

The design of the emblem of the National Federation of Music Clubs was presented by Mrs. John Leverett and unanimously accepted as the official emblem of the Federation.

PART THREE

Footnotes to History

FROM THE GRASS ROOTS...

1

As provided in that first charter and bylaws adopted by the newly organized National Federation of Musical Clubs, the "object" was "to bring into communication with one another the various musical clubs of the country, that they may compare methods of work and become mutually helpful."

Clubs submitting applications for membership were required to include a copy of the club's "constitution and bylaws" as proof that they were "officered by women only" and that their purpose was "musical culture".

Geographically the United States was divided into four "sections" – the Northern Middle Section, the Eastern Section, the Southern Middle Section, and the Western Section.

The officers, who were elected by the official delegates were: a president; six vice presidents including first and second vice presidents elected from the membership at large, and a vice president from each of the four sections; a recording secretary; a corresponding secretary; a treasurer; and an auditor. Two directors were elected from each section.

The Executive Committee consisted of three members, including the president as chairman and two elected members.

Dues were five cents per capita annually on all classes of membership.

There was only one membership classification – the Senior Division, however the bylaws provided, "children shall be admitted to the Federation as Study Clubs, without power to take part in discussion or vote." It was not until 1919 that the bylaws were changed to include the second membership classification – the Junior Division. In 1936 the Student Division was founded and named the third membership classification.

The first recorded junior club to become a member of the Federation was the Vivace Junior Group, in 1902, sponsored by the Beethoven Club of Memphis, Tennessee.

2

ACCEPTANCE FOR MEMBERSHIP

(National Federation of (Musical Clubs

Southern Middle SECTION

State *Alabama*

City *Mobile*

Name *Clara Schumann*

Date *March 27th 1899*

Total Number of Members *58*

Cor. sec *Miss Ruth Wilkinson*

Vice President *J. M. sec.*

Mrs. Napoleon Hill

Mrs. Eugene F. Verdery

Mrs. Isabelle S. Perry

Directors

Amount of dues *2.90*

For seventeen years, in the early history of the Federation (1898-1915), clubs became members before their states were organized or federated. Such was the case of the Clara Schumann Club of Mobile, Alabama, which is still a member of the National Federation of Music Clubs today.

When clubs applying for membership in the Federation were accepted, they received certificates as the one photographed. This certificate approved membership of **The Clara Schumann Club** of Mobile, Alabama, issued March 27, 1899 – approximately one year after the Federation was organized formally.

The certificate of The Clara Schumann Club, located in the Southern Middle Section, is signed by the National Vice President of the Section, Mrs. Napoleon Hill, and the two national directors, Mrs. Eugene F. Verdery and Mrs. Isabelle S. Perry.

The Schumann Music Club, as it is known today, celebrated its 100th Anniversary on Sunday, September 18, 1994 with a "100th Anniversary Concert" followed by a reception.

MILESTONES

1

The first Biennial Convention of the National Federation of Musical Clubs was called to order May 3, 1899 at 11:00 a.m. in the Union Club Hall, St. Louis, Missouri, by the president, Mrs. Edwin F. Uhl. Prayer was offered by Reverend F. L. Hosmer, after which the audience joined in singing *America.* The address of Welcome was given by "Mrs. James L. Blair, President of the Local Biennial Board," in which she said in part:

"... Indeed, when it is considered with what sacrifice of time and convenience many of you have come hither and by what a high and unselfish purpose all are actuated, our welcome may well expand into an enthusiastic congratulation upon this most auspicious beginning of our life as a national institution. We are fully justified in believing that with so fair a promise, most valuable results will follow, and that the intelligence and enthusiasm gathered here will infuse into our common purpose a new life and energy... The value of such an association cannot be overrated whether it be considered with reference to individual growth or the increased efficiency of united effort in the dissemination of culture in the most elevated as well as the most beautiful of all the arts....

"For many weeks our entire musical community has looked forward with pleasurable anticipation to your coming... to fittingly celebrate this event which we regard as the beginning of a new era in the musical history of St. Louis."

Mrs. Edwin F. Uhl, the national president, then, for the first time, addressed the group. She said in part:

"We are indeed, fortunate that, gathered from the East and West, North and South, on this, the occasion of our First Biennial, we are the guests of the musical clubs of this fair city...

After several attempts, with much labor on the part of the pioneers of this movement, the National Federation of Musical Clubs is fairly launched, and its most ardent supporters and enthusiastic believers in the efficacy of united effort cannot fail to be cheered and encouraged on this beautiful May day by the gathering here of so many faithful workers in the spreading abroad of the knowledge of all arts – music... Unlike the more tangible arts – plastic art and painting – music has to be reincarnated on every occasion... and the written composition without the life breathed into it by the (performers) is like the finished statue enduring perfect in outline, but dead, imprisoned in marble... and only when the people in general begin to take a lively interest in music and art as they now take in these more material matters, will the arts come to their own... each club belonging to the federation can, in its own vicinity, be one of the centers of musical development, for so old a philosopher as Plato has said,

'Music, that perfect model of elegance and precision, was not given to men by the immortal Gods, with the sole view of delighting and pleasing the senses; but rather for appeasing the troubles of their souls and the sensations of discomfort which imperfect bodies must necessarily undergo.'

"Many ask the question, 'What good will joining the organization be for us, and how can our societies be benefitted?'... Much is expected of this Federation by its friends. Its motto should be the 'greatest good to the greatest number'... its first duty to cultivate and create a taste for the highest quality of music, and to bring us within hearing of all, whether rich or poor...."

Mrs. Uhl closed by saying:

"At the convention in Chicago in 1893, of which your Honorary President, Mrs. Theodore Thomas, was the moving spirit, at which time a National recognition of this department of educational work was given, the wish was expressed, that out of that beginning 'might grow a permanent organization, which should be the best friend of musical art in America.' We can wish no higher mission for this National Federation of Musical Clubs than the fulfillment of that hope."

Mrs. Uhl called for the report of the Recording Secretary, Mrs. Thomas E. Ellison, who included in her report the organizational meeting in Chicago and each of the three meetings of the Board of Management.

Mrs. James Pedersen, Corresponding Secretary in her report said:

> "The history of the sixteen months that have elapsed since the organization of the National Federation of Musical Clubs is full of encouragement for the present and promise for the future. Of the nineteen members of the Board of Management elected at the Chicago meeting, all, save one, accepted the duties of their offices with earnest enthusiasm." (Mrs. Clara Korn, elected Vice President of the Eastern Section, declined the office.) "The first circulars... after the organization, were sent out the middle of March 1898... to the 322 clubs contained in the Directory of Musical Clubs prepared by Mrs. Virgil, also to officers of the Federation and Musical magazines. As a result of these announcements of the Federation, by July 1, 1898, thirty clubs had paid their dues and were listed as members... By January 1, 1899, this number had increased to forty-five... In March 1899, circulars were sent announcing the Biennial Meeting – to both federated and non-federated clubs, resulting in swelling the ranks of federated clubs at the present moment, to seventy-eight."

Mrs. Pedersen continued by saying:

> "The question has often been asked me by professionals and laymen, 'What is the value of the National Federation of Musical Clubs?'... Let me remind such clubs of the history of our nation during the past year, and see if they cannot draw a parallel. Let us as an organization take 'Expansion' of our Cantus Firmus and for a counterpoint use the theme, 'It is more blessed to give than to receive.'"

The treasurer, Mrs. Eugene Verdery reported $560.10 collected from January 1898 to April 1899, there remaining a balance of $384.43 after $175.67 had been paid for expenses for the sixteen months.

The Credentials Committee chairman, Miss Grace Taussig, reported the number of delegates registered were 106; forty-five clubs represented by seventy-four officers and delegates.

The officers elected for 1899-1901 were:

 the Creole of Martinique.

Highlighting the entire six days of concert programs was the Kneisel Quartet of Boston, who was presented by the Union Music Club of St. Louis.

There were two concerts given by "Representatives of Federated Clubs". Some of those clubs participating were: the Rubinstein Club of St. Louis, Missouri; Mozart Club, Dayton, Ohio; St. Cecilia Society, Grand Rapids, Michigan; Schubert Club, St. Paul, Minnesota; Ladies Musical Club, Topeka, Kansas; Fortnightly Club, Cleveland, Ohio; Amateur Musical Club, Chicago, Illinois, and many others.

Among the many engraved invitations received by members for attendance at concerts and social events was the following:

The Wednesday Club
of St. Louis
invites you to be present
at a lecture by
Mr. Henry E. Krehbiel,
of New York

on

"Folksongs in America."

in honor of

National Federation of Musical Clubs,

May the third, at three o'clock.

Cor. of Grand and Franklin Avenues.

2

At the invitation of one of the largest women's musical organizations, the Fortnightly Musical of Cleveland, Ohio, the National Federation of Musical Clubs held its second Biennial Convention and Music Festival in that city April 30 – May 3, 1901 in the Colonial Club House.

"Two years ago the first Biennial Convention set the first milestone on a road which we had walked but a short way. We came away with renewed enthusiasm, fresh purpose and high ideals," were the words with which Mrs. John Howard Webster greeted the opening session of the convention. Mrs. Webster who was first vice president of the National Federation of Music Clubs and convention chairman found herself in the dual capacity – the convention chairman and as first vice president, the presiding officer. The national president, Mrs. Edwin Uhl was prevented from attending because of the death of her husband. Again, as at the beginning, so in the ending of Mrs. Uhl's three year administration, fate prevented her from being present.

The Federation during this biennium had reached a peak of 128 clubs in thirty-three states with a membership of 11,086, and the treasurer's report showed a healthy growth with $1239.04 receipts in club dues.

The first federation pins were sold at this convention – a total of sixteen. Mrs. Charles B. Kelsey purchased the first pin.

Not only was there an increase of clubs in the states, but enthusiasm had spread to Canada, and their citizens were asking to be admitted. In attendance were officers of the Matinee Musical of Montreal, and they, along with a club in Kingston, Ontario wished membership in the National Federation.

The first scholarships to be offered by the Federation came at this second biennial when the D/Angelo Bergh School of Singing of New York City offered four – each worth $250, covering four months instruction to candidates with "marked talent" under thirty years of age.

The convention programs were outstanding; excellent programs presented by the host club, the Fortnightly Musical, as well as the Rubinstein Club of Cleveland; three concerts by the Pittsburgh Symphony Orchestra under the baton of its distinguished conductor, Victor Herbert, and featuring the American pianist, Madame Fanny Bloomfield-Zeisler. The third concert brought to a brilliant close the 1901 Biennium Music Festival when the beloved Madame Ernestine Schumann-Heink was presented in roles from Wagner's operas *Tristan and Isolde* and *Das Rheingold*.

The Cleveland Biennial gave to the Federation its second president, Mrs. John Howard Webster (Helen Curtis). Mrs. Webster was one of the founders of the Fortnightly Musical and was its president when the Call came for the permanent organization of the National Federation in Chicago. She attended as a delegate from the Fortnightly Musical.

3

On May 19, 1903 the third Biennial Convention of the National Federation of Musical Clubs opened in "Powers Hall" in Rochester, New York with the national president, Mrs. John Howard Webster presiding. Mrs. John N. Steele, president of the host club, the Tuesday Musicale of Rochester, extended a welcome to Rochester. She pointed out that the organization of the Tuesday Musicale preceded the organization of the National Federation but "gladly" admitted that much of the success of the Tuesday Musicale was due to the Federation's "influence and broader vision."

Members of eighteen federated music clubs from twelve states accepted the invitation of the Biennial Program Committee to furnish a musical program. These member groups were presented in concerts on

May 19 and 20, 1903.

Concluding the musical program of the federated clubs, the host club presented an evening concert featuring a "stirring performance" of *Hiawatha's Wedding Feast* by Samuel Coleridge Taylor.

The American Symphony Orchestra under the baton of Sam Franko, presented an evening of symphony music featuring Madame Gertrude Stein, soloist. Closing the third biennial convention on May 22, the delegates were honored with a piano recital by the eminent pianist, Rafael Josefly.

Mrs. John Howard Webster refused re-election for a long residence abroad; thus ending six years of intensive, active service to the National Federation of Musical Clubs during its formative years.

4

We are amazed at the wisdom, courage and vision our first presidents and their official families possessed! As members of the Federation our eulogy to them is best said in our Federation Collect – "Through us, as channels of Thy grace, may this blessed legacy be shared with all mankind."

Each of the biennial conventions has been important and unique to the history of the Federation – some more than others. The fourth convention in Denver, Colorado was one of those. On the morning of June 7,1905 the first national vice president, Mrs. Russell Ripley Dorr, presiding in the absence of the president, Mrs. Winifred B. Collins, who was ill, opened the convention and responded to the address of welcome given by Mrs. George McCartney, vice president of the host club, the Tuesday Musicale of Denver.

This convention was unique in the action taken to amend for the first time, the Certificate of Incorporation granted by the State of Illinois in 1898. The convention in executive session, voted to strike from the "object" – Section II which read: "Constitutions of clubs applying for membership must show that they are officered by women only, and their purpose is universal culture." Maude Frey, recording secretary notified the Secretary of State, of Illinois, of the action taken June 10, 1905, and on October 7, 1905, Mrs. J. E. Kinney, national president, affixed the corporate seal of the Federation to the Certificate as amended. For the first time the Federation would admit clubs officered by men.

One of the most startling and dramatic events came in the closing hour when Mrs. C. B. Kelsey of Grand Rapids, and one who was to become the sixth national president, rose and said:

"Realizing that the proof of the adage 'In union there is strength' is older than the Republic of Rome and as enduring as even our glorious American Republic, and believing that the work of the National Federation of Musical Clubs will be greatly enlarged and made more efficient in its own immediate and individual sphere by affiliating with the General Federation of Women's Clubs, I therefore move the adoption of the following: 'Resolved, that the National Federation of Musical Clubs become affiliated with the General Federation of Women's Clubs.'"

The motion was seconded, and although a "strenuous" effort was made to induce members to approve affiliation, it met with even more "strenuous" opposition. The motion was lost by a decisive vote.

This remarkable occurrence demonstrated that those present had not forgotten the Founders and their abiding faith in the purpose of the National Federation of Musical Clubs, as well as their dedication to this purpose – to make it the one organization in America whose sole purpose is to raise musical standards and promote musical opportunity. Today – the Federation has no apology to make!

The late Theodore Thomas, who had passed away on January 4th of 1905 was eloquently eulogized and a memorial resolution passed in honor of his memory:

"Whereas, We, together with the people of Chicago and the cultured of the entire nation, have suffered irreparable loss in the death of Mr. Theodore Thomas; and

"Whereas, This has brought deep distress and affliction upon our Honorary President, therefore, be it

"Resolved, that the National Federation of Musical Clubs, the beloved child of Mrs. Theodore Thomas, extend to her our deepest sympathy and our loving greetings; and further be it

"Resolved, That the National Federation of Musical Clubs give expression to its adoption of these resolutions by sending a copy of them to Mrs. Thomas."

The invitation of the Beethoven Club of Memphis, Tennessee to hold the next biennial in that "hospitable Southern city" was accepted enthusiastically.

Mrs. Dorr was elected and introduced as the fourth president of the National Federation of Music Clubs.

Shortly after the Denver Biennial Mrs. Kinney resigned the Second

Vice Presidency to which she had been elected.
Mrs. Dorr served two months and resigned the presidency the last of
July by mail ballot. On the same ballot she nominated her successor.
Her resignation was accepted by the Board of Management and Mrs. J.
E. Kinney of Denver was elected the fifth president.
This was the Federation's first mail ballot.

5

The highlight of the 1907 Biennial Convention in Memphis, Tennessee during the administration of Mrs. Julius Eugene Kinney, was the emphasis on American music, and American Music was made a department of the Federation. A resolution had been passed whereby there would be submitted to the clubs at this convention the plan of placing the Federation behind the American composer and artist in a helpful way. This resolution was carried unanimously. The American Music Department was established and a standing committee, consisting of Mrs. Susan B. Walker, chairman, Mrs. Emerson Brush, Mrs. D. A. Campbell, and Mr. Arthur Farwell, was appointed to develop the work.

The establishment of the biennial competition for American born composers seemed the best way. The Federation had no false hopes or mistaken ideas about the value of the works that would be submitted, but they knew there were men and women in our country striving to express themselves through the art they loved, and it was their wish for them to know and feel that the music clubs of America were glad to give their works recognition and encouragement.

One winning composer said, "It is not only the prizes in the monetary way that appeal to us... but it is the thought that there is a strong body of splendid, earnest women, lovers of music, back of us, watching with interest the growth and development of our work. That is the comfort and inspiration."

How little did those dedicated ladies attending the Memphis convention realize the sound waves of American music which they set in motion would reverberate from the shores of the Pacific to the roaring waves of the Atlantic for generations to come.

It was voted that the National Federation of Musical Clubs would offer its first prizes for composition – three prizes in three different classifications, to be awarded at the Biennial Convention two years hence in Grand Rapids, Michigan in 1909.

AN ERA OF BEAUTY AND GRANDEUR

Stan Hywet Hall

1

Members of the National Federation of Music Clubs point with pride to the 16th century English Tudor mansion, Stan Hywet Hall (Stan Hee~wet) in Akron, Ohio, the home of the Federation's ninth president, Mrs. Frank A. Seiberling (Gertrude Penfield), for it was here that much of the history of the Federation was written.

Stan Hywet is Anglo-Saxon meaning "stone quarry" which referred to the rock from which the mansion's basement was carved, and to the private quarry nearby.

The magnificent English Tudor Manor house was built by Frank A. Seiberling, founder of the world's largest rubber company, the Goodyear Tire and Rubber Company, and the Seiberling Rubber Company. Because of his interest in the grace and dignity portrayed in the Elizabethan era of English culture, the Seiberlings visited England, drawing inspiration from Haddon Hall, Wyngate and Ockwell Manor, thirty miles from London. From the beginning Stan Hywet was intended as a musical and cultural center.

On an original 3,000 acre estate the "castle" was begun in 1911 and completed in 1915 at a cost of $2,000,000.

The furnishings were acquired from a dozen castles in England and Europe – antique silver, della Robbia plaques, 16th century Flemish tapestries, priceless original paintings and sculptures, rare porcelains, floors of teakwood and rosewood – treasure upon treasure, seen as one wandered from room to room in the 65 room Stan Hywet Hall.

The Music Room was considered by many architects and interior designers to be one of the most beautiful rooms in America. This room, seating 250, was the setting of three meetings of the Board of Managers of the National Federation of Music Clubs during and before the presidency of Mrs. Seiberling. The 18th century harpsichord, acquired from

Ockwell Manor was once owned by Handel and played by Haydn. There is an old Aeolian organ, and the grand piano is the same piano played by Paderewski. Casting a glow over all the beauty and eloquence are crystal chandeliers with hanging prisms of amber and amethyst.

The crest inscribed above the main entrance of the mansion, "Non Nobis Solum" meaning "Not for us Alone" was translated into reality by the Seiberling family. Four presidents of the United States were entertained here; Will Rogers swapped stories with his industrial host; and from here James Melton announced his engagement. It was in the Music Room that Paderewski, Percy Grainger, Marian Anderson, Leopold Stokowski, Madame Schumann-Heink and many other international artists performed and were guests. The Seiberling daughter, Irene Seiberling (Mrs. Milton Harrison) tells the story, "I shall never forget the night that Paderewski stole in here (Music Room) in the dark and sat at the grand piano, moonlight streaming over his shoulder, playing the *Moonlight Sonata.*"

It was in the Music Room that Mrs. Seiberling (NFMC president, 1919-1921) entertained members of the National Board of Managers for the first time on December 4-7, 1917, only two years after the completion of Stan Hywet Hall. The 11:00 o'clock meeting was called to order by the president, Mrs. A. J. Oschner. Present were Mesdames Oschner, Hinckle, Davis, Oberne, Leonard, Morris, Steele, Middelschutte, Seiberling, MacArthur, Yager, Campbell, and Foster.

After Mrs. Seiberling was elected the Federation's ninth president in 1919 at Peterborough, New Hampshire, she again entertained the Board of Managers at Stan Hywet on October 25-31, 1919, and on November 10-16, 1920. The meetings always opened with the group singing songs as *Blest be the Tie that Binds, Come Thou Fount of Every Blessing, Onward Christian Soldiers, Battle Hymn of the Republic, America* and others. They usually closed with *God be with you 'til we Meet Again* or *Auld Lang Syne.*

Federation history was written in the Music Room of Stan Hywet Hall. The Board voted to give "$2,000 from the national treasury for the erection of permanent seats for the Outdoor Theatre at Peterborough, New Hampshire to serve as a memorial of the 1919 Biennial Convention"; Mrs. Seiberling called attention to the beautiful gavel of ivory and gold presented to the Federation by the Fortnightly Musical Club of Cleveland, Ohio "in honor of three national presidents this club has given the National Federation of Music Clubs"; the official music clubs magazine, *Official Bulletin* was born at Stan Hywet in the "wee hours." Could the Board of Managers in this beautiful setting, have been looking through "rose colored glasses" when they voted to offer $5,000 for the best musical setting for an oratorio, *The Apocalypse* – a project that proved very hard to finance?

The minutes of November 10, 1920 at the Stan Hywet meeting named Mrs. Robert I. Woodside, Greenville, South Carolina, "representing South Carolina" as one of those in attendance. Mrs. Woodside, who was one of the founders of the South Carolina Federation of Music Clubs in 1920, was to tell this writer thirty-five years later:

> "... In 1919... Mrs. Lucas (Mrs. Cora Cox Lucas, first president of the South Carolina Federation of Music Clubs) asked me to represent the state at a National Board Meeting in Akron, Ohio. ... We were most splendidly entertained by Mrs. Seiberling who was our national president. Her home was, and still is, one of the twelve handsomest homes in America. All of our meetings and the concerts of an entire week were held in her Music Room which is 40 by 100 feet, and in which she had several grand pianos, and a magnificent Aeolian organ. It was after my attendance at this meeting that South Carolina became affiliated with the National Federation of Music Clubs."

Mrs. Seiberling attended an organizational meeting of the South Carolina Federation in Columbia, South Carolina, in 1921 and the convention in Greenville in 1923 when she was the house guest of Mrs. Woodside.

Stan Hywet, today is a symbol of beauty and grandeur of an era which probably never will return.

Mrs. Seiberling in the garden of her home, Stan Hywet in Akron, Ohio.

BACKSTAGE

1

History records that about twenty years after the organization in Chicago in 1898 there arose confusion and misunderstandings. Many women claimed the honor of being recorded as a founder of the National Federation of Music Clubs.

Following Mrs. Sutro's defeat for the presidency in Chicago in 1898 she was not heard from again in the Federation until Dr. Frances Elliott Clark observed and called to the attention of Mrs. Russell Ripley Dorr, NFMC historian, that the American Supplement to *Grove's Dictionary of Music* carried the information that Mrs. Theodore Sutro of New York City was the founder of the National Federation of Music Clubs.

Immediately Mrs. Dorr corresponded with Dr. Waldo S. Pratt, editor of the *Grove's American Supplement*. Dr. Pratt replied that his information was derived from the statements made in the first volume of *Who's Who in America*, and in *Baker's Dictionary of Musicians*, third edition, 1919. He added that he was quite unaware that these assertions were "matters of dispute," and he wished a better statement, so that in the future edition the matter might be set right.

He had accepted the statement "of the last mentioned author, and of Mrs. Sutro herself as truthful and therefore made no effort to confirm them". Mrs. Dorr requested a conference with Dr. Pratt at which time she might show him evidence to the contrary – in letters, newspaper articles, and written statements of those who served the temporary organization. Mrs. Clark suggested the matter be referred to Mr. Lawerence Erb, Director, Metropolitan School of Music. Mr. Erb wrote Dr. Pratt, in a letter dated May 12, 1923, "The idea of a Federation seems to have originated with Mr. and Mrs. Theodore Thomas...."

In Mrs. Dorr's words, a meeting "was arranged and all proof was laid before him. After several days of careful study he was convinced *Grove's Dictionary*, *Who's Who* and *Baker's Dictionary* were all in error... The evidence plainly disclosed that six women, Mrs. Chandler Starr of Rockford, Illinois; Miss Frances Marion Ralston of St. Louis, Missouri; Mrs.

James Pedersen of New York City; Miss Rosalie Balmer Smith of St. Louis, Missouri; Mrs. Russell Ripley Dorr of St. Paul, Minnesota; and Mrs. Charles Virgil, of Long Island, New York were the founders...."
    Mrs. Dorr tried to get the information changed in *Grove's Dictionary*, but said she would make no effort to correct it in *Who's Who* and *Baker's Dictionary*. Mrs. Dorr was later on occasions introduced as a "founder of the National Federation of Music Clubs."
    In her "Excerpts from Reports of the National Historian, Mrs. Russell Dorr", the Secretary of the National Federation of Music Clubs, 1935-1939, stated "I take it that only six persons referred to by Mrs. Dorr, assembled for the organization. There are some discrepancies in Mrs. Dorr's reports".

2
The daughter of Mrs. Edwin F. Uhl, first NFMC president, claimed that her mother was the founder of the Federation. In a letter from Lucy Uhl Wood to "My dear friend", dated October 23, 1919, Mrs. Wood said:

"... I have been trying for nearly two years to get in touch with the Historian of the NFMC in order to give her the data about mother's connection with the starting of the Federation for I understand that there was some confusion or misunderstanding about it all.
    "I happen to be the only one who can furnish reliable information on the subject... At that time (Columbian Exposition) mother and Mrs. Thomas, after talking the matter over... decided it would be an excellent idea to try to form a Federation of Musical Clubs... I have letters pertaining to the effort on her (Mrs. Uhl's) part, including one from Mrs. Thomas stating that she had no time nor strength to give to the enterprise, but gave her hearty approval and urged mother to do it. Therefore, mother is alone responsible for the initial movement to formulate the NFMC....
    "If there are any questions Mrs. Dorr would like to ask me, I would be very glad to write her....

3

Ten years of research for this history have failed to reveal ANY evidence indicating that prior to the Music Festival at the World's Columbian Exposition in 1893 there ever had been any thought or action taken toward organizing the music clubs in the United States into a National Federation. Neither is there any evidence that any of the aforementioned "founders" had expressed any thoughts or taken any action in this direction.

Rose Fay Thomas, president of the Amateur Musical Club of Chicago, envisioned the possibility of inviting all of the music clubs in the United States to convene for a Musical Festival with the possibility of uniting in a Federation to work for one common goal – American music. Working with Mrs. Thomas as Vice-Chairman was Mrs. William S. Warren, also a member of the Amateur Musical Club.

Mrs. Thomas secured the names and addresses of every music club in the United States, and each was sent a special invitation to attend the Festival.

During these four days the ladies in attendance were inspired and expressed their feelings that from this convention there might be a permanent organization – a National Federation. All of this was evidenced in the many clubs' tributes and expressions of appreciation to Mrs. Thomas. The seed had been planted. It was she who had "laid the groundwork" for what was to come later.

Rose Fay Thomas was a lovely, gracious and talented lady – yet very modest in her many accomplishments – preferring always to remain out of the spotlight. She wished no recognition for her accomplishments.

The following is excerpts from a letter written by Mrs. Thomas to Mrs. Helen Harrison Mills, Editor of the *Official Bulletin*, dated October 5, 1925. This was written in explanation to a certain point in Mrs. Dorr's (historian) story which had appeared in a previous copy of the *Bulletin*.

"The facts of the case are as follows: I had gathered together delegations from the Women's Amateur Musical Clubs, of all sections of America, at the Chicago World's Fair in 1893 for a four-day convention. It was the first time these clubs had been brought into association with each other and the meetings proved so interesting and helpful that at the closing session Mrs. Edwin F. Uhl, of Grand Rapids, suggested that the temporary organization thus called together should be perpetuated in a National Federation of Women's Musical Clubs.

"I have never claimed for myself the honor of being the founder of the Federation. In fact, I hardly think that anyone of us could justly make that claim. My part in the work was to find the clubs and interest them in taking part in the Chicago convention. Mrs. Uhl proposed to perpetuate the convention in the form of a National Federation, and took the initial steps for its creation. Mrs. Sutro and her committee continued the work and brought about the meeting for organizing and elections. Each of us, *and our committee members*, shared in the great work, and to me it is a pleasanter thought that so many talented women in all parts of America united in its organization than if it had been the achievement of a single "founder." There is glory enough for many founders, as well as for those brilliant women who have carried the little Federation of 1898 to its present splendid and important development in the musical world."

The Federation would take none of the honor from those brave women who played such a vital and indispensable role in the early days of the Federation, for without them and their perseverance the National Federation would not be the great organization it is today.

For one hundred years, both Federation members and non-members alike have honored and revered the memory of Rose Fay Thomas as the Founder of the National Federation of Music Clubs. And to her is due all the credit of envisioning, planning and executing that first convention when the idea of a National Federation of Musical Clubs originated. News periodicals through these 100 years have given recognition to the fact that Rose Fay Thomas was the Founder of the National Federation:

"The idea of a Federation of Women's Musical Clubs had its origin in the convention under Mrs. Theodore Thomas at the World's Fair in Chicago in 1893, but until now there had been no opportune time for carrying it into execution."
—*New York Tribune*, June 29, 1897

"Set in motion by Mrs. Theodore Thomas at the Columbian Exposition, a great wave of musical activity in the line of women's musical clubs has swept over the country."
—*Etude Magazine*, February 1898

"The national organization (NFMC) effected in 1893 (by Mrs. Thomas)... grew in power and influence under splendid executive administration."
—*Delineator*, September 1910

"The National Federation of Women's Musical Clubs was the natural outcome of the convention I (Mrs. Thomas) had organized for the World's Fair."

—The Musical Monitor, 1913

"Many readers may have overlooked the interesting fact that the promotion of American Music was first fostered by Mrs. Theodore Thomas, wife of the orchestra leader, who founded the National Federation of Music Clubs."

—Chicago Tribune, December 9, 1938

"More than 300 leaders in Chicago's musical world met yesterday at a White Breakfast... held in memory of the founder of the Federation and wife of the first conductor of the Chicago Symphony Orchestra."

—Chicago Daily News, June 15, 1940

That seed sown in 1893 might be likened to a grain of rice, which when cast into the water, floats for a time, apparently without much purpose, then sinks out of sight as if lost forever. In time it bursts up through the water to greet the early springtime, without effort, thought or ingenuity. It grows into a beautiful, tall, flowery, grassy plant – in due time bearing fruit.

That "grain of rice" thrown into the water by Rose Fay Thomas in 1893 at the World's Fair, "floated for a time" and then with one of the greatest depressions this country has ever known – the great Panic of 1893 – it "sank out of sight as if lost forever."

In 1898 that seed "burst without effort, thought or ingenuity" to grow into one of the most beautiful "flowering plants" of all time, working for the promotion of music – The National Federation of Music Clubs.

PART FOUR

Extending Our Horizons

CHAPTER ONE

GREAT INVESTMENTS

Junior Division

1

According to Miss Etelka Evans, NFMC Junior Counselor, 1937-1941, "The inspiration for the Junior Division seems to have come from the editorial work, done by Mrs. Anna Heurermann Hamilton of Missouri, for the Junior sections of music periodicals such as the *Musical Observer* of New York and *The Clef* of Kansas City, during the years 1896-1916." The Junior work of the National Federation of Music Clubs began in 1902 during the administration of the second president, Mrs. Curtis Webster when she began the Junior movement with the first recorded junior club – the Vivace Junior Group, sponsored by the Beethoven Club of Memphis, Tennessee.

It was during the presidency of Mrs. A. J. Oschner, 1915-1919, that the Federation acquired an official medium for its publicity in *The Musical Monitor*, and Mrs. Hamilton became the editor of the Children's Construction Page.

In 1916 Mrs. Hamilton suggested to Mrs. Oschner that a Junior Division be made a part of the National Federation. One year later in 1917, at the Biennial Convention in Birmingham, Alabama, Mrs. Hamilton presented the recommendation that a Junior Division be incorporated as a part of the National Federation of Music Clubs. The recommendation "appealed to Mrs. W. D. Steele of Missouri", who was at that time the NFMC chairman of the Department of Education.

At the second meeting of the Missouri Federation of Music Clubs in 1919, a Junior Division was organized, thus making Missouri the first state to include Junior work as a department. Mrs. Hamilton became the first state Junior Counselor.

It was in that same year – 1919, that the president of the Missouri Federation, Mrs. J. H. Rodes, brought before the Biennial Convention in Peterborough, New Hampshire, Missouri's slogan, "Junior Clubs are

Missouri's Speciality." She reported that "twelve clubs at the first meeting now have increased to twenty-five." As a result of Mrs. Rodes report, the convention voted to "recognize Junior work as a regular department of the organization" and thus the Junior Division of the National Federation of Music Clubs "was born in the summer of 1919." Mrs. Grace Porterfield Polk of Florida was appointed the first National Junior Counselor.

At the Davenport, Iowa Biennial in 1921, two hundred- twenty-seven clubs were reported in twenty-six states. Mrs. William John Hall of St. Louis, succeeded Mrs. Polk as the second Junior Counselor.

The Department of Education of the Junior Division had its beginning in the articles written by Mrs. Hamilton for the Children's Construction Page of *The Musical Monitor*. These were considered to be the Official Course of Study for the Junior Division. In 1921 during the counselorship of Mrs. Hall, the first Course of Study to be printed was written by Dr. Frances Elliott Clark.

At Missouri's third annual convention in 1921 Mrs. Hall inaugurated the first state Junior Contest. In that same year, Junior Contests, or the Junior Festivals as they are known today, were established as a national event. The following year in 1922, the South Atlantic District held the first annual Junior Contests.

Mrs. Hamilton was the "leading spirit" in the first steps toward national Junior growth.

In 1937 at the Indianapolis Biennial Convention Mrs. Phyllis Lations Hanson recommended that the official title of the "Junior Contests" be changed to "Competitive Festivals", and that the "rating" rather than the "winner" system be adopted officially. "Competitive Festivals" remained the name until 1961 when it was dropped and became the "Junior Festivals".

At this same meeting in Asheville, North Carolina in 1961, Mrs. Doris Allbee Humphrey suggested the 5-3-1 GOLD TROPHY CUP PLAN for the Junior Festivals, and it was listed for the first time in the 1962-1964 *Junior Festival Bulletin*. The theme for the festivals became, "Not to earn a prize, nor defeat an opponent, but to pace each other on the road to excellence." The festivals always have had as a goal the highest standard of achievement.

In 1925 Miss Julia E. Williams of New Jersey was appointed NFMC Junior Counselor by Mrs. Edgar Stillman Kelley, president, and it was she who began the *Junior Bulletin* in 1927. It retained the name *Junior Bulletin* until 1939 when it became the *Junior Magazine*.

In February 1928 a Harmonica Department was added to the Junior

Division. Harmonica Bands became very popular with the Juniors. In 1929 the Harmonica Band of Dayton, Ohio performed for the Ohio state convention playing *Sextette* and Percy Grainger's *Country Gardens*.

In Pennsylvania there were thirty-seven Rotary Club Harmonica Bands who competed in a contest at the Allentown 50th District Rotary Club Conference.

The work of these bands was combined with church services, brass bands and symphony orchestras. A Harmonica Jubilee was held in Philadelphia to aid financially the Philadelphia Harmonica Band, its summer camp, and the Harmonica Movement.

In addition to the above mentioned Harmonica Bands, others noted in the 1929 *Junior Bulletin* were:

> Westbrook, Maine Harmonica Band
> Northside Junior High School Harmonica Band, Richmond,
> Virginia
> Dothan, Alabama Harmonica Band which played at the
> Alabama State Convention

In 1928, the *Official Junior Song*, with words by Mrs. Abbie L. Snoddy and music by Mrs. Anna Heurermann Hamilton, was adopted. In 1932 Miss Julia E. Williams wrote the Junior Pledge, and had it printed and distributed. In 1938 the Junior Collect, by Mrs. Thomas J. Cole of Amory, Mississippi, was adopted. In 1939 the *Junior Hymn* – words by Irena Foreman Williams and music arranged by Mrs. Crosby Adams – was adopted for use in the Junior Division.

The design of the Junior pin, is based on the design of the Senior pin. In 1942 a musical setting for the Junior Collect was written by Olive F. Conway and adopted by the Federation.

The first exhibit of *State Scrapbooks* at a National Convention was at the 1931 San Francisco Biennial when Texas gave $25.00 in gold for first prize, calling it the *Grace Godard Prize* in honor of the National Counselor.

During World War II the contributions of the Juniors were outstanding – many junior clubs contributed musical instruments to the war efforts. The Allentown, Pennsylvania Junior Club musically equipped a ship to bring back wounded servicemen. About $300 was received which was sent to the Federation. This purchased for the ship, four victrolas ($44.40), one record kit ($55.88), one chaplain's kit ($12.50), and one Gretsch kit (musical instruments). The surplus was used toward the equipment of another ship.

Equipment for each ship consisted of an instrument kit, including a guitar, banjo, ukulele, violin, two and one-half dozen ocarinas, twelve nose flutes, and the requisite song books, pitch pipes and replacement parts; also four phonographs with needles, 100 popular records, a set of classical records, and an album of religious records at a cost of $237.79.

During the restoration of the Eden-Talbott House in Indianapolis, Indiana, in 1979-1980 as the Official Headquarters of the National Federation of Music Clubs, the Junior Division, under the leadership of Mrs. Doyle P. Smith (Ruth) of Jackson, Mississippi, National Junior Counselor, 1979-1983, raised $3,000 which paid for the pictures of all the national presidents to be hung in the Presidents' Parlour. Twenty-four pictures were hung, and three have been added since that time.

Since the beginning in 1919, the purpose of the Junior Division has remained the same: "to bring together young people for regular group study of music, for performance before others, and for social enjoyment; to train future club leaders; to cultivate courteous and appreciative audiences; to stimulate interest in creative music; to provide incentive for high standards of performance through festival events; to encourage service through music; and to broaden the vision, and the ability of members through understanding of, and cooperation with the state and national goals."

Thus – the formative years of the Junior Division were built on a firm foundation. Many wonderful achievements have been undertaken and accomplished, which at the beginning of the twentieth century was only "a toddler at the Federation's knee"- its strength and stature having grown from one club in 1902 to approximately 5,000 clubs today. It is in looking to the future that the Federation's faith and trust is placed in the Juniors, for they will be the wise and dedicated Federation leaders of tomorrow.

Some of the most outstanding achievements which have been undertaken follow.

2

One of the earliest projects undertaken by the Junior Division was begun seven years after the Division was organized – the Children's Crusade for the MacDowell Colony.

Aaron Copland tells of the founding of the Colony which is located in southern New Hampshire, a place described as "tranquil and serene."

"In 1906 the American composer and pianist, Edward MacDowell, had expressed the wish to found a center where artists in various fields could live and work without interruption, exchanging ideas with one another in a tranquil country setting. Mrs. Marian MacDowell, also a pianist, had purchased a summer place in Peterborough, New Hampshire in 1896, where the couple spent their summers. 'Hillcrest', as the place was called, seemed the perfect setting for an artist colony."

During MacDowell's last illness he fretted unceasingly at the thought that his beloved old farm with Deep Woods and Log Cabin, soon would fall into the hands of strangers. "If only in someway it could be kept," he said, "to give to other artists the joy and inspiration it has given to me." Mrs. MacDowell made a solemn promise that his wishes would be carried out.

In 1907, a year before the composer's death, Mrs. MacDowell established the Colony and "it was she who was responsible for everything," said Aaron Copland. In a handwritten letter to the Juniors from Mrs. MacDowell, written in 1947, she wrote:

"Thank you for your warm letter, and I am going to jump into the subject you wanted me to tell about... THE LOG CABIN.

"We bought Hillcrest in 1896... Hillcrest alone seemed all anyone could desire, but... I said to myself – 'conditions are still not quite perfect for composing.'

"I talked it over with a carpenter (and foreman)... and we decided that we were going to surprise MacDowell in 1897 with an isolated workshop... a log cabin... on a small hillside among great pines which were there long before the white settlers came to Peterborough... so often, I went ahead, not quite sure where I was going to find the money for it, but of course I did!... Some of you who saw it later may remember how MacDowell wrote one name on the hearth while the cement floor was still soft and damp.

"Of course I was scolded as well as praised for what I had done... but he was happy at what the little building was going to mean to him... He really had it so few years, but in it he wrote so much of his music best known to the world.

"This place was the seed from which grew the MacDowell Colony. MacDowell learned to know how much such an isolated workshop could mean to creative writers....

"With warm affection and love to all of the Juniors."

Dear to the hearts of Federation members – and in particular the Juniors – through the years, has been the MacDowell Colony as has been evidenced through support and gifts.

That first support came before the Junior Division was "born" – when in Birmingham, Alabama in 1917, at the Biennial Convention, the Federation voted to hold the 1919 Biennial Convention in Peterborough, New Hampshire. Later at the Board meeting in the Music Room at Stan Hywet, the home of Mrs. Frank A. Seiberling in Akron, Ohio, on February 4, 1917, Mrs. MacDowell told the members of the "interest manifested by citizens and musicians of Peterborough... her plans for the entertainment... and what it would mean to the MacDowell Association to come in close touch with an organization which was represented by such a noble body of women."

Upon a motion by Mrs. Seiberling, the following December, 1917, the Board voted "that $2,000 be appropriated... for the erection of permanent seats for the Outdoor Theatre at Peterborough, New Hampshire, and that these seats serve as a memorial of the 1919 Biennial Convention." It was at this same meeting that Mrs. Albert J. Oschner, national president, asked for the "privilege of developing a department whose chief object would be to assist Mrs. MacDowell in carrying on the work of the MacDowell Memorial Association, and that she (Mrs. Oschner) be the controlling head for five years." The Board acceded to Mrs. Oschner's proposals, but before long misunderstandings and hard feelings arose. Mrs. Oschner wished the monies received sent directly to the MacDowell League, and the Federation wished contributions to go through the national treasurer.

At the meeting in Chicago in 1918 Mrs. MacDowell reported progress on the permanent seats and it was voted to have a "strong box placed in the cornerstone of the permanent seats, containing the names of members of the Board and such archives as may be deemed valuable."

The Peterborough convention was in the nature of a pilgrimage to Edward MacDowell's home. The official opening came on Monday afternoon, June 30th in the Town House of Peterborough with President Mrs. Albert J. Oschner presiding. The week was filled with outstanding speakers and musicians, with MacDowell's music taking precedent throughout. Highlighting the week's program was a tea given for the 500 guests by Mrs. MacDowell at her beloved "Hillcrest", and the Peterborough Pageant seen on Tuesday and Thursday afternoons.

The program of the Pageant, originally produced in 1910 was written and arranged by Professor George P. Baker of Harvard University. With one single exception of that for the Irish dance, the music was drawn entirely from the works of Edward MacDowell. Performed against a backdrop of tall pines, forest glades the stage wings, the earth the stage floor, through which poured the scarlet sun, Peterborough's sons and daughters brought to life eleven scenes drawn from the history of the sleepy little town and its people. One guest said he "had never been so profoundly moved by the stage spectacle as he was by this presented by the homely folk of a little New England town."

Sunday afternoon witnessed the dedication of the Pageant Stage seats presented by the Federation to the Edward MacDowell Memorial Association. The gift was presented by Mrs. Oschner in "a gracious address" to which Mrs. MacDowell responded. Dr. Norman Bridge outlined the work of the Association, after which Christine Miller sang a "touching solo" of the third stanza of the *Battle Hymn of the Republic*.

The bronze memorial tablet which was the personal gift of Mrs. Frank A. Seiberling, was presented by Mrs. Seiberling, to be placed on the peristyle, and bearing the inscription:

"A Testimonial from the National Federation of Musical Clubs, in loving Remembrance of Edward MacDowell and His Ideals. The Eleventh Biennial, June 30 - July 5, 1919."

Mr. William D. Paddock, sculptor of the tablet, and Mr. F. Edson Moon and Mr. George Edwards, contractors, were given words of appreciation.

The August 1919 issue of *The Musical Monitor* carried "The Perfect Tribute" to Edward MacDowell, for back of all of this was MacDowell's "pressing spirit."

THE PERFECT TRIBUTE

The spirit of Edward MacDowell pervaded the thoughts and actions of the Biennial week. So it was altogether fitting and proper that at the week's end homage was paid America's noblest voice in music. With heads veiled in white the delegates gathered in the twilight around the composer's final resting place. Bowed heads spoke unspeakable adoration while the orchestra under Mr. Barlow's direction played the "Constancy."

But adoration merged into jubilant song and "Onward, Christian Soldiers" woke the hills. MacDowell's spirit marched in majesty to his own "A. D. 1620" and in pantheistic love "To a Wild Rose."

Night fell and silence succeeded, silence broken only by the natural sounds of MacDowell's own hillsides or by the smothered sob of some indistinguishable individual moved for the moment by that moment's impressiveness.

Then swelling from orchestra and assembled voices rose the solemn lines of "Nearer, My God, To Thee," and to its singing the multitude moved in a long recessional down the leafy pathway that leads back to the sterner walks of life.

There is a just sufficiency in all things. In every manifestation of reverence for the great that are passed the danger line is that of over-indulgence. Be it, therefore, to the everlasting credit of those who that Friday evening in the shadow of New Hampshire hills paid homage to MacDowell's shrine that they at no time violated the spirit of poetic reverence. Not Christian Soldiers alone and Nearer to God—for the moment at least—but holding in the love of nature communion with her inmost self, they paid the perfect tribute.

Due to the increase in prices brought on by World War II the convention ended with an unexpected deficit, and the amphitheatre seats cost more than twice the amount estimated – approximately $5,000. It was not until two years later, in 1921, that the Federation through individual pledges and a loan, was able to pay the remainder of the amount owed to Mrs. MacDowell. And – the MacDowell League, headed by Mrs. Oschner, was dissolved after only four years.

In 1926 when the Junior Division was only seven years old, the MacDowell Children's Crusade was organized by Mrs. Edgar Stillman Kelley, national president, for the preservation of the Log Cabin and the grave of MacDowell. She was assisted by Miss Nan Stephens of Atlanta for the Seniors and Miss Julia Williams of New Jersey for the Juniors. Each Junior was asked to give a penny or a nickel. The workers were called "Crusaders", but after the first amount was given a Crusader became a "Minnesinger", and the second amount made the Minnesinger a "Minstrel". "Troubadours" were appointed to collect the money. The largest contributor to the fund was Mrs. Leonidas R. Dingus of Lexington, Kentucky who gave $1,000.

One of the triumphant features of the Children's Crusade was the MacDowell Festival at Willow Grove Park, Pennsylvania. According to the *Official Bulletin* of October 1927, "such a large number of children musicians has never before assembled at any one time and place, and the elaborate preparations assured the tremendous success of this significant music event. The 5,000 seats, although priced at only twenty-five cents each, netted the cause a considerable sum." The music of MacDowell, alone, was featured on the program.

In Mrs. Kelley's *Memoirs* she wrote:

"It is not fitting that I should here indulge in too much comment on my own activities (the most of the *Memoirs* was about her illustrious composer husband Edgar Stillman Kelley), but one of my projects was a penny drive among our junior club members for a special MacDowell Fund. The announcement of this drive swept the country. Real pennies rolled into my office in great quantities, besides checks, money orders, etc.

"The president of a Boys Junior Club in the West sent their pennies in a cigar box by express, with a note saying that their pennies had been gathered in various ways, and that they had insisted on sending 'real pennies,' not a piece of paper with the amount written on it.

"Ten thousand dollars was gathered in three months. In fact,

the little copper discs would still be rolling in had they not been
stopped by the MacDowell Colony Treasurer (and wisely) for
fear of lessening the interest in much needed larger gifts."

As a result of one years work, $10,000 was presented to Mrs. Mac-
Dowell at the 1927 Biennial Convention in Chicago. In 1934 under the
counselorship of Mrs. Julia Fuqua Ober, the MacDowell Junior Fellowship Fund of $3,000 was begun for the purpose of financing an Ameri-
can artist at the Colony. It was completed and over-subscribed by more
than $500 under the counselorship of Miss Etelka Evans of Ohio. The
$500 was given to Mrs. MacDowell to apply to the *Fund for the Per-
petual Care of MacDowell's Grave*. Since that time the Juniors have
contributed annually to this Fund and to the Fellowship. Toward the
support of MacDowell's grave the Juniors also sold Presidential Gavels
made from the wood at Peterborough.

In a letter from Mrs. MacDowell written at the age of ninety-five, she
wrote of her love and deep appreciation to the National Federation of
Music Clubs for its loyal support for almost fifty years.

The Federation worked for about twenty years for the election of
Edward MacDowell to New York University's Hall of Fame. This project
became a reality in 1961, and Mrs. Clifton J. Muir represented the organization at the ceremony at which she made the presentation. In 1963
the Federation helped finance an $11,000 bronze bust of the composer,
which was placed at the University's Hall of Fame.

Edward MacDowell's last composition was *From a Log Cabin*, and
the inscription from the title page of this composition is graven on the
huge boulder which marks the last resting place of the composer in
Peterborough:

> *A house of dreams untold,*
> *It looks out over the whispering tree tops*
> *And faces the setting sun.*

The Federation takes pride in the fact that Peterborough, New Hampshire is being maintained as a home for artists-composers, painters, sculp-
tors, writers – where they may live close to the lovely scenes which
MacDowell loved, and carry on their artistic creative work. *Porgy and
Bess* was written there. According to Tim Clark, writing for Yankee magazine, Thornton Wilder's *Our Town* was "written while he was a guest at
the MacDowell Colony, two miles down the road" from Grover's Cor-

ners, the setting for *Our Town*. The list of musicians goes on and on –
Charles Wakefield Cadman, Gena Branscombe, Edgar Stillman Kelley.
And – even though the part played by the National Federation of Music
Clubs may have been a small one, still all members feel as if they have a
"close tie" to the MacDowell Colony in Peterborough, New Hampshire.

It has been said that one never can shake the dust of Peterborough.
And – it was in this setting in 1919 that the Junior Division was born.

3

From an humble beginning on a hot July afternoon in 1935 – five
copper pennies placed in the center of the table around which sat five
dedicated women – has grown the Stillman Kelley Scholarship, today
offering awards annually to two Junior instrumentalists, $1,000 to the
first place winner and $500 to the winner of second place.

Miss Etelka Evans, National Federation of Music Clubs Junior Counselor (1937-1941), and Musicology teacher at the Cincinnati Conservatory of Music, invited to her home, Mrs. John A. Hoffman, Mrs. Alfred
Hahn, Mrs. R. A. Herbruck and Miss Margaret Lockwood. She presented
the idea of a scholarship fund for the Junior Division, at which time
each of the five ladies contributed one penny. In deciding on a name,
Miss Lockwood said "We could think of no other people but Jessie and
Edgar Stillman Kelley, our dearest friends living in Oxford, Ohio to be
so honored."

On September 7, 1938 Miss Evans presented the recommendation to
the National Board of Directors, meeting in Chicago, Illinois, and it was
approved wholeheartedly, "That whereas Edgar Stillman Kelley and his
wife have always been so vitally interested in the Junior Division of the
National Federation of Music Clubs, this new project shall be known as
the Edgar Stillman Kelley Scholarship Fund."

The scholarship carried the name of "Edgar Stillman Kelley Scholarship" honoring Dr. Kelley, eminent composer, music educator, and at
that time Dean of Composers. Later in recognition of his wife's accomplishments as the eleventh president of the National Federation of Music Clubs (1925-1929) the title was changed officially to the "Stillman
Kelley Scholarship" honoring both of this husband-wife team, Edgar
Stillman Kelley and Jessie Gregg Kelley (often compared to Marian
and Edward MacDowell, and Elizabeth and Robert Browning).

According to Miss Evans, "this scholarship was begun to provide
funds for talented Juniors under the age of sixteen who would not other-

wise be able to continue their musical education." She liked to call it her "brainchild", and to it she devoted herself loyally.

Varied means were used to increase the scholarship endowment to the amount it is today: Miss Evans suggested that Juniors drop a penny a month into the "Wishing Well" for ten months; in 1939 the Juniors sold Christmas seals to increase the fund; Dr. Kelley gave a New York performance of his "New England Symphony", from which he gave the proceeds to the endowment; and in 1971-1973, Miss Margaret Lockwood of Hamilton, Ohio, the only living founder of the scholarship – offered in memory of Miss Evans, $100 to the state making the largest contribution to the Fund.

The scholarship was given for the first time in the Northeastern Region, with fifteen year old David Smith, pianist from Cincinnati, Ohio, the winner. David made his New York debut in Town Hall on November 5, 1944. Given annually, the scholarship rotates among the four regions of the United States.

4

For years – in the safe deposit box of the National Federation – there has been a little black velvet box containing a bright, shiny, little gold coin – a twenty dollar gold-piece. From whence it came, was a question asked frequently, but never answered. Administrations, presidents and treasurers came and went, but no one seemed to know the answer.

Only the research and the writing of this history have unfolded the mystery. Soon after the Stillman Kelley Scholarship was established in 1938, Mrs. Edgar Stillman Kelley gave a twenty dollar gold piece to the Federation – the exchange of which was to be added to the Scholarship Fund. Who knows what happened? Was it carelessly overlooked – or forgotten? Or, was it prized too much to give up?

Lo, for these fifty years or more it has remained in the little black velvet box. Because of her love for young people and the Juniors, it was given by the Federation's beloved eleventh president, Jessie Stillman Kelley.

SPOTLIGHT ON YOUTH

Student Division

1

Although student clubs had not been made officially a membership classification of the National Federation of Music Clubs, they were recognized as far back as 1913, when according to the minutes, "Moved by Mrs. Smith (Mrs. Ella May Smith, the daughter-in-law of Carrie Jacobs Bond) and seconded by Mrs. (Emerson) Brush, that the chairman of the Student Department be empowered to organize a National Students Club, dues to be one dollar a year."

Members realized a very real need in the Federation's program for a Student Division. According to the bylaws, "The membership of the National Federation of Music Clubs shall be classified as Senior Members and Junior Members." Many young musicians outgrowing the Junior Division had "no place to go." They were too old for Juniors, and too young for Seniors. An organization of a Division to parallel the Junior Division was the answer.

On October 16, 1936, during the administration of Mrs. John Alexander Jardine, thirteenth president, at the meeting of the Board of Directors in Dallas, Texas, when the Federation's emphasis was on musical youth, the Student Division was established. The bylaws were revised to read, "The membership of the National Federation of Music Clubs shall be classified as Senior Members, Student Members, and Junior Members, in each of which there may be active Members, Associate Members, and Honorary Members. The National Extension Chairman shall be known as the National Student Sponsor."

The age limit for the newly created Student Division included "members between the ages of eighteen and twenty-five." Two days later, on October 18, Miss Julia Williams moved to STRIKE OUT the word "sponsor"... and insert "Advisor"... Seconded by Mrs. (Walter) Knerr" and carried.

The first National Student Advisor was Mrs. Reid Lancaster, Montgomery, Alabama. As president of the Alabama Federation of Music Clubs she had realized "the necessity of a connecting link between the Junior and Senior Departments...."

According to Mr. John E. Howard, Student Advisor, 1938, the Gewandhaus Club at the Arizona State Teachers College at Tempe was the first club organized in the NFMC Student Division. It was sponsored by Mr. Carl Hoyer, teacher of band music at the college. Soon to follow were four clubs organized in Atlanta, Georgia: The Evelyn Jackson Students; Young Artist Music Club; Pi Mu Club; and the Student's Concert Guild. Pennsylvania followed with five clubs: The Crescendo Music Club, Philadelphia; Horseshoe Choral of Woods School, Langhorne; Monday Evening Musicale, Canton; and Grace Choral, Butler. The Fargo (North Dakota) Student Music Club was organized with all the meetings at the home of the past national president, Mrs. Jardine, in whose administration the Student Division had been founded.

The activities of the Student Division at once became tremendously varied. Members participated in: Symphony orchestras, choral societies, chamber music groups, opera, oratorio, folk songs and dancing, composition, hymn sings – the list could go on and on.

The Student Division made a remarkable record during the war years, 1942-1945. Many students, both men and women answered the call to service. Others had to help maintain homes where parents took on war jobs. All of this meant little or no time had been left for the study of music.

The age limit for the Student Division was lowered from eighteen to sixteen as a "duration" measure. It proved so successful that on recommendation of the Board of Directors, the change in age limit was made permanent.

The War Benefit program given by the New Jersey Student and Junior Ensemble in the Arts High School, in April 1943, received one of the $50 War Bond Awards in the Donald Voorhees Contest. Outstanding features of the project included the Upsala College Choir in a group which included the *British Children's Prayer* by Jacque Wolfe, and a ballet, complete with scenery and costumes, *Les Millions D'Arlequin*, given by a newly federated group, the New Jersey Civic Ballet.

The Student Musicale of Allentown (Pennsylvania) Music Club gave its second War Service Fund concert at which $65 was raised. An earlier concert netted $70 making a total of $135 sent to the War Service Fund. There was no end to the outstanding accomplishments of the Students toward helping win World War II and making musical opportunities available to returning service men and women.

The wonderful news of victory in Europe in 1945 brought to special attention the ex-service men, many having been attached to branches of the service where they could not use their musical abilities. Many of the schools and departments of music adjusted their schedules and curricula to meet the demands of the returned music students. Such a plan as this was the Yale University plan whereby students who had previous college training, or training while in the Service, were credited on a college level and were put in classes which were designed especially for them.

The first Young Composers Contest in the Student Division was inaugurated in 1943 – a contest which has continued for these fifty plus years. During these last few years, the Victor Herbert-ASCAP Young Composers Awards have been made possible for Students, by the American Society of Composers, Authors and Publishers, honoring one of the organizations founders, Victor Herbert, who in the words of Morton Gould, past president of ASCAP, "took the dream of ASCAP and made it a reality."

The Victor Herbert-ASCAP Awards are given biennially in the amount of $1,000 for first place winner; and $500 to each of the second and third place winners.

Supplementary Young Composer's Awards are: the Devora Nadworney Award made possible by a gift from Devora Nadworney, 1921 Young Artist winner, Woman's Voice. She gave the Federation the full credit for her having pursued a concert career.

The Nancy and Russell Hatz Special Recognition Award is given by Mr. and Mrs. Hatz of Pennsylvania.

Dr. Merrills Lewis, Student Advisor, 1944 said, "From this group of thousands of young musicians must come the seniors of tomorrow and the music of America. From America will come the music of the world, therefore, let us be practical visionaries and look well to our Students."

2

In 1951 Mrs. Royden J. Keith, sixteenth president of the National Federation, was honored by the establishing of a scholarship in her name – the Marie Morrisey Keith Scholarship, given annually to either instrumentalists or vocalists. This rotated among the four regions until 1992 when it became a biennial scholarship – in the Student auditions.

Mrs. Robert E. L. Freeman, who has done extensive research on NFMC scholarships said of this scholarship, "As if it were leaven, the presence of this one 'starter scholarship' in the Student Division created an ever rising number of new opportunities. First there were the Federation funded auditions with separate competitions for the various instruments and man's and woman's voices. In the beginning the monetary awards were small but over the years the scholarships have been increased by means of bequests namely: the legacy of Mr. Clifton J. Muir, honoring his wife, Mrs. Clifton J. Muir, the nineteenth president of the Federation; and a bequest from Miss Agnes Fowler from Ohio".

In addition to the Marie Morrisey Keith Award, in the Student Division, there are four other awards honoring Past National Presidents:

Dorothy Dann Bullock Music Therapy Award
Irene S. Muir Voice Awards in Man's and Woman's Voice
Hinda Honigman Scholarship for the Blind
Ruby Simons Vought Organ Award

Added to the scholarships given by the National Federation in almost every classification in the Student Division, are scholarships and awards which have been endowed by gifts and legacies.

PART FIVE

Gems of a Musical Heritage

FEDERATION INSIGNIA

1

The National Federation of Music Clubs first pins, designed by Mrs. John Leverett, were accepted on April 19, 1899, and sixteen pins were sold at the second biennial convention in Cleveland, Ohio, the first pin being purchased by Mrs. Charles B. Kelsey.

It was the Federation's fourteenth president, Mrs. Julia Fuqua Ober of Norfolk, Virginia who interpreted the meaning of the design of the blue and gold emblem:

> "The encircling band of blue is the loyalty that holds us together within the Federation.
>
> "It is tipped with gold that is enduring in our friendship and our music.
>
> "The eagle of supremacy, with outspread wings, stands guard above us – supreme in the power of music and goodness.
>
> "Across all rests our symbol, interpreted, we read – My Country 'Tis of Thee.
>
> "It is with faith in friendship, country and God that we stand secure within the bonds of our Federation through music."

The Federation pin may be worn by any member of the Federation. It may be either plain or set with jewels. The policy of the Federation has been that only those who have served as state – or national presidents may wear a diamond pin. The small gold gavel, which may be attached as a guard, is worn with the head of the gavel pointing upward if the wearer is serving at the present, or the head pointing downward when the president has retired from the office.

The president of the National Federation of Music Clubs wears the Federation pin of past national president, Mrs. Guy P. Gannett of Portland, Maine.

This – her personal pin which she had made, was willed to the Federation to be worn by the incumbent president, who upon her retirement pins it on her successor.

Another of the Federation's beautiful pins was a gift to Mrs. Frank A. Seiberling of Akron, Ohio, by members of the board who had been her house guests at Stan Hywet during a meeting of the Board of Management.

The pin as described by Mrs. Leverett, was "very handsome". "The eagle done in platinum, set with fourteen diamonds; three larger diamonds are set in the buckle at the bottom." The pin was engraved with the name of Mrs. Seiberling, "from her house guests of the National Federation of Musical Clubs, October, 1919." The enclosed card carried the inscription – "To dear Mrs. Seiberling – From her house guests of the NFMC, October, 1919" with the names of the donors.

In reply, Mrs. Seiberling wrote that upon her return from an important engagement in New York – in time to celebrate her January 23rd birthday, she found a great birthday surprise – "the beautiful velvet jewel case and... therein, the wonderful pin."

She continued, "I remember how the announcement was made the night of our banquet. I was told that being 'Conductor' of the 'Sunshine Express' I must have a 'headlight' which would keep the track well in view, and that the headlight would be this beautiful pin whose brilliant diamonds would illuminate my way... It will give me courage in moments when I may feel dismayed or uncertain... and will clear my mind and make more firm my belief that this great body of women devoted to the cause of music is in a way ordained by Divine Providence to bring the blessing and harmonizing power of music to this great country."

The twenty-fourth president of the National Federation of Music Clubs, Mrs. Jack C. Ward, prizes as one of her most valued possessions the magnificent diamond Federation pin formerly owned by Mrs. Conway Jones, Sr. of Fountain Inn, South Carolina – a gift to Mrs. Ward by Mrs. Jones's family. Mrs. Jones, Sr., inspired upon seeing the pin worn by the national president, designed and had the pin made – with diamonds in a band encircling the emblem, set with five larger stones – all attached to a diamond encrusted gavel guard. The presentation was made by Mrs. Conway Jones, Jr. at the banquet of Mrs. Ward's last convention in Columbus, Ohio in 1983.

FEDERATION COLLECT

We praise and thank Thee, Father, for the gift of music. Through us, as channels of Thy grace, may this blessed legacy be shared with all mankind. Grant that we may exemplify in our own lives the harmony of Thy great purpose for us.

Give us magnitude of soul, and such understanding hearts that we who make music may be as players upon rightly tuned instruments responding to Thy leading.

Let us with renewed consecration dedicate ourselves to the purpose of our Federation, to bring the spiritualizing force of music to the inner life of our nation. Open our minds that divine knowledge and wisdom may teach us how best to execute our pledge.

—Mrs. Thomas J. Cole
Excerpts from *A Musical Ritual*,
Mrs. Frank A. Seiberling

1

The minutes of the early history of the Federation record that on more than one occasion the meetings were called to order by "reading" the "Collect for Club Women." There was no official Collect for the National Federation of Musical Clubs:

October 20, 1919, "Mrs. Campbell opened the meeting by reading the 'Collect for Club Women.'"

And – in 1921, "After the reading of the 'Collect for Club Women'... the minutes of the previous meeting were read...."

In 1927 Mrs. Frank A. Seiberling, past national president, 1919-1921, wrote *A Musical Ritual* used at the Chicago Biennial Convention in connection with the "Singing Biennial Collection of Songs." It was recommended that *A Musical Ritual* be used not only by the Federation, but at "Formal opening exercises of Music Clubs." The *Ritual*, a responsive reading consisting of prayers, a memorial service, choral responses, etc. – beautiful for a scheduled program, was much too long to be used as a

Collect to open meetings.

Mrs. Thomas J. Cole (May Belle) of Amory, Mississippi loved the Federation and the *Ritual*, and from its phrases she arranged a prayer. It was at the meeting of the Mississippi Federation of Music Clubs in Gulfport, in 1929 that the prayer was read for the first time.

In attendance, as the official guest of the National Federation was Helen Harrison Mills of Illinois, editor of *Music Clubs Magazine*. She was so impressed by the "beauty and adequacy" of Mrs. Cole's arrangement of the phrases from the *Ritual* and the resulting prayer, that she requested the privilege of taking the original manuscript to the National Federation of Music Clubs.

Time passed. The words became so much a part of all Federation assemblies that no one knew who had been the author. During her national presidency, Mrs. Julia Fuqua Ober attended a convention of the Mississippi Federation in Meridian, and there met Mrs. Cole, who was a dynamic Federation leader in her state. The story of the Collect was told. Because Mrs. Ober had recommended the creation of a Student Division, and because she loved Juniors for whose Division she had served as National Junior Counselor, she wished each division – Senior, Student, Junior – an equally beautiful prayer by the same author. Therefore in 1938 at the request of the national president, Collects for the Student and Junior Divisions were written by Mrs. Cole.

2

From the Chicago Fall Session in 1938 we read in the minutes, "The National President announced that the Federation is indebted to Mrs. Thomas J. Cole... for arranging the Federation Collect now in use. Mrs. Cole culled this beautiful prayer from the Club *Ritual* which was prepared for the *Chicago Biennial Convention Song Book* by Mrs. F. A. Seiberling, Past President of the NFMC...." The minutes continued:

"The Chair requested the Secretary to read a prayer written by Mrs. Thomas J. Cole for the use of the Student Division of the Federation. The Secretary read as follows:
'Dear God and Giver of all things good,
Grant us the grace of truly hearing Music.
Release us to the divine idea beneath its
*   sonant forms*
And quicken us to the inmost beauty of it

> *That we may perceive Thee, patterned in the*
> *   miracle of Song;*
> *Teach us to discern above Earth's discord*
> *The purposed Melody of Thy eternal love*
> *And transpose our lives to tones of higher*
> *   impulse*
> *That, through us, as ministers of Music*
> *Earth's birth-right of Harmony may be*
> *   redeemed*
> *And Men's hearts may sing again together*
> *In the concord of fellow-service*
> *And the great Amen of universal peace.'"*

Mrs. Jardine moved that the Federation recommend the prayer written by Mrs. Thomas J. Cole, to the Student Division for its use. It was seconded and carried.

The national president read a prayer also written by Mrs. Cole for the use of the Junior Division. The prayer follows:

> *We Thank Thee, our Father,*
> *For all things beautiful.*
> *Open our minds to the Beauty that is Music*
> *And teach us to remember it*
> *As part of Thy great goodness to us.*
> *Help us to grow each day*
> *Unto the stature of Thy grace*
>
> *And keep our hearts so tuned with Thy heart*
> *That our lives may re-sound*
> *Thy very Music*
> *In the melody of lovely living*
> *And in service that is Song.*

Miss Rudy moved that the prayer written by Mrs. Thomas J. Cole for the use of the Junior Division be adopted. The motion was seconded and carried.

The year of adoption of the Senior Collect is not clear, however it is believed that "the prayer 'culled' by Mrs. Cole to be used as the Senior Division Collect would date from the same year" as *A Musical Ritual*, which was 1927. Thus the Collect which is a prayer became a part of the National Federation's "Ritual" according to Mrs. Julia Fuqua Ober, national president, 1937-1941.

May Belle Pugh Cole (Mrs. Thomas Jefferson) was a lover of beauty and music, serving actively on the local, state and national levels. She was a member of the National Federation of Musical Clubs before her own Mississippi Federation was organized. After its organization she served as the second president, 1918-1919. Mrs. Cole passed away in 1965 without ever having the recognition of her name being carried on the Collect as its author.

3

Historical records reveal that from time to time numerous musical settings of the Collects have been adopted by the National Federation of Music Clubs as the "Official Musical Setting". The year the Federation adopted the three part women's chorus musical setting, written by Gertrude M. Rohrer, of Pennsylvania, is unclear. It was copyrighted in 1945 and "Dedicated to Dorothy Dann Bullock, President, Pennsylvania Federation of Music Clubs 1944-1948 – Elected national president 1959."

In 1942 a "Musical Setting" for three part treble voices was adopted "by the National Federation of Music Clubs" Junior Division – words by May Belle Cole and music by Olive F. Conway.

"Gratitude for Music" another musical setting for the Junior Collect, for two part treble voices, words by May Belle Cole, music by Mary Mann Hepburn, was "adopted in 1970 as the Official Junior Musical Collect by the National Federation of Music Clubs."

OFFICIAL INVOCATION

1

At the 1953 Biennial Convention in New York City, a pleasant custom was initiated – that of featuring an invocation by a woman composer at each session. It was continued at the 1955 convention in Miami, Florida when the Official Invocation, "Great Land of Mine" by Mary Howe, a prolific composer and member of the NFMC Board of Directors, formally opened the convention on April 22, 1955. Others whose invocations were selected for the Miami convention were: Glad Robinson Youse, Mabel Daniels, Olive Dungan, Laura Howell Norden, Lillian Anne Miller, Gena Branscombe and Elinor Remick Warren.

The custom was continued for the 1957 Biennial Convention in Columbus, Ohio when invocations of the following composers were heard: Ruth Bradley, Gena Branscombe, Mabel Daniels, Vera Eakin, Hazel Dessery Gronert, Gladys Washburn Fisher, Eusebia Simpson Hunkins, Dale Asher Jacobus, Frances McCollin, Ruth Taylor Magney, Lillian Anne Miller, Laura Howell Norden, Doria A. Paul, Bessie Whittington Pfohl, and Glad Robinson Youse.

It is not clear whether or not the custom of featuring an invocation by a woman composer at each session was continued after these three biennial conventions.

2

For the national biennial convention held in New York City in 1967, the national chairman, Dr. Merle Montgomery, wished to present a song by Julia Smith, eminent composer, lecturer, pianist and life member of the National Federation of Music Clubs. An Invocation was needed. Miss Smith did not have time to compose one so she took one of her published songs which A. Walter Kramer had just published when he was with Galaxy, and wrote Invocation words to it. It was at once a success. Mrs. Ada Holding Miller, past national president, who heard the composition, agreed that it was perfectly suited to be the Official

Invocation of the National Federation of Music Clubs.

On August 28, at the 1967 Fall Session of the Federation in St. Louis, Missouri, Miss Smith's *Invocation* was adopted as the Official Invocation of the National Federation.

A native of Denton, Texas, Julia Smith came to national fame with the performance of her first opera, *Cynthia Parker* which was premiered in Denton. She also composed operas, a symphony, a piano concerto, orchestral suites, choral and chamber music, and piano works.

Remember the Alamo was commissioned of Julia Smith by Lieutenant Commander Anthony A. Mitchell, Leader of the United States Navy Band, for the band's Inaugural Concert on January 15, 1965, honoring and dedicated to President Lyndon B. Johnson.

FEDERATION BANNER

1

The November 9, 1920 minutes of the National Federation of Musical Clubs in session at Stan Hywet Hall, the beautiful home of Mrs. Frank Seiberling, president, recorded:

> "A Federation Banner is to be designed, using the national emblem and colors – royal blue and gold being the colors of the Federation."

The Federation Banner was designed and made according to specifications, and at the 1921 Biennial Convention in Rock Island, Illinois, it was displayed for the first time, when according to the minutes: The "Banner was borne by the National Federation of Music Clubs President, Mrs. Frank A. Seiberling, in the Processional."

FEDERATION HYMN

To Thee our God, Creator, King,
To Thee our Hymn of thanks we sing Alleluia, Alleluia.
Thy boundless mercy crowns our days,
Thine be the meed of joyful praise.
Alleluia, Alleluia, Alleluia, Alleluia, Alleluia!

Thy truth and patience make us know,
Toward Thy perfection let us grow, Alleluia, Alleluia.
Thy providence our path has led,
By Thy good grace our souls are fed.
Alleluia, Alleluia, Alleluia, Alleluia, Alleluia!

Free stands our country, blessed by Thee,
Bless Thou our souls with liberty, Alleluia, Alleluia.
From selfish pride, oh, set us free!
With single hearts to worship Thee.
Alleluia, Alleluia, Alleluia, Alleluia, Alleluia!

On Thy strong arm Thy people lean,
Grant vision clear and purpose keen, Alleluia, Alleluia.
Our lives to Thee we dedicate,
Thy truth to keep inviolate.
Alleluia, Alleluia, Alleluia, Alleluia, Alleluia!
—Irena Foreman Williams   Geistliche Kirchengesange,
Cologne, 1623
arr. by Peter Lutkin

1

"I tried to write something that could be sincerely sung by all musicians – or even non-musicians – regardless of their creed or denomination, and if it has met that need, I am more than happy to have had a part in it," said Irena Foreman Williams of the *Federation Hymn*, she had written at the request of Mrs. Crosby Adams.

The *Federation Hymn*, set to the tune of "Vigiles Et Sancti" from the Cologne Gesangbuch and arranged by Peter Christian Lutkin, was sung for the first time at the Chicago Biennial Convention in 1927.

Mrs. Williams, who had been a language and literature tutor at Davidson College in North Carolina, wrote secular and religious poetry throughout her life. Several of her poems have been set to music and are used in religious services in Montreat, North Carolina, where she grew up and lived the last years of her life. At the time of her death Mrs. Williams was one of the last two living original residents of the Southern Presbyterian Mountain retreat Montreat.

The inspiring words of Irena Foreman Williams official *Hymn* of the National Federation of Music Clubs will perpetuate her memory wherever Federation members gather.

OFFICIAL BENEDICTION

1

"It is heartwarming to know that my *Bless Us O God* is to be the Official Benediction of the National Federation of Music Clubs. The work was written as an expression of my deep interest and appreciation of all the NFMC means to me," wrote Glad Robinson Youse upon being notified that her composition had been made the Official Benediction of the Federation at the 1969 Fall Session in Charlotte, North Carolina. It was her wish to give the proceeds from the composition to the Headquarters Building Fund. She continued, "I trust the work will prove lucrative for the project."

Glad Robinson Youse of Baxter Springs, Kansas, internationally acclaimed composer, was not only a dedicated member of the National Federation but also a dear friend, a loyal supporter and one of the Federation's foremost women composers. She served as both faculty member and composer-director of music conferences throughout the United States. She was particularly interested in the sacred and educational fields of music. Although many of her texts are her own poems, others were taken from the scriptures, and still others from the writings of Grace Noll Crowell, Ralph Spaulding Cushamm and Edith Hope Genee.

Mrs. Youse was honored with a National Federation of Music Clubs Presidential Citation at the 1981 Biennial Convention in Birmingham, Alabama, presented by the president of the National Federation, Mrs. Jack C. Ward.

OFFICIAL MAGAZINES

1

The real history of the Federation cannot be written without knowing the story of the official magazine. The official news media of any organization reveals its character, power, strength, weakness and its "reason for being". Mrs. Rose Fay Thomas in her last address to the Federation in Chicago in 1927 said "the *Official Bulletin* is the ribbon that binds the clubs together."

The first reference we find for having an official news magazine for the Federation was on May 4, 1901 when "Mr. Wilcox", editor of the *Concert Goer* appeared before the Board of Management "to explain his proposition for making his paper the *Official Organ* of the Federation." Mrs. Moore moved that the Federation adopt no official organ for the next two years.

It is believed that *The Musical World*, printed from 1911 until 1913, carried news of the Federation, for in the Federation Archives in the Library of Congress those issues are complete except for the first.

The Musical Monitor, printed by Mrs. David A. Campbell, a charter member of the Federation, was founded shortly after the 1911 convention in Philadelphia, and from 1913 until 1915 *The Musical World* and *The Musical Monitor* merged using both titles, continuing to carry news of the Federation. The December 1913 issue carried an article entitled, "The Several Hundred Music Clubs which for 16 years have been moulding local Musical Sentiment in every State of the Union."

The meeting of the Board of Management in Chicago October 22-24, 1912, recorded, "The National Federation of Musical Clubs chose as the official magazine for the Federation, *The Musical Monitor*, a monthly magazine published in New York by Mrs. David A. Campbell."

On December 4, 1917 at the Board meeting, Mrs. Campbell suggested that the Federation own a department in *The Musical Monitor*. The Board voted to purchase a share of the magazine for $2,000 which entitled the Federation to have the use of ten pages. Even those who had doubted the wisdom of this became very happy with it as is evidenced by a letter from Mrs. Russell R. Dorr:

> "... *The Musical Monitor* is a constant delight to me. I like its make-up... the excellence and arrangements of your 'cuts'. Your correspondence and contributions are first rate and all the literary matter, including your editorials, dignified, timely and true. May you live long and dream for us.
>
> (Signed)
> Louise Dorr"

The "honeymoon" was short-lived however, when the March 1921 issue of *The Musical Monitor*, in one of its editorials, attacked one of the Federation's beloved and highly esteemed charter members, and chairman of the Education Department, Dr. Frances Elliott Clark. At the meeting of the Board on the following November 9, 1921, Mrs. Frank A. Seiberling offered a resolution and moved its adoption:

> "The relation previously existing between the Board of Directors, NFMC and *The Musical Monitor* was dissolved in November 1921... the Board hereby demands the immediate removal from the coverage and columns of *The Musical Monitor* all reference to any connection whatever with the NFMC; and be it further Resolved, That Mrs. David A. Campbell's place on the Board be and is hereby declared vacant."

Mrs. Lyons, president of the Federation wrote Mrs. Campbell who had not been present at the meeting, informing her of the Board's actions. The Board voted, also to:

> "discontinue use of the *Monitor* as the official organ after January, 1922. As evidence of appreciation we present you the $2,000 *Monitor* stock with best wishes for success of the magazine.
>
> (Signed)
> Mrs. John F. Lyons, President"

2

Reluctance to give up the pages assigned to the Federation in *The Musical Monitor*, the Federation's first news venture was finally overcome in midnight Board sessions at Stan Hywet Hall, Akron, Ohio. The independent first *Official Bulletin* was born in 1920 with Helen Harrison Mills as editor. It made its official debut in May 1922 in Peoria, Illinois, the home of Mrs. Mills.

It is to Mrs. Worcester R. Warner, Tarrytown-on-the-Hudson, New York for her far-sightedness and generosity that the official organ of the Federation received its initial financial wings through the benefactions of this devoted friend and member. Mrs. Warner wrote:

> "Out of the survey of the Federation's growing activities and pressing needs of inner-communication grew the *Official Bulletin*. Because I like to think of myself as its sponsor, I exercise at this time the grandmotherly right to remark on some of its engaging qualities and commend it to the affection of all clubs and all other Federation members."

In 1927 during the presidency of Mrs. Edgar Stillman Kelley, two "unique" publications were added – the *Church Music Bulletin*, setting forth the outstanding work of the Department of Religious Education, and edited by the chairman, Mrs. Grace Widney Mabee of Los Angeles, and the *Junior Bulletin* edited by the Junior Counselor, Miss Julia E. Williams of Philadelphia. The *Church Music Bulletin* reported the progress of work pertinent to church music as well as articles from the pens of religious educators and the music of the hymns of special significance, including information on the Hymn Contests. Mrs. Elmer James Ottaway, president, realized that because of the depression, it became practical to synchronize all Federation activities into one magazine presenting all branches of work under one cover. The three were combined and given the name *Music Clubs Magazine* in 1929. They were again separated in 1954 – one magazine, *Junior Keynotes* for the Juniors, and *Music Clubs Magazine* for the Seniors.

In 1931 Mrs. Paul J. Weaver of Ithaca, New York became the managing editor whose duties were managing the office and editing the magazine. The publications office was moved from Peoria, Illinois to 320 Wait Avenue, Ithaca, New York in 1931. Mrs. Abbie L. Snoddy assumed the editorship of the Senior section of *Music Clubs Magazine*, with Mrs. Mabee continuing her editorship of church music affairs, and Miss Williams in the office of Junior editor.

When the publications office opened in Ithaca, the Federation owned practically no office equipment. Only through personal arrangements was a working space and the necessary equipment made available. For four years the office force struggled with an antiquated Elliott addressograph lent by the Cayuga Press. Two card cabinets were the only purchases by the Federation. Not until 1935 did the Federation find itself in a position to purchase modern equipment, including an addressograph, graphotype and a cabinet for stencils.

The first Editorial Board of five members was appointed September 8,1937 at the Chattanooga, Tennessee Fall Session. In about 1960 the name of *Music Clubs Magazine* was changed to *Showcase*. This lasted approximately three years when the members in 1963 changed it back to *Music Clubs Magazine*.

The National Federation office was moved to New York City in 1951 where it remained until 1960 when it was moved to Chicago. In 1980, with the hard work of the office chairman and her husband, Vera and Lynn Turner, the office was moved for the last time to Indianapolis, Indiana to the newly purchased and restored Eden-Talbott Mansion, the headquarters for the National Federation of Music Clubs. Today, the modernized headquarters office occupies the entire second floor of the headquarters building – the Eden-Talbott Mansion at 1336 North Delaware Street.

The first Office Committee was appointed in 1951 for the purpose of managing the business of the office.

3

Cartoon from First Junior Magazine

Miss Julia E. Williams of Wilmington, Delaware became the third National Junior Counselor – appointed in 1925 by Mrs. Edgar Stillman Kelley, president. She founded the *Junior Bulletin (Junior Keynotes)* in 1927 and served as its first editor and publisher. In her own cheery words she writes:

> "The start of the magazine was a thrill… Dot (her sister) and I had fun planning the cartoons for my 'serials'. Father, who did the artist work, did not approve of Dot's free drawings and several times said he just could not take them to the Beck Engraving Company where he worked as a 'finisher'. However he did take them, and the men had a good time laughing at some of them."

Pictured above is a cartoon from the first *Junior Bulletin* in 1927.

Mrs. Crosby Adams of Montreat, North Carolina, was the first subscriber to the *Junior Bulletin*.

In 1954 a title contest was held by the Federation to choose an official name for the junior magazine. A cash prize was offered to the club who came up with the winning name. This was won by the B Sharp Club of Elgin, Illinois who suggested the name – *Junior Keynotes*. It was that same year that the junior and senior magazines were separated.

PART SIX

The Cornerstone: American Music

THE JEWEL OF THE FEDERATION TIARA

American Music

1

Rock-a-bye baby in the tree top,
When the wind blows the cradle will rock.
When the bough breaks, the cradle will fall,
And down will come baby, cradle and all.

American music composition predates the National Federation of Music Clubs by approximately 200 years, according to an article in the May 17, 1917 issue of *The Musical Monitor*. The story carried in *The Musical Monitor*, which at that time was the official magazine of the Federation, tells that the first poem to be set to music in America was the lullaby *Rock a-bye Baby*. A young Englishman upon his arrival in the new world saw an Indian papoose strapped to a "cradleboard" and swinging from a tree. He wondered what kept the "cradleboard" and infant from falling as the wind blew. He wrote the words to the lullaby on his shirt cuff, and later set it to music. The name of the young Englishman is unknown.

The first convention of the National Federation of Music Clubs was called to order May 3, 1899 in the Union Club, St. Louis, Missouri, by the president, Mrs. Edwin F. Uhl, with eighty-nine accredited delegates from fifty-one clubs present. Among the policies and procedures set by the group was "to make Biennial Conventions great gala musical festivals with emphasis on American music and American musicians."

"From the first biennial program in 1899 to the present day the works of the American composers have been featured." The first biennial program set the pattern for all time by featuring a lecture recital, "Folk Songs in America" by Henry E. Krehbiel, lecturer and Mrs. Krehbiel, vocalist. The program given "In Honor of the National Federation of

Music Clubs" featuring folk songs throughout the United States opened with *Nobody Knows* (slave song) and ended with *There was a Little Boy* (a nursery song from Connecticut). Programs by representatives of federated music clubs and by professional musicians, included compositions by American composers, "along with the world's great masters."

Even though the Federation sponsored American music since its beginning, it was not until seven years later in 1905 that they "abandoned their attempt to establish a national artist committee." Instead, a resolution was passed by the National Board of Management "to submit to the clubs at the 1907 Biennial Convention the plan of placing the Federation behind the American composer and artist in a practical and helpful way." The resolution was carried unanimously at the convention in Memphis, Tennessee in 1907. The American Music Department was established and a standing committee, consisting of Mrs. Susan B. Walker, chairman, Mrs. Emerson H. Brush, Mrs. David Allen Campbell, and Mr. Arthur Farwell, was appointed.

To the committee it seemed the best way to arouse interest and carry forward "a propaganda already begun" in native creative art was the "establishment of a Biennial Competition for American-born composers." Accepting the motion made by Mrs. J. E. Kinney, the Federation offered its first cash prizes – three prizes in three classifications to American composers – the winning composition to be announced and performed at the 1909 Biennial Convention in Grand Rapids, Michigan.

Two years later in 1909 in Grand Rapids, the prizes were announced:

> Class I – Henry Hadley, Sommerville, Massachusetts, a Rhapsody, *The Culprit Fay* for orchestra $1,000
> Class II– Arthur Shepherd, Newton Center, Massachusetts, *The Lost Child*, a vocal composition $500
> Class III – Arthur Shepherd, *Sonata of the Turtle*, a piano composition $500

The Culprit Fay was performed on the Grand Rapids convention program by the Theodore Thomas Orchestra (today the Chicago Symphony Orchestra) with the composer, nineteen year old Henry Hadley, conducting.

How little did the National Federation of Music Clubs Board of Management realize in Memphis in 1907 that they were setting in motion sound waves of American music that would echo and re-echo from the roaring waves of the Atlantic to the peaceful shores of the Pacific, for a century to come.

Henry Hadley, who was to become one of the foremost of American composers and conductors in both the United States and throughout Europe, was born in Sommerville, Massachusetts in 1871. A pioneer among American conductors, as well as an indefatigable composer, his entire life was devoted whole-heartedly to music, having composed in almost every musical form – vocal and instrumental. It is said, that to Henry Kimball Hadley must go the credit of producing the first genuinely American school of musical composition – perhaps the only American "school" worthy of the name.

These competitions continued with some of America's most outstanding musicians declared winners – Horatio Parker, George Chadwick, Charles Wakefield Cadman, Deems Taylor and many others.

2

Through those early years there was much support for the American music program. In 1923 the Board voted to endorse the newly formed American National Orchestra in New York City which had been founded for the purpose of stimulating greater support of the American musicians, "both creative and interpretive." The orchestra, composed exclusively of American born professional musicians, headed by an American-born conductor, pledged to play an American composition on every program.

In the 1930's there was great emphasis on American music:

> Arizona – all clubs featured American music, one sponsoring four artist concerts with all American talent.
> Connecticut featured American composers in lecture recitals of the composer's own works.
> Louisiana – all clubs studied American music – one club presented a series of sixteen weekly broadcasts.
> Mississippi – all clubs used American music on 50% of their programs.
> North Carolina offered a silver loving cup to the club doing the most outstanding work in American music.
> Virginia – twenty-one of twenty-four clubs studied American music during the entire season.

3

During the intervening years since 1907 at the Memphis convention when the American Music Department was organized, participation has been widespread, but in 1955 the Federation was to reach an historical milestone in American Music. It was the sixteenth president, Ada Holding Miller, who during the last year of her administration originated the Federation's first nationwide Parade of American Music to be staged during the month of February each year. Mrs. Miller wrote:

"February will prove to be one of the most momentous months in our whole musical history... for through coordinating programs we shall prove to the entire musical world (and to our own composers) that we are truly musical patriots. One waits with keen expectation and hope, the results of the Parade of American Music, which is being organized by the National Federation of Music Clubs for the purpose of having no less than 5,000 programs presented over the length and breadth of the land during the month of February, to quote the words of Frank Conner, President of Carl Fisher, Inc., 'The eyes of musical America are upon us!' We will rise to meet that challenge!"

Cooperation of orchestras, radio and television stations, music departments of colleges and universities, and every type of musical media, raised the total of all American programs presented during the month to more than 5,000.

The plan as it has been carried out through the years since 1955, has been that each entrant present at least one entire program during American Music Month, to give the American composer recognition, encouragement, and support through a wider hearing of his work... and to impress on the American public that we have a musical culture equal to that of any country. We have composers today who can hold their own with any in the world.

Mayors and governors throughout the United States issue proclamations declaring February American Music Month. The governor of North Carolina was the first to issue a proclamation to this effect in 1956, and the idea was quickly endorsed by the National Federation.

The Parade during each president's administration, down through the years has been successful, effective and well known. Its tremendous impact each February turns the eyes of America and other nations to the Federation's creative artists. Through this concentrated effort hundreds of fine contemporary works are performed in addition to music of the past heard again and again. The American composer through the Federation's Parade of American Music is known and respected as never before.

4

In 1965 a stellar innovation in the parade, during the administration of Mrs. Clifton J. Muir, was the participation of the United States Army throughout the world – a project set in motion by the chairman, Mrs. C. Arthur Bullock. That first year twenty-nine Special Awards of Merit went to Army divisions, and the highest American musical "Recognition Award for the Advancement of National and World Culture Through Distinguished Service to Music", was awarded at the 1965 convention in Miami Beach, Florida.

The following year in 1966 fifty-nine Special Awards went to Army units. The Army honored the Federation and Parade by dedicating the twenty-fifth anniversary volume of their monthly publication, *Armed Forces Song Folio* to the Parade. Through their participation, the Army has communicated America's traditions and music of American composers across the world through the Federation's Parade of American Music.

Among the many works composed especially for this Parade was a "full scaled symphony" entitled *Sinfonia da Chiesa*, a prayer for strength in defending freedom of the Vietnamese people, by twenty-four year old PFC James M. Prigmore, stationed at Fort Monroe. Private Prigmore, holder of a Fine Arts degree as pianist, had written over fifty compositions and was resident composer at Pasadena Playhouse before entering the service. The symphony was premiered by the Continental Army Command Band at Fort Monroe.

In the words of an Army communique, "Wherever United States military men are found, you will find American music – whether it is coming from a dance band, a local radio station, the USO or the guy with the guitar in the next bunk. The Armed Forces have proved to be a natural setting for the creation and perpetuation of music that is distinctly American."

5

During the administration of Mrs. Ronald A. Dougan in 1957, the Federation offered for the first time an award of $1,000 to the individual artist or musical ensemble who had done the most to further the performance of American music abroad. The first award was won by William

Strickland in 1957 when he introduced a total of twenty-eight American works in concerts given by European orchestras which he conducted. Runners-up were Eugene List, pianist; Alfred Wallenstein, conductor, Los Angeles Philharmonic; the New York Woodwind Quintet; and the After Dinner Opera Company.

The 1958 award went to the Westminster Choir, who on a tour of twenty-two countries gave 147 concerts, and presented forty-one American works, each of which was heard sixty to seventy-five times.

6

It was in recognition of outstanding works by Army composers that prompted Mrs. Maurice Honigman, national president, to offer in 1969 an Annual Composers Competition specifically for the Army. A single prize of $200 was offered initially by the National Federation of Music Clubs, but the Army Entertainment Branch suggested that two $100 prizes be given – one for a choral work and the other for an instrumental work.

The first Annual Army-NFMC Parade Composers Contest, open to all U.S. Army personnel on active duty for more than ninety days, was launched in December 1969. The winning choral work was *Psalm 47* by Specialist James C. Dearing, U.S. Army European and Seventh Army. Specialist Dearing, who had studied composition with Zoltan Kodaly, was the Assistant Conductor of the famed Seventh Army Soldier Chorus who had sung in concerts all over Europe and this country.

In the instrumental category, a tie was declared: *Voyage to the Seventh Star* by First Lieutenant Richard B. Wallick, a graduate of the University of Ohio, who was attached to the Sixth Army stationed at the Presidio in Monterey, California; and Specialist David R. Holsinger, a graduate of Central Methodist College, Fayette, Missouri, for his *Fanfare for Those Conceived in Sorrow*.

The Army professed itself highly honored, and expressed its appreciation to the National Federation of Music Clubs. The Federation was pleased and proud that it could extend further the influence through music to many talented young men in the service of their country.

7

Two awards offered by the National Federation of Music Clubs, administrator, in cooperation with the American Society of Composers, Authors and Publishers (ASCAP), donor of the monetary awards, are the Award Program for Summer Music Festivals and the Awards to Educational Institutions. Both are offered annually to increase programming and performance of American music, and to broaden the knowledge of American repertory for artists, students and performing groups.

The Summer Music Festival Award was offered for the first time in 1967. The $500 award is available to Summer Music Festivals, Centers, and Camps in the United States and Territories whose program includes the most American music between May 15 and September 1.

Two awards of $500 each are given to Educational Institutions in the Federation's award program. The two categories in which these are awarded are 1) to a privately supported college, university or school of music, and 2) to a state or municipal college or university. These awards are based on the performance and promotion of activities and programs featuring American composers from June 1 to May 31. This has been an annual project supported by ASCAP since its inception in 1962.

CHAPTER TWO

KEEPERS OF THE PAST

Folk Music

1

"Folklore: the oral tradition channeled across the centuries
through human mouths."

—Richard Dorson, Folklorist

Thomasine McGehee describes folk music as "a mirror held up to
people; it gives a true reflection of what they are. Folk music reflects the
customs and disposition of a nation... This music of the heart we call
'Folk Music.'" We should begin by recalling that the great art music of
every nation has grown out of its folk music, some of the greatest being,
Bach, Brahms, Mozart, Chopin, Liszt, Grieg and numerous others.

John Tasker Howard said that folk songs are usually most common to
those people whom civilization has touched the least. Hard labor and
isolation from others are factors that create and nourish folk music. In
many of the more remote mountain areas have been unearthed some of
the choicest folk music. Sometimes called "the wildflowers of music it
is also music involving the creator, the interpreter, and the listener.

Since the late 1920's or early 1930's the National Federation of Music
Clubs has worked to keep folk music alive by singing it, playing it, dancing to it, and listening to and recording it. One of the Federation's most
active workers in the field of folk music was the chairman of the American Music Department, Annabel Morris Buchanan of Virginia, and it was
she who was successful in the establishment of the Federation's National
Folk Music Archives in the Library of Congress in Washington, D.C.

The first state federation of music clubs to contribute to the National
Archives was Tennessee, Mrs. Hal Holt Peel, president, through her composer archivist, Charles Iler of Chattanooga; Alice and Ross Whitmire –
"a singing cowboy" of Wyoming, contributed songs, ballads, and dance
tunes; Kentucky archivist, Edith Fitzpatrick James sent some of the oldest

folk music in America; Rhode Island contributed early tribal chants of the Narragansett Indians through Princess Red Wing and Mrs. Carl Kaiser. These are only a few of the states making valuable contributions.

The first state to set up its own Archives was Wisconsin, Mrs. Morton Hull Starr of Madison, chairman. Mrs. Starr also wrote the National Federation's booklet, *Let's Have a Folk Festival* which continues to be used today.

The first Folk Festival in miniature (made up entirely of Federation members) was presented at the Wisconsin State Fair's Little Theatre in 1952.

2

Under the organization and direction of Annabel Morris Buchanan, in 1931 more that 20,000 people "climbed or drove" to the mile high summit of Whitetop Mountain near Marion, Virginia to attend the annual, of at least five Folk Festivals. Through these the mountain people of the Appalachians experienced a new respect and love for what Cecil Sharp of England designated as the most beautiful and alive folk music of the English-speaking world. In attendance was the First Lady, Mrs. Franklin D. Roosevelt, who awarded contest prizes. Loud speakers carried the music to the throngs who tented on the broad mountain slopes, enjoying the beautiful entertainment and magnificent view. (Mrs. Roosevelt's family once owned a part of Whitetop). Adding to the enjoyment were the sword dancers of Kentucky. Addresses were heard from DuBose Heyward, author of *Porgy*; Mrs. J. A. Jardine, national president; Mrs. Elmer J. Ottaway, past national president; and other folk authorities and celebrities.

3

On June 11, 1933 Kentucky sponsored its third annual American Folk Festival founded by Jean Thomas, Kentucky author and president, at her cabin "Traipsin Woman". Quoting from the Louisville *Courier Journal*:

> "Strains from ancient dulcimers and an old valve accordion echoed through the vale in the Cumberland foothills... Composers, librettists, and musicians interested in native music dotted the crowd – standing or seated on the ground under a hill orchard. The scent of mint came from a nearby stream as the singers in native mountain dress called up the ghosts of Bar-

bara Allen, one of the 'glamour girls' of America. Sweet William lay on his death bed pining for 'Barbara Allen' who, when she was sent for and arrived at Sweet William's home, looked coldly upon him and remarked, 'Young man I think you are dying!' He agreed. She would do nothing to help the situation because he had once slighted her. Sweet William died and hard hearted Barbara died soon after – he of love, she of sorrow for her misdeeds. And so – from his grave there grew a red rose, and from her's a briar, which twined themselves on the old church wall."

Toward the closing of the folk festival the entire cast sang *Down in the Valley* to the strumming of a dulcimer, guitar and ancient fiddle.

The Federation continued to place a special emphasis on folk music and folk music festivals. In 1936 for Arkansas's celebration of their centennial, Mrs. Dusenberry, a blind folk singer was brought from the mountain section of the state as a guest artist at the Centennial Music Festival in Little Rock. Over 100 records of her mountaineer songs were made and placed in the Federation's Congressional Archives. Mrs. Dusenberry was featured on many centennial programs.

4

In 1939 Pennsylvania reported forty-one folk music festivals. Pennsylvania abounds in folk music. The coal miners in the anthracite coal belt were isolated for many years before the days of cars and good roads. After a week's work, there was a "day when the sunlight was their own." They sang of tragic love, mine disasters, strikes. It was these races made up of Welsh, Irish and English, that mined most of the coal. One of the choicest songs from that coal region of Eastern Pennsylvania was *The Shoo Fly* which tells of trouble of an old Irish woman. Times were hard and they had struck a bad vein of coal in the Shoo Fly mine, and the old furnace had been condemned. The old lady owed much money to many, each of whom she called by name. She consoled herself that she had children and "if God spares them until next summer," out of their earnings she "will build a snug house" at the fork of the Plane, and "forget the days she was poor."

Folksongs are the root of American music and the Federation has endeavored not only to unearth songs yet undiscovered but to make America aware of the folklore which is the root of music in America.

Some who have made great contributions toward preserving America's folk music are: Burl Ives, John Jacob Niles, John Powell, Carl Sandburg, and many others.

Possibly the Federation member who did more than any other to promote and preserve folk music was Annabel Morris Buchanan of Marion, Virginia. After serving as the Federation's chairman of American Music and Folk Music, she continued as Folk Music Archivist.

Carl Sandburg dedicated his volume of *The American Song Bag*: "To those unknown singers – who made songs out of love, fun, grief – and to those many singers – who kept those songs as living things of the heart and mind – out of love, fun, grief."

President Franklin D. Roosevelt's message to the National Federation's first National Folk Festival said in part: "We are amazingly rich in the elements from which we weave a culture. In binding these elements into a national fabric of beauty and strength, let us keep the original fibers so intact that the fineness of each will show in the complete handiwork."

And – as an Oriental poet once wrote, "The blossoms of tomorrow are in the seeds of today."

Jean Thomas on the stoop of her cabin the "Traipsin Woman".
Photo courtesy of Jimenez Maggard Studio, Ashland, KY.

MUSICAL ACCENTS

Oratorio and Opera

1

With World War I raging in Europe since 1914, there was general unrest throughout the world, and war clouds hung heavily over the United States. On December 4, 1917 following the United States declaration of war on April 6, 1917, the NFMC Board of Management meeting in the Music Room of Stan Hywet listened intently to the report of Mrs. Pauline Arnoux MacArthur, chairman of the American Music Committee.

Mrs. MacArthur "stated it was the desire of the committee to have a dramatic oratorio given, which could be inspiring and uplifting in its influence, and in perfect accord with the demands of the present national crisis (WWI), the suggestion for which was to be taken from the Books of Daniel and The Revelation of St. John." The suggestion was approved by the Board.

The libretto for the new dramatic oratorio, the *The Apocalypse* was selected and arranged by Pauline Arnoux MacArthur and Henri Pierre Roche.

Mrs. Ella May Smith of Columbus, Ohio, brought to the Board the information that her mother-in-law, Carrie Jacobs Bond, would write a song, the proceeds from the sale to be used by the Federation to pay the $5,000 prize offered for a musical setting of the *The Apocalypse. Ten Thousand Times Ten Thousand* was written and placed in the hands of music dealers.

Very little money was realized from the sale of the song. The American Music Committee, of which Mrs. Smith was now chairman, found itself with a "difficult inheritance". The prize of $5,000 had been announced and would have to be given. "The Bond Shop had been informed of the situation."

At the September 3, 1920 Board of Management meeting, it was announced that "a telegram had been received from Mrs. Smith stating that Mr. Smith (Mrs. Bond's son) had threatened suit for seventy-five dollars against the Federation unless immediate payment was made. (Although not specified, it was assumed the amount of the threatened suit was the cost of publication.) It was admitted that the song had been a failure." The Federation had hundreds of copies it could not sell, but it was deemed wise "to close the matter as amicably as possible." A check was sent Mr. Smith and the incident closed.

The following January 15, the Executive Committee decided that *The Apocalypse* would be produced at a big banquet for the President's Night at the next biennial convention.

Approximately one month later on February 26, the judges decision was announced. Dr. Stillman Kelly, Rubin Goldmark and Mollineur had declared Paolio Gallico of New York City the winner of the $5,000 prize for the musical setting of *The Apocalypse*. Victor Herbert, the fourth judge gave an adverse ruling, but the majority ruled in spite of the fact that Mrs. MacArthur, co-writer of the libretto, had insisted that no winner be declared unless the decision of the jury was unanimous."

Mrs. Smith notified Mr. Gallico, and *The Apocalypse* was performed in 1921 at the twelfth Biennial Convention in the Tri-Cities: Davenport, Iowa, and Moline and Rockford, Illinois – four years after the idea was conceived.

Note: *One copy of* Ten Thousand Times Ten Thousand *was found in the National Federation of Music Clubs Archives. The return address was from attorneys in Fresno. California and addressed to Ruth Heagy in Fresno. It carried the notation, "This music was found in an old house in San Francisco."*

2

Even though the prize of $5,000 had been given for the musical setting of *The Apocalypse* it was not until 1961 that the first oratorio was commissioned by the Federation. *Reflections on Christmas* was commissioned of Dr. Bethuel Gross, and was premiered at the 1961 Biennial Convention in Kansas City, Missouri by the Chancel Choir of the Community Christian Church, under the direction of Lucy Lemley.

Oratorio has continued to be important in the musical program of the National Federation of Music Clubs. Through the generous contribution of Mr. Louis Sudler of Chicago, philanthropist and Honorary Member of the Federation, an oratorio award was added to the Young Artist Competition in 1962. The "Young Artist Oratorio Award Honoring Louis Sudler" was given biennially from 1963 through 1985.

3

The Federation's Opera Department was not officially established until 1955, however the history of opera in the organization dates back to its early years when Horatio Parker was paid $10,000 for his opera *Fairyland*, premiered at the 1915 Biennial Convention in Los Angeles, California.

At the meeting of the Board of Management in Chicago, October 22-24, 1912, they empowered the Executive Committee and American Music Department to investigate offering special prizes to be competed for in 1915. It was their feeling that with the Panama-Pacific Exposition coming to the west coast, some western city might be willing to offer a prize through the Federation.

At first thought it was staggering, but was much too big a thing for Los Angeles to reject. The offer of $10,000 for a grand opera, written by an American composer was made by the American Opera Association of Los Angeles to the National Federation of Music Clubs at its 1913 "biennial festival" in Chicago, and Los Angeles was chosen as the convention city.

The "Grand Prize of America" of $10,000 was offered by the Federation to a "composer of the United States" with the Federation reserving the right to produce the Prize Opera for the first sixty performances, "thereof without royalty to the composer." Fifty six entries were submitted, and the panel of distinguished judges voted unanimously in favor of Horatio Parker's *Fairyland* with the libretto by Brian Hooper.

Fairyland was world premiered on July 1, 1915 at Clune's Auditorium Theatre. Three successive performances followed on July 2nd and 3rd. Los Angeles not only gave the $10,000 prize, but financed the elaborate production, engaging artists of high rank, sparing no effort with both orchestra and chorus, and securing as director a man of national recognition.

In appreciation to Mr. F. W. Blanchard, president, American Opera Association, Los Angeles, he received from the Federation numerous accolades, and resolutions "embodying the sentiment of the Board of Managers." He was elected an honorary vice president of the Federation with a rising vote of appreciation, and was presented a Federation pin.

Horatio Parker, born in 1863, was considered by many to be the greatest American composer. He was for forty years Dean of Music at Yale University, to whom he willed the original manuscript of *Fairyland*.

In 1940 Robert Hill, Music Archivist at the Library of Congress, lamented the fact that the National Federation's archives in the Library did not contain a copy of Horatio Parker's *Fairyland*. This was taken care of when in 1989 at the Biennial Convention in Philadelphia, Dr. Marion Richter presented to Mrs. Glenn L. Brown, national president, a copy of *Fairyland* to be placed in the National Federation of Music Clubs Archives. It is now in the Library of Congress.

A special voice prize in Opera in the amount of $1,000 was offered by the National Opera Club of America to a "female voice of outstanding quality" at the 1927 Biennial Convention in Chicago.

In 1967 the National Federation of Music Clubs and the American Society of Composers, Authors and Publishers (ASCAP) sponsored jointly an original opera contest, chaired by Mrs. Martha Sykes. Of the seventy-four entries from twenty-three states, Joyce Barthelson, of New York, was the winner with a one act comedy fantasy, "Chanticleer" which was performed at the 1969 Biennial Convention in Albuquerque, New Mexico.

4

The idea of Grass Roots Opera had its beginning in the belief that the present supply of talented singers was much greater than the demand for them. Thus began the movement to give all qualified singers the opportunity to gain experience before the footlights for the development of their talents and/or a professional career, and to acquaint the public with the beautiful music to be found in opera.

The person responsible for developing this movement was Mr. A. J. Fletcher, lawyer and businessman of Raleigh, North Carolina. It all began with the North Carolina Federation of Music Clubs in 1948, and very soon he was appointed Chairman of the Opera of the National Federation. From there the movement "spread like wildfire throughout almost every state."

Accepted, was the theory that opera should be sung in English, something for which the Federation had worked since the beginning of the century. "To accept the theory that opera should not be sung in English is to deny its primary function as an art in English-speaking countries." Each club was requested to perform opera in concert form or a standard opera. The rating sheets carried "fifteen points for public opera produced in costume."

Mr. Fletcher insisted that Grass Roots Opera groups of whatever size or status should be federated with the National Federation of Music Clubs from whom they could gain wider publicity and prestige, which only membership in the Federation could offer. The Board of Directors accepted and published Mr. Fletcher's Handbook, *Grass Roots Opera* which was made available to clubs. Included was an extensive list of Grass Roots Operas of twenty to sixty minutes duration. His television station in Raleigh was the first commercial station in the nation to present opera in prime time.

Mr. Barre Hill of National Music Camp at Interlochen, Michigan who succeeded Mr. Fletcher in 1962, published a booklet *Grass Roots Operas* which was even more inclusive in listing the operas available than had been the first.

Possibly among Federation members one of the most prolific writers of Grass Roots Operas was Eusebia Hunkins of Ohio who wrote and published fifteen chamber operas. On checking with her publisher, Carl Fisher, it was learned that "over 5,000 copies of *Old Smokey* had been purchased, and it was second place in the catalog only because Eusebia's *Child of Promise* had outsold it!" *Old Smokey* was performed at the 1959 Fall Session at Interlochen, Michigan, Mrs. C. Arthur Bullock, president, and *Child of Promise* was performed at the 1980 Fall Session in Sun Valley, Idaho, Mrs. Jack C. Ward, president. All of Eusebia Hunkins compositions are in the Library of Congress where they are available to the generations that will follow.

The Community Opera idea which had as its core "Grass Roots Opera," was conceived by Gladys Mathew, opera chairman of the New York Federation of Music Clubs, with numerous performances – free to all – in music halls, museums, and Town Hall Community Clubs.

In the Federation's promotion of opera, one of its aims has been to reach out to those singers, engaged in other lines of endeavor, who never expect to pursue singing as a profession, but who wish to sing as an avocation.

5

To quote Mr. A. J. Fletcher: "Opera will never become a means of mass entertainment unless you reach the children."

On April 1, 1978 the Opera for Youth Workshop brought together at the John F. Kennedy Center for the Performing Arts in Washington, D.C. concerned citizens to explore the feasibility of opera for children, with children themselves performing. This came as the outgrowth of Mr. Fletcher's program in North Carolina. Initiating the movement was the District of Columbia Federation of Music Clubs, Miss Marian McNabb, president.

Dr. Emily Hammood, third vice-president of the D.C. Federation, saw the need for an Opera for Youth Association and she worked unceasingly toward the organization of the project. Also interested were many members of the Federation, including Dr. Merle Montgomery, past national president, Eusebia Hunkins, composer, and other outstanding experts.

There were panels and discussions and a program of excerpts from opera performed by the children themselves. The Federation contributed not only physically but financially to the project. The workshop proved to be a great success. Very soon Opera for Youth was made one of the projects of the National Federation of Music Clubs, with an Opera for Youth Chairman appointed. Miss Marian McNabb was the first to serve in this chairmanship.

Mrs. Dwight D. Robinson, national president (1983-1987), commissioned the Federation's first Opera for Youth, and on April 26, 1987, *The Minion and the Three Riddles* by Joseph Robinette and James Shaw, was world premiered at the Biennial Convention in Miami, Florida.

6

Toward the Federation's promotion of opera it has commissioned many operas. Highlighting the "Decade of Women" project (1975-1985), Mrs. Frank A. Vought, national president, commissioned a Triple Bill Opera – three one act operas by women composers. Produced and performed at the Hunter College Playhouse in New York City on December, 2nd and 3rd, 1978 were:

> *The King's Breakfast* – Joyce Barthelson (libretto, Maurice Baring)
> *The Shepherdess and the Chimney Sweep* – Julia Smith (libretto, C. D. Mackey)
> *The Nightingale and the Rose* – Margaret Garwood (music and libretto)

Musical director and conductor of the New Amsterdam Symphony Orchestra was Victoria Bond.

Reviews were outstanding as from Abram Chasins, eminent pianist-composer: "... The afternoon I heard The American Opera Gala was a delight, dramatically, vocally, and orchestrally... All the little operas impressed me for their human warmth, humor and directness... Everything was accomplished with ease and style and with unpretentious musical invention... It was a first class event... I salute you all."

7

The Charleston, South Carolina Fall Session, Mrs. Jack C. Ward, national president, proved to be a veritable feast for history buffs and lovers of opera. This historical city, with America's first legitimate theatre – the Dock Street Theatre – dating back to 1736, was the perfect setting for a reproduction of *Flora or Hob in the Well*, the first opera produced in America in 1735.

Colley Cibber, actor, comedian, theatrical manager and play-wright was poet laureate of England, 1730 until his death in 1757. It was after John Gay's *Beggar Opera* proved so successful in England that Colley Cibber decided to try his hand at the new art form. And it was through his ingenuity that he was successful in getting the opera produced in America with the first recorded performance in the courtroom of Shepherd's Tavern in Charleston, South Carolina on February 12, 1735.

On August 11, 1979, again *Flora or Hob in the Well* played to a full house at the Dock Street Theatre, with the Governor of South Carolina, The Honorable Richard W. Riley and Mrs. Riley; and the President of American Society of Composers, Authors and Publishers, Mr. Stanley Adams and Mrs. Adams heading the list of distinguished guests seated in one of the theatre's thirteen boxes.

The opera was produced by the Opera Department of the Brevard Music Center of Brevard, North Carolina with John Richards McCrae, Producer-Director, and Dr. Henry Janiec, Conductor. A cast of fifty Brevard summer music students took part in the production of the 250 year old opera to make it a huge success.

8

Covered in these pages is only a small part of the Federation's contribution to the promotion of opera in America during these 100 years. Julia Smith wrote many operas, including *Daisy* in 1973, based on the life of Juliette Gordon Low, of Savannah, Georgia, founder, Girl Scouts of America.

In 1973 the Ruth Freehoff Opera Award was established. Designated by the Federation for study at the Santa Fe Opera Program in Santa Fe, New Mexico, the award was endowed by a legacy "for assistance to talented youth" left by the late Ruth Freehoff.

"The National Federation of Music Clubs Opera Award Honoring Past President Dr. Merle Montgomery" is given to Young Artist winners in Man's Voice and Woman's Voice.

The National Federation of Music Clubs gives an annual $500 opera award, the "Alpha Corinne Mayfield Opera Award" for young musicians, ages 18-35. This award was endowed by a legacy left by Dr. Mayfield and established in 1989.

"Opera in the Ozarks" at Inspiration Point Fine Arts Colony in Arkansas, described as "a mountainous place not too far from heaven," has been supported by the Federation since its beginning by Dr. Henry Hobart in 1959.

9

The Federation has worked for the promotion of American music since its founding in 1898, however it always has worked for the highest standards in American music.

At the meeting of the Board of Directors in Louisville, Kentucky in 1960, Mrs. C. Arthur Bullock, president, there was much concern about the possibility of an opera being written by Marc Blitzstein, and produced by the Metropolitan Opera Company, portraying two convicted criminals – both of whom had been executed – as martyrs. Mrs. Ronald A. Dougan, past president, read the following resolution, which had been brought to the meeting by Mrs. J. A. Alexander. Mrs. Dougan moved its adoption and the motion carried.

A RESOLUTION
Adopted by NFMC Board of Directors
August 27-31, 1960, in Louisville, Ky.

WHEREAS: Nicola Sacco and Bartolomeo Vanzetti were found guilty of the murder of Frederick A. Parmeter and his guard, South Braintree, Massachusetts, were sentenced and electrocuted for the crime (August 1927) (Crime committed April 1920);

WHEREAS: Said Vanzetti and Sacco were known to be draft dodgers and radicals, and they confessed to radical activities;

WHEREAS: Jurors, trial Judges, and men reviewing the case (namely Gov. Alvan T. Fuller with an advisory committee of leading citizens and the then associate Justice of the Supreme Court, Hon. Oliver Wendell Holmes, and others) were convinced that the verdict was just;

WHEREAS: From the time of the trial and up to the present time the Sacco-Vanzetti case has been a Communist *cause celebre* – a propaganda weapon – to discredit the United States of America through presenting America not as a free spiritual nation but rather as a nation materialistic and barbaric where the capitalist and he alone matters – "where the working man is the victim of total injustice, atrocious abuse, even condemnation to death";

WHEREAS: Efforts are being made to portray the two men (Sacco and Vanzetti) as martyrs and victims in a war of "reactionaries" against "liberals" by telling about the case in an opera, purporting to be American Folklore;

WHEREAS: Marc Blitzstein, who is being paid (in part with funds from the Ford Foundation) to compose the opera, admitted to members of the House Committee on Un-American Activities (May 1958) that he had been a member of the Communist Party (1938-49) and his record shows that for years he has been associated with numerous organizations listed as subversive by the U.S. Attorney General's Office;

WHEREAS: We believe that exploiting the criminals through the media of opera is not in good taste, will provoke undeserving emotional display if it is produced, is an encroachment on the field of American Art and not representative of American Folklore;

WHEREAS: Permitting the exploitation of government and/or foundation funds to produce a work which, when performed abroad, can serve but to jeopardize American prestige which the United States Government, through the Voice of America, the United States Information Agency, and other agencies at a cost of hundreds of millions of dollars is continuously striving to maintain; and

WHEREAS: The Metropolitan Opera Company is the Opera Center of the Western World, having earned that reputation by producing works of the highest standards for three-quarters of a century; therefore

BE IT RESOLVED: (a) That while we applaud the Metropolitan Opera Company for their productions of American Opera in the past, and their desire to produce other American Operas in the future, we oppose the opera being written by Marc Blitzstein, we protest its production and performance for any audience within the United States of America (all 50 of them); (b) That we register our disapproval of the use of funds from any American Foundation for the benefit of a person of proven subversive character; (c) That we respectfully request the Manager of the Metropolitan Opera Company, Mr. Rudolph Bing, and the Company's Board of Directors to cancel its scheduled (or intent to schedule) production of any opera which attacks the American system of Government, Judicial, and/or political, and in particular the opera being written about the Sacco-Vanzetti Case; (d) That a copy of this RESOLUTION, approved by the members of the Board of Directors of the National Federation of Music Clubs, in session at the Brown Hotel, Louisville, Kentucky, August, 1960, be mailed to: Mr. Rudolph Bing; Members of the Board of Directors of the Metropolitan Opera Company; American Society of Composers, Authors and Publishers (ASCAP); Ford Foundation; the State Department; Members of the House Judiciary Committee; Rep. Joel T. Broyhill; Rep. Carroll D. Kearns; Rep. Elmer J. Holland; Rep. Francis E. Dorn; Rep. Louis C. Rabaut; Rep. Herbert Zelenko; Music Educators National Conference; National Music Council; the National Council of Arts and Government; the General Federation of Women's Clubs; the National Education Association; the American Legion; Veterans of Foreign Wars; the Daughters of the American Revolution; and the Guardians of Our American Heritage.

CHAPTER FOUR

I HEAR AMERICA SINGING

Choral Music

1

Dr. Walter Damrosch is quoted as saying, "Don't call yourself musical until you can play at least three instruments." Few can play three musical instruments, and many cannot play even one. But there is an avenue of musical expression open to all - singing.

Since the inception of Choral Music in the early history of the National Federation of Music Clubs, it has encouraged participation in choral activity in musical life generally, by encouraging choral music as a project through choral singing in the clubs, church choirs, civic clubs, schools and industrial centers. Leadership for this has been provided when needed, and publicity has been given through the press.

The Federation has encouraged American composers to continue their efforts in the choral field, and to build toward a permanent library which might be available in the future. Through the encouragement of choral clinics and choral contests the Federation has worked to raise the standards of amateur choral effort.

For the three years, 1918 until 1920, the National Council of Women of the United States sponsored at their national convention "A Memorial Sing" under the guidance of several organizations, including the National Federation of Music Clubs. The entire nation was asked to sing on November 11, in "memory of the signing of the Armistice... in memory of our Fallen Heroes... and in memory of a Victorious Army." The program which everyone throughout the United States was asked to sing at the same hour – eleven o'clock on November 11 – in 1920, was:

Star Spangled Banner   *Our Tribute*
Battle Hymn of the Republic   *Ring Out Sweet Bells of Peace*
Lest We Forget   *America the Beautiful*
Nearer My God to Thee

The February 1923 *Official Bulletin* (the Federation's official magazine) reported the extensive choral work being done by the clubs:

- The Choral Department of the HARMONY CLUB OF DOTHAN, ALABAMA, Mrs. Addie Anderson Wilson, president, presented Gaul's *Holy City* with orchestra accompaniment. For six years "Christmas carols on the street and in the hospitals have been a feature of the club's work."
- The TUESDAY MUSICALE OF PITTSBURG's chorus of eighty women gave its midwinter program, beginning with German's *O Lovely May* and closing with *Come Sister Come* by Mackenzie.
- The TREBLE CLEF CLUB OF NIAGARA FALLS, NEW YORK, was heard in a well chosen program of Christmas carols from "different countries, including St. Saen's cantata, *Night.*
- The COMMUNITY CHORUS OF BELOIT, WISCONSIN gave a program of "unusually good character" on December 5, the "most important number being Samuel Coleridge-Taylor's *Hiawatha's Wedding Feast.*"

The 1927 Biennial Convention in Chicago was called the "Singing Convention". The "happy idea" of holding a Singing Biennial was conceived by Mrs. Frank A. Seiberling, past national president. As Biennial Choral Chairman for this convention she had labored unceasingly helping to compile the two "charming souvenir" Song Books used by the chorus and delegates for the massed Choral Concert. In the words of Mrs. Seiberling:

> "The crowning glory of the entire event... was the element of singing which entered so largely into each day's program – singing by the assembly at every occasion, singing every morning and afternoon by one of the fourteen outstanding choruses which came from all directions at their own expense to participate, and who helped to create an atmosphere so literally tinged with the spirit of music that the convention assumed the nature of a glorious and uplifting paean of song."

The first of the outstanding musical events was in Orchestra Hall by the Apollo Club of Chicago, one of the oldest choral organizations in America, who gave a brilliant interpretation of Edgar Stillman Kelley's oratorio – *Pilgrims Progress* – assisted by an orchestra of players from the Chicago Symphony Orchestra.

It was for this Singing Convention that Mrs. Seiberling wrote *A Musical Ritual* (consisting of much choral singing) from which Mrs. Thomas J. Cole of Amory, Mississippi gleaned many of the phrases which she used in writing the Federation's official Collect.

The fifty dollar prize and banner, offered by Mrs. Seiberling to the state having the largest percentage of clubs sending "Singing Delegates" was won by the Wisconsin Federation of Music Clubs.

On May 14, 1939 the National Federation of Music Clubs observed Federation Day at the New York World's Fair. One of the most important events of the day was the massed Federation Chorus with John Warren Erb directing more than 1,000 singers. The New York Federation of Music Clubs served as host.

Maintaining morale through Music in Industry during World War II was truly a valued patriotic service rendered by the Federation. In Brunswick, Georgia, shipyard workers with the J. A. Jones Construction Company constituted the main membership of the Brunswick Choral Society. The shipyard employees worked on the first and third shifts so that they were able to be free to rehearse. Major musical events included performance of the oratorio, *The Messiah*, the opera, *Carmen*, and weekly community sings.

In 1947 at the Biennial Convention in Detroit, Michigan, big industry's contribution to the development of choral singing was demonstrated for Federation members. From the Chevrolet plant came the Glee Club, and the Dow Chemical Company sent its male chorus from Midland. Huge choruses and small groups were active long before industry began to explore the value of music to the production of machines.

In 1981 the "American Music Festival Chorus" was revived by the national president, Mrs. Jack C. Ward, for the Biennial Convention in Birmingham, Alabama. Miss Ernestine Ferrell was named director and Mrs. Josephine Bryan, accompanist. This has continued to play an important role on biennial convention programs since that time, with both men and women singing in the chorus.

FROM SONG TO SYMPHONY

Crusade for Strings

1

There are many legends connected with the early history of strings according to the 1973 NFMC *Crusade for Strings* chairman, Mrs. Martin E. Grothe: According to the Greek legend, it was the twang of the bowstring that first made Apollo aware of the musical properties of a vibrating string; An Egyptian legend credits Hermes with the discovery. One day as he was walking along the bank of the Nile, his foot chanced to strike the shell of a dead tortoise, causing the dried sinews to vibrate; An Irish tradition maintains that it was the playing of the wind on the dried muscle fibers of a dead whale that presented man with the first idea of a stringed instrument.

Before the mid 1950's strings had been stressed very little in the Federation – and very little had been accomplished. With two world wars and a great depression the attention was focused to the more pressing needs of the day. There was a Department of Orchestra and Chamber Music, but the accent on strings hardly reached beyond that. In the summer of 1941 during the presidency of Mrs. Guy Gannett, when the Little Red House was begun at Berkshire Music Center, the Federation initiated a contest to select three string players for scholarships to the Music Center. This was initiated because of the pronounced shortage of strings available to the orchestra. Two boys and a girl were chosen, and had the enviable experience of playing with Dr. Serge Koussevitzky's famous Youth Orchestra in the summer of 1942.

It was in that same year, that because of the shortage of string players, the National Federation of Music Clubs instituted in collaboration with the Julliard School of Music and the National Broadcasting Company Orchestra, under Leopold Stokowski, a plan to select a violinist for a Julliard scholarship. A young California girl was selected.

It was not until Mrs. Ronald A. Dougan's election to the national presidency in 1955 that something was to be done about the shortage of string players in the United States. One of the first crises which claimed her attention was the limited number of students studying strings both in schools and with private teachers. This threatened the deterioration of the quality of performance of the orchestras in the United States, especially the outstanding ones which had done so much to enhance American prestige abroad.

Mrs. Dougan gave much of the credit of her promotion of strings to the states throughout the nation to whom she had been invited to visit during her vice-presidency and presidency. One who influenced her decision greatly was the visit of Mrs. Ada Holding Miller to the South Carolina Federation of Music Clubs convention in Spartanburg, in 1951. On the convention program was a gala concert featuring strings directed by the outstanding violinist and teacher of strings, Peggy Thomson Gignilliant. It was this visit and others like it from which she received the inspiration for the National Federation of Music Club's *Crusade for Strings* to take top priority when she assumed the presidency. It was founded during the first year of her administration.

Mrs. Dougan tells the story of how, early in January, 1956 when she was at the Gotham Hotel in New York City, she again began wondering what could be done by the Federation to alleviate the "dearth of strings" in the United States. It was then the title, *Crusade for Strings* came to her. She immediately telephoned Thor Johnson in Cincinnati, who was "thrilled" with the idea, the title and the list of achievement goals which she outlined. Dr. Johnson accepted the chairmanship, and Dr. Lena Milam became the vice-chairman. In four brief months seventy-six entries were received with twenty-eight states represented.

In Dr. Johnson's first Plan of Work, he wrote, "Concern is voiced daily over the shortage of string players capable of membership in our great orchestras... There are two simple solutions... (1) encourage school boards... to establish first class elementary string programs; (2) create a greater demand for the private teacher of stringed instruments."

Since 1956 the *Crusade for Strings* has been one of the most important projects sponsored by the Federation. Awards of Merit and Rating Sheet credit are given clubs and individual members who are successful in inaugurating string programs of high caliber in schools; who present outstanding string programs; who establish orchestras of String Ensembles and contribute to their support; who federate musical string groups; who give string scholarships and/or awards; and who in other ways promote the study and performance of strings.

Each year as the *Crusade* has grown in scope and influence, and the Federation has been recognized for "originality", strings have been accented in several summer music centers. In addition to the scholarships given, including four cash awards given by Broadcast Music Incorporated (BMI) in 1965, strings are included as one of the four classifications in the Federation's Young Artist Auditions, awarding to the winner $7,500. A supplemental award of $1500, should the winner be a violinist, is given by the National Federation of Music Clubs in honor of past president, Vera Wardner Dougan (Mrs. Ronald A. Dougan).

THEY FOLLOW THE BATON

Bands and Orchestras

1

Before the founding of the Federation's *Crusade for Strings* program, orchestras in the United States were few because of the lack of string players. The support of orchestras and bands, however, always has been uppermost in the hearts of Federation members. Many symphony orchestras have been organized by clubs in the local communities.

Since the earliest years the Federation has featured major orchestras on the biennial convention programs. In 1909 the Theodore Thomas Symphony Orchestra (Chicago Symphony Orchestra) in Grand Rapids, Michigan performed the Federation's first prize winning composition, *The Culprit Fay* by Henry Hadley; the open-air concert by the San Francisco Symphony Orchestra, in San Mateo, California when San Francisco hosted the 1931 Biennial Convention; the Chicago Symphony Orchestra, under the baton of Frederick Stock at the 1927 convention; the 1933 Philadelphia Biennial Convention when the Philadelphia Symphony Orchestra performed with Leopold Stokowski, Director, and José Iturbi, Conductor. Appearing on the same convention program were The Women's Symphony Orchestra of Philadelphia, and the High School Girls Orchestra. The 1947 Biennial Convention program in Detroit, Michigan included the Detroit Symphony Orchestra, Paul Kruger, conducting and the program highlighted John Powell's *Symphony in A*, the Federation's first commission, which was based on American folk themes.

The historical files reflect that through the years there have been many commissions for orchestrated music. In addition to the first commissioned orchestral work, *Symphony in A*, which was premiered at the 1947 Biennial Convention in Detroit, in 1955 Mrs. Ronald A. Dougan, national president, commissioned Peter Mennin to write an orchestral work for the opening concert for the Columbus, Ohio convention. *Canto for Orchestra* was written and performed.

In 1959 Mrs. Dougan again commissioned Lucas Foss to write an orchestral work to be world-premiered at the San Diego convention. Mr. Foss's work, entitled *Variations*, originally was to have been heard at the San Diego Biennial but was not completed. It was premiered at a later date.

The latest among the many commissions of the Federation is *Piano Concerto 11* by a popular contemporary composer and Pulitzer Prize winner, John La Montaine. It was commissioned by Mrs. Jack C. Ward, president, in 1983, and was world-premiered on December 9, 1994, by the Eastman School of Music Philharmonia Orchestra, with David Effron conducting, and Barry Snyder, soloist.

During the great depression following the collapse of the stock market in 1929, the WPA (Works Progress Administration) was founded for the purpose of giving jobs to the unemployed. Through the work of the WPA music project, many orchestras were organized, chiefly for the purpose of serving as relief projects for the unemployed musicians. Federation members gave unstintingly of their time and energy on behalf of this program – many serving on advisory boards governing the project.

In the 1930's, among the Juniors there were many toy orchestras and rhythm bands organized and federated, and countless juvenile and junior clubs were using toy orchestra works as a part of their regular club programs. Delaware had a state chairman of Toy Orchestras and Rhythm Bands; Maine had annual Toy Orchestra contests with a silver loving cup as an award; Georgia made the Toy Orchestra contest a permanent feature; and state newspapers in Texas, New York and Massachusetts gave space to toy orchestra activities.

2

Unique among the orchestras and bands which were members of the Federation in the early 1920's, were "bands in the workplace – in industry." The Central of Georgia Railroad maintained two splendid bands – the Central of Georgia Shop Band in Macon, Georgia, organized in 1923, and the Right Way Band of the Savannah Shops organized in 1924. There also was an orchestra at both the Macon and Savannah shops – as well as numerous glee clubs and quartets at various points in the system.

These musical organizations all had a prominent part in events for the recreation and entertainment of employees. The Macon band of fifty-five members was under the leadership of Professor W. C. Dean, an accomplished musician, who won fame as director of the "Old Grey Bonnet Band" during World War I. The Macon band won fame throughout the nation when two concerts were broadcasted by the radio station of the Atlanta Journal.

The Right Way Band, composed of workmen in the Savannah shops, was made up largely of young men who were taking individual lessons in addition to mass practice. The band was under the leadership of Professor I. C. Davis, an experienced band leader in Savannah.

It was the belief of Mr. Downs, president of the Central of Georgia Railroad "that there is no over-estimating the value of music as a stimulus for morale among workers." He encouraged this form of musical organization "of every nature by all possible members."

In 1927 a unique hospital band was the Moody Hospital Saxophone Players of Dothan, Alabama which was directed by Mr. D. G. Farnum. The band, as a member of the Federation, afforded many happy hours for the Moody Hospital.

The Toy Orchestra, Tampa, Florida.

MUSIC HATH CHARMS

Music in Prisons

1

Everyone is aware of the effects of music upon the inmates of the
prisons. It is a well-known fact that bands and orchestras help uplift the
atmosphere in these places.

In the early 1920's and well into the 1950's the Federation was aware
of the effects of music upon the inmates of the prisons, and the members
worked untiringly toward helping to bring music to these penal institutions. The first prison band in America to federate was the United States
Disciplinary Band and Orchestra of San Quentin, California – D. G.
Gallur, director, and J. F. Brennan, Drum Major.

In 1926 the Federation received a letter of appreciation from Mr.
Gallur, in which he stated that their prison band of thirty-six members,
and the "orchestra of less number, are both doing fine work, and having
the orchestra play in the dining room during meals has changed the entire atmosphere of the prison, giving the inmates moments of real joy."
He continued by saying, "After working hard all day, to hear good lively
music is a treat for the inmates, and it has helped to ease the sorrow that
all of the boys are burdened with, and I believe I am safe in saying that
it has been the means of curbing the turbulent spirit that exists in all
institutions of this kind."

Many musical instruments were presented to the prison by Federation members. Mrs. H. H. Koons presented a number of instruments on
behalf of The Friday Morning Music Club of Los Angeles, California.

The prison on Governors Island, as well as other prisons, had bands
and orchestras, all of which were in need of musical instruments. Pleas
went out to members and state presidents to supply the musical needs of
those penal institutions within their own states.

Among other prisons to benefit from this program were singing groups
in the Central Prison for Men, and the Woman's Prison, in Raleigh, North

Carolina. Under the sponsorship of the Raleigh Music Club, Mr. and Mrs. John D. Holmes worked unceasingly in this program of social rehabilitation.

There were many problems. In the Woman's Prison Mrs. Holmes faced: women who had run afoul of the law, were hostile and socially maladjusted; many were full of resentment. But as the weeks went by, the chorus grew steadily. Within three months they had developed into a creditable choir, and in March 1951 they presented their first program of Easter Music. They made their own vestments, and when they marched down the aisle to the processional, *Christ the Lord is Risen Today* they would have "done credit to any church or college choir".

A special feature of this program was a violin solo by a girl named Betty. When committed to the institution she was emotionally upset and avoided contacts with others. When it was discovered she played a violin, one was provided. Soon they became inseparable companions and gradually she played with pleasure for her companions and grew daily more congenial. When she left the prison she was heard to say, "As long as I can have my violin, I am sure I can make a go of things."

ONE COMMON TIE – MUSIC

American Society of Composers, Authors and Publishers

1

The twenty-sixth biennial convention of the National Federation of Music Clubs in Salt Lake City, Utah, May 20-27, 1951, was one of the largest and one of the most brilliant in the Federation's past fifty-three year history – outstanding speakers and musical programs in the city's Mormon Tabernacle.

But this was more than a convention – this was the beginning, as Stanley Adams, president of ASCAP said when he addressed the National Federation in 1979, "of a love affair between the National Federation of Music Clubs and the American Society of Composers, Authors and Publishers (ASCAP)" which has lasted for these past forty-two years, and as he continued, "hopefully divorce proceedings will never be initiated by either party."

Mr. Otto Harbach, president of ASCAP, was a guest of the Federation and its president, Mrs. Royden James Keith at the Salt Lake City convention. He was very much inspired and in sympathy with the work of the organization, and felt the two organizations had one common "tie" binding them – their love of music and its promotion in America. Upon his return to New York he conveyed his feeling to his colleagues who supported him.

During these intervening years since Mr. Harbach visited Salt Lake City in 1951 this wonderful and gratifying association has continued through the administrations of six presidents of ASCAP – Otto Harbach, Stanley Adams, Paul Cunningham, Hal David, Morton Gould, and today's Marilyn Bergman, Chairman of the Board, who continues to serve with the same dedication as her distinguished predecessors – all who have worked closely with ten presidents of the National Federation of Music Clubs.

The National Federation of Music Clubs is deeply grateful to ASCAP.

Because of their loyal support for forty-four years, the Federation has made possible many opportunities to America's young musicians – opportunities which otherwise would have been impossible.

The two organizations have been co-workers in their work for legislation affecting music and musicians in America, often appearing side by side before the Senate Judiciary Committee on behalf of America's composers and performers – the Copyright Law, the Juke Box Bill, and on and on.

Otto Harbach, a native of Utah and president of ASCAP visits with another fellow Utahn, Dr. Frances Elliott Clark, charter member of the National Federation. Mr. Harbach's visit to the 1951 Salt Lake City convention marked the beginning of a close friendship between the Federation and the American Society of Composers, Authors and Publishers.

PART SEVEN

A Musical Showcase

AN ONGOING LEGACY

Scholarships and Awards

1

"Had you (the Federation) commissioned me to make for you a report of survey of performance of American Music, you would have cause for rejoicing – Moreover the Federation is entitled to feel an especial gratification over the changed state of affairs, for it has been a valiant crusader in the cause of American Music, one of the truly important factors in giving a sympathetic hearing for native composers."

—John Tasker Howard

According to Dr. Frances Elliott Clark, one of the charter members of the National Federation of Music Clubs, "The National Federation was the first to offer prizes in a large way to American composers." There was much criticism, with many asserting it was wrong, "impossible", "no worthy work could be produced to order", but the Federation members went "serenely along" offering prizes and giving the works "public production".

It was not long before the giving of prizes for American composition was begun by orchestras, opera associations, schools of music, clubs, newspapers, colleges and individuals – and today it is accepted universally as a way of promoting the American composer and American music. Mrs. Clark continued, "Perhaps again the Federated music clubs may feel that their efforts have borne such fruit that they may turn their strength to pioneering in still other fields."

2

The Siren Song

Out from far places,
Where the grey sea
Meets the grey sky,
And a dim moon has lost the line thereof –
Softly, the siren song.

Half fainting on his deck, the wanderer
Feels the soft fingers of the soulless voice
Along his body's length;
And on his lips, a mouth
Clinging so close, he feels the pressing
 teeth.

Then must his soul wing forth,
And in that void of stricken grey,
Another voice wail endlessly.

And if some soul that will not die, fight
 back –
Once more the tumbled blue,
With rainbows in the stinging spray,
And overhead, great sun-draped banks of
 white.

But ever, on his eyes, the stricken grey;
And in his ears, the aching song;
And underneath the lips of his true love,
The pressing teeth – unto the end.
—Joseph Tiers, Jr.

Deems Taylor, composer and past president of ASCAP tells the story of the part the National Federation of Music Clubs played in his life, in an article entitled, "My Second Prize Start" in *Music Clubs Magazine*, in which he says:

"It was the early fall of 1912, and I was, as they say, at loose ends. Two years before I had had a musical comedy produced on Broadway, and was prepared to settle down to a career of fame and affluence. Unfortunately things didn't turn out that way. The musical comedy, after a brief New York run, had taken to the road, where it had quietly passed away. My first invasion of Broadway had been a failure – struck out first time at bat....

"Then, in my darkest hour, I read a paragraph in the Musical Courier. It announced that the National Federation of Music Clubs was offering a substantial prize for the best symphony or symphonic poem by an American composer....

"'If Broadway doesn't want me,' I said to myself, 'I'll try Carnegie Hall.'

"So I went out and bought a quire of music paper, found a poem with a mood I liked, and set to work. The piece, which I christened *Siren Song*, was finished and shipped off to Chicago... in November, 1912.

"Ten suspenseful weeks went by, the longest ten weeks of my life. Then at long last, dated March 14th, came a telegram from Mrs. Jason Walker, Chairman, American Music Committee:

'JUDGES HAVE SENT DECISION FOR CLASS ONE YOUR "SIREN SONG" AWARDED SECOND PRIZE THREE HUN- DRED DOLLARS CHICAGO ORCHESTRA WILL CON- SIDER RENDERING AT BIENNIAL IF YOU SEND PARTS BY WEDNESDAY NINETEENTH ABSOLUTELY (sic) NEC- ESSARY TO SEND AT ONCE DIRECT TO MR. STOCK WIRE HIM ACCEPT CONGRATULATIONS AM WRITING YOU.

(Signed)
MRS. JASON WALKER'"

The following day the promised letter arrived. It stated that the judges were very slow in sending their decision, as at first there had been some difference of opinion, but the final agreement was to make no award in Class I for the first prize, but *The Siren Song* should receive second prize. Mrs. Walker continued by inviting him to attend the Biennial Fes- tival in Chicago, April 21-26, "as you are now an Honorary Member of the National Federation of Musical Clubs."

Mr. Taylor continued:

"Of course in my innocence, it had never occurred to me to have the parts extracted. So, needless to say, *The Siren Song* was not played. No matter, I was a composer. The judges (one of whom was Leopold Stokowski) had said so.

"And that is how the National Federation of Music Clubs
changed my life."

The second place winner was awarded a cash prize of $300.00.

One last word about *The Siren Song* – In 1924 Mr. Taylor revised
some passages of it and had the parts copied. The New York Philharmonic gave it two performances under Henry Hadley.

The original manuscript of *The Siren Song* is in the Library of Congress. When this writer was there doing research, she was asked by a
guard to accompany him to the desk. Not knowing why, she followed
with fear and trembling. After showing her credentials she was seated. It
was then learned – the original copy of *The Siren Song* was brought to
the table, and with the guard standing watch, the writer had the thrill of
seeing the original manuscript of *The Siren Song* – the composition to
which Deems Taylor gives credit for his having become a composer.

3

In early 1943 the Federation, Mrs. Guy Patterson Gannett, president,
motivated by the banality of much of the war music, in collaboration with
the National Broadcasting Company, launched a contest to secure a patriotic song which was hoped would have more merit than the current ones.

The type of song sought was one of easy range that might be adopted
to community singing with original words and music. "In other words,"
according to Mrs. Gannett, "it might be a musical setting to lyrics which
would have the inspiring qualities of *Battle Hymn of the Republic* or a
simple stirring patriotic song like *Over There.*"

The award was to be a premiere on an NBC network, and published
by Mills Music Inc. on a royalty basis. The song also was to be given
consideration for the "Army Hit Kit."

More than 8,000 manuscripts, from many of the best known composers
in America, were judged by a committee of four judges: Leopold
Stokowski, Lawerence Tibbett, Ernest LaPrade and Lt. Colonel Howard
Bronson. None seemed to have quite the quality or spirit desired. The four
receiving honorable mention were selected for world premieres on the
NBC network, and one of the four was published by Mills Music Inc.

Wednesday evening, May 10, 1944 was an auspicious occasion, for
in the studio in the RCA Building, a fine concert orchestra under the
baton of Dr. Frank Black, an excellent chorus, and two distinguished

soloists – Nan Merriman, 1943 Federation Young Artist winner, and Robert Merrill, baritone – gave the songs their first performance. Miss Merriman sang *America United* by Paul Kirby, conductor of leading orchestras in the United States and abroad, and *A Beacon in the Darkness* by Sergeant William Carty, A.A.F. Mr. Merrill sang, *Where Men Are Free*, written by Mrs. Doris L. Jackson of Garnett, Kansas, and *Americans All* by Wallace G. Anderson, leader of the dance band at the Hotel Olympic in Seattle.

4

Dr. Hazel Post Gillette had no idea in 1965 when she founded the Adult Non-Professional Composers' Contest, to what proportions it would grow, or the influence it would have on music in America. The competition, founded during the administration of Mrs. Clifton J. Muir, was intended to give encouragement to adult composers who had never had their compositions published.

The first winner of the competition in 1965 was Harriett Bolz of Columbus, Ohio, whose winning composition was entitled, *Floret – A Mood Caprice for Piano*. Since winning that first competition the list of Harriett Bolz's accomplishments are endless. In corresponding to this writer she wrote, "This was the start of my success as a composer, and so I owe a great deal to the National Federation of Music Clubs... I have performed all over the country and expect a performance in Italy."

The award of fifty dollars for the Adult Non-Professional Composers' Contest held biennially was made possible by Mrs. Robert W. Roberts of St. Petersburg, Florida, benefactor of the Federation. Through a legacy left to the Federation by the late Glad Robinson Youse, the award was raised to $500 to be given biennially and called the Glad Robinson Youse Adult Composers' Award.

5

"In appreciation of the dedication required from a person accepting the responsibility of volunteer service as the national president of the Federation of Music Clubs," says Mrs. Robert E. L. Freeman, "each president, upon retirement, is honored with the establishment of a scholarship or award of her choice." Beginning in 1962, the goal of endowing each of these scholarships seemed almost unattainable. But success in reaching their objectives was not to be denied the committee members.

"In 1983, for the first time, the total amount needed to endow a Past National President's Scholarship was raised by the end of the administration, and the completion of the endowment announced upon the occasion of the retirement of the president, Lucile Parrish Ward. This has continued in subsequent years."

National presidents have shown great variety in their choices of scholarships or awards established in their honor. Many selections reflect the needs of the times; others show deep personal interest.

- Since 1937 the NFMC **Agnes Jardine Scholarship** has been awarded to International Music Camp, Peace Gardens, North Dakota.
- The NFMC **Anne M. Gannett Award for Veterans** emphasizes Mrs. Gannett's war time presidency, 1941-1947.
- The **Marie Morrisey Keith Scholarship** is offered biennially in the Student Division in orchestral woodwinds and orchestral brass.
- The scholarship honoring **Ada Holding Miller** is awarded to Kneisel Hall, Blue Hill, Maine for the study of strings or piano.
- The **Vera Wardner Dougan Award** is a biennial award given in the Young Artists Auditions as a supplemental award to the winner of violin.
- In 1963 the **Dorothy Dann Bullock Music Therapy Award** was established as an annual student scholarship.
- The **Irene Steed Muir Scholarship**, in 1967 was designated for summer study of students of instruments and voice at the Stephen Collins Foster Music Camp, Richmond, Kentucky.
- 1971 brought the opportunity for a blind student, when the **Hinda Honigman Scholarship for the Blind** was initiated to be given annually in the Student Division.
- The **Merle Montgomery Opera Award** which was begun in 1975, is given as a supplementary award to the man's and woman's voice winners in the Young Artist Auditions.
- The **Ruby S. Vought Scholarship in Organ** is given in the Student Division biennially.
- The Lucile Parrish Ward Piano Young Artist Award (1983) became the **Lucile Parrish Ward Award for American Music Performance** in the Ellis Duo-Piano Competition in 1991.
- 1987 highlighted ballet when the **Thelma A. Robinson Ballet Award** was established in the Junior Division as a biennial award.

- The **Mary Prudie Brown Award** is given a student at Inspiration Point Fine Arts Colony to be used to further his/her musical education.

The National Federation of Music Clubs Scholarships Honoring Past National Presidents, are funded by the earnings from endowments which assure their continuance, and attests to the firm conviction of its members and its presidents that the organization has an obligation to provide opportunities for future generations.

6

The National Federation of Music Clubs gives thousands of dollars each year in scholarships and awards to the musically talented Juniors, Students and Seniors – all in the promotion of American music – the composer and performer. Almost all of the scholarships given by the Federation – have been endowed by either individuals or the Federation. Included are awards in almost every musical classification – piano, voice, strings, organ, opera, composition, music education, music therapy, music for the blind and handicapped, summer music camps and many more ranging from $50.00 to $10,000.

The first scholarships offered by the National Federation were in 1901 at the second Biennial Convention in Cleveland, Ohio. The scholarships were given by D/Angelo Bergh School of Singing in New York. Eight months later the Federation held the competition and four scholarships of $250 each were given covering four months instruction in the Special Singers and Teachers Course.

Since those first scholarships in 1901, the number of scholarships has continued to increase. In many instances there have been scholarships given on a one year, two year or possibly three year basis by individuals or others in which the Federation was the administrator. Some of these include:

- In 1928 the Hollywood Bowl inaugurated an annual prize composition award of $1,000 for a concert overture, the winning work "to be performed by the Hollywood Bowl Symphony Orchestra."
- The Atwater Kent competition in 1929 for the "best young singers" was offered. The awards – $17,500 in prizes, plus tuition was offered to ten national winners. The ten finalists

were announced at the NBC Studio on Fifth Avenue in New York City by Mr. Atwater Kent at a ceremony witnessed by members of the Federation, headed by Mrs. Edgar Stillman Kelley, chairman. The two winners of the top awards of $5,000 each were: Miss Agnes Davis, lyric soprano, Denver, Colorado, and Wilbur W. Evans, bass baritone, Philadelphia, Pennsylvania. The contest continued for a second year with approximately 60,000 soloists competing.

- In 1938 the Federation accepted Vick's Chemical Company's offer to sponsor a violin contest in which four violins valued at $1,000 each, were awarded with all publicity subject "to Federation supervision on Tony Wons radio program."

- The Donald Voorhees contest in 1944 was administered by the Federation. A $500 war bond given for the best patriotic concert was won by the Music Club of Vernon, Texas.

- The Paul Lavalle $1,500 scholarship given by the distinguished orchestra leader, conductor of the Cities Service program, heard on NBC, was administered by the National Federation. Lavalle was prompted to offer the scholarship "because of his keen interest in young people and his sympathy with those who might have a struggle to finance their musical studies." The winner of the first scholarship in 1947 was Donald Gramm, bass, of Milwaukee, Wisconsin.

- 1954 marked the 100th Anniversary of the Steinway Piano Company. Included in their one year celebration was the announcement of a Centennial Award of $2,000 for advanced study for a pianist of concert calibre – to be administered by the National Federation of Music Clubs. Theodore Steinway announced the winner, 20 year old John Browning.

- It was only five years later, at the Biennial Convention in San Diego, California in 1959, that Van Cliburn presented to Mrs. Ronald A. Dougan, president, a check for $1,000 for an award to be given in memory of Theodore Steinway. In 1961 the Steinway Memorial Award was presented to James Mathis, runner-up in piano in the NFMC Young Artist Competition.

These are only a few of the many scholarships which have been administered by the National Federation of Music Clubs for "music-loving" donors. There were many others as: Readers Digest Foundation, Fred Waring, Peabody Conservatory, Eastman School of Music, the Arthur J. Bitkner offered by Music by Muzak, and more.

ON WINGS OF SONG

Young Artists

1

The mention of the names of certain concert artists – Rosalyn Tureck, Shirley Verrett, Gary Lakes, Kathleen Battle and on and on – has a special and personal meaning for members of the National Federation of Music Clubs. Such expressions as, "I heard her when she won the Young Artists Auditions" or "He is one of ours" are heard. Members of the Federation take great pride in the accomplishments of their Young Artist winners. Being chosen a winner in the National Federation's Young Artist Auditions serves as a stepping stone to an illustrious musical career, for no winner is declared unless the judges consider the finalist ready for a concert career.

Only seventeen years after its founding in 1898, the National Federation launched this ambitious project – first a state winner was chosen to compete in the district – the district winners proceeded to the national auditions. The first national chairman was Mrs. Louis E. Yager.

In that first year – 1915, no national contest was held, but four district winners in each of the three classifications – voice, piano, and violin, performed at the national convention in Los Angeles, California.

Two years later in 1917 the Board voted that "after further consideration of plans for the Young Artists contest" the Federation hold a national contest in addition to state and district contests, and that a prize of $150.00 be given each of the three national winners. Mrs. Frank Seiberling offered to provide the prize for the national vocal winner, to be known as the James H. Rogers Prize, and to be given in perpetuity. In addition it was decided that each district winner should receive "a gold pin of the Federation Insignia."

At the Peterborough, New Hampshire convention, in addition to the prize offered two years previously by Mrs. Frank Seiberling to the winner of voice, additional prizes were offered in perpetuity by individuals:

Mrs. A. J. Oschner $150 given in memory of Edward MacDowell to the winner of piano; $150 given by Mrs. Christine Miller as the William L. Whitney violin prize; and $150 given by Mrs. Grace Porterfield Polk for a voice prize for women.

Through eighty years the Young Artist Awards have increased from the $150 in 1915 to $7,500 with supplemental awards in the four classifications – piano, strings, man's voice and woman's voice. (In 1974 the violin classification was changed to "strings" with one award to be given for violin, viola, violoncello or string bass.) In 1961 a Young Artist Oratorio Award was given by Louis Sudler, friend and Honorary Member of the National Federation of Music Clubs, with Dale Moore, baritone, Granville, Ohio, declared the first winner. The award was discontinued in 1987.

Beginning with the 1985 competition, the second place winners in the national competition were awarded prizes of $500 each, with these increasing to $1250 each with the 1991-1993 biennium.

At the Biennial Convention in Buffalo, New York in 1993, in addition to the $7,500 given each of the four winners in the classifications of piano, strings, man's voice and woman's voice, there were supplemental awards to each:

WOMAN'S VOICE:
- The National Federation of Music Clubs Award honoring Dr. Merle Montgomery, past president – $750.00
- Mary Kimball Hail Award honoring the Chaminade Club of Providence, Rhode Island – $250.00

MAN'S VOICE:
- The National Federation of Music Clubs Award honoring Dr. Merle Montgomery, past president – $750.00

STRINGS:
- The Lily Peter String Award – $1,000.00
- The National Federation of Music Clubs Violin Award, honoring Vera Wardner Dougan, past president – $1,500.00

PIANO:
- The Edwin B. Ellis Award – $1,000.00
- The Samuel Sorin Piano Award – $1,000.00
- The Claudette Sorel Piano Award – $500.00

3

In addition to the supplemental cash awards, there have been many promotional awards, which the artists many times appreciate even more than the cash awards. Some include:

- The Schubert Memorial Award offered for the first time in 1929, which gave the Young Artist Competition greater significance in the professional world of music. The gift was announced by the president, Ossip Gabrilowitsch, and the secretary, Madame Olga Samaroff Stokowski. It offered through the Philharmonic Symphony Society, "to the best instrumentalist Federation National winner, an appearance with the Philharmonic Symphony Orchestra in Carnegie Hall, New York, and also (unless plans change)... an appearance at a pair of concerts with the Philadelphia Orchestra in Philadelphia". This award continued for many years.
- In 1939 the Firestone Tire and Rubber Company offered a $500 supplemental cash award, together with an appearance with a "radio orchestra from Firestone". Harvey S. Firestone, Jr. presented the award to 1939 Young Artist winner, Martha Lipton.
- In that same year – 1939, Dr. Nikalai Sokoloff offered "the winner in violin classification, the winner in the voice classification, and if one of the pianists fails to receive the Schubert Memorial Award, to that one also, a special appearance to be known as the NFMC program in four major cities, New York, Philadelphia, Chicago and Boston," with Dr. Sokoloff conducting the orchestra, making it a very festive and special occasion for the winners.
- In 1951 a managerial contract was given by the National Concert and Artist Corporation to a young artist winner. Claudette Sorel was the first winner, with Naomi Farr winning in 1953.
- In 1959 in San Diego, California, Mrs. Ronald A. Dougan, president, accepted a check for $1,000.00 from Van Cliburn, given in memory of Theodore Steinway and designated as an award toward a Town Hall appearance for a Young Artist winner in piano.

The Van Cliburn-Theodore Steinway Award was presented to James Mathis, runner-up in the 1961 auditions.

James Mathis made his debut as the winner of the Cliburn Award in Carnegie Hall on January 17, 1962, and the exceptional brilliance of the audience attested to the importance of this debut. "A lustrous new star is added" said the *New York Herald Tribune*.

The program was broadcast on WNYC and taped for the Voice of America.

4

In view of the fact that Paderewski, Fritz Kreisler and Albert Spalding had resumed their concert careers after World War I, the Federation took steps to insure that the talented musicians who served in World War II might do likewise. In 1943 the Board of Directors passed a recommendation allowing young artist applicants who had served in the Armed Forces, "without fee" to file applications which "will be held until such time as the applicant will be considered eligible, regardless of age, to compete in a contest held not later than three years after the completion of the war."

During World War II, and the administration of Mrs. Guy Gannett, no national conventions were held. Upon the "advice of concert managers and other authorities in the music world" for the first time the Young Artists finals were held in New York City. It was felt that the winners, if they possessed exceptional qualifications, would in this way be attracted more readily to the attention of artist managements. The facts that Nan Merriman, 1943 winner, was signed to a five year contract with the National Broadcasting Company on the day of the finals, and that heavy concert schedules were carried out by the 1945 winners would appear to justify the experiment.

At the Fall Session in Memphis, Tennessee in 1965 it was agreed that the Federation adopt a People to People project and pay $1,000 toward the transportation of one of the Federation's Young Artist winners to go abroad as a means of promoting good will. This was arranged in cooperation with the People to People Music Committee of the United States Information Agency and under the sponsorship of the United States Embassy. Elaine Skorodin, violinist, was chosen for the first concert tour to Japan. Again in 1966 Joseph Fennimore was given a good will concert tour to Japan.

These were the beginning of several Artists Foreign Goodwill Tours. Brenda Rucker-Smith, 1981 Artist winner, soprano, was sponsored on a three week good will tour to countries of the Caribbean and Central America. In each of the countries visited, the reviews were proof that "music is the international language of mankind".

5

"Our Young Artists Speak Out…"

Most of the Young Artist winners are grateful to the Federation for having ignited that spark which made possible for them concert careers.

- 1921 Artist winner, Devora Nadworney, voice, gave the Federation all the credit for having had a successful concert and operatic career. In appreciation she left a legacy to the Federation with which her sister, Mrs. Robert Wakefield, in 1944, endowed the Devora Nadworney scholarship in composition which is given annually in the Student Division.

- Margaret Harshaw, 1935 winner, voice, said: "I had great singing aspirations, but few practical hopes prior to my entering the Federation of Music Clubs biennial auditions." She had sung for local musical auditions in Philadelphia, "but," she said, "I was earning my living as a stenographer for the telephone company, and at that time it looked sadly as though I would continue a career of taking dictation all my life. Never did I anticipate winning the contest… I was bored and discouraged with the repetition of my daily working routine. The contest, I felt would force me to a decision… Somehow I found myself the winner… heaven sent as the money was, it was nothing compared to what winning the contest meant to my morale….

"My life changed with the Federation Award. I knew a career was possible… José Iturbi was one of the judges… he asked me to appear as soloist in El Amor Brugo, under his conductorship at the Robin Hood Dell, Lewisohn Stadium, and with the Rochester Symphony the following summer. My appearance at the Lewisohn Stadium resulted in an offer of a scholarship to the Julliard School of Music… Hans Kindler also suggested me to sing with the National Symphony Orchestra following the Federation contest… In the years that have gone by, wonderful things have happened: study at the Julliard School, my first management, winning the Metropolitan Auditions of the Air, my debut as a contralto at the Metropolitan Opera in 1942 and nine years of opera until I sang my first soprano role at the Met in 1951. Now – two years later I am singing Isolde, Donna Anna, Bruennhilde and Ortrud regularly… all of which might never happened had I not tried out, against my better judgement, for the Young Artist Auditions, and won… If any other winning artist added one-half as much to her life as I did as the result of the Federation prize, then she knows what I mean when I say gratitude is not enough. Only by constantly doing our best can we show the Federation that its faith and support have been cherished and needed and used."

- Martha Lipton, the 1939 twenty-four year old winner from New York, said: "Of course being the winner is the magnificent fulfillment of many dreams and much work... there is something which is even a greater gift to the many hundreds who compete, and that is the assurance that we, as young artists, American and not yet 'box office' are wanted and that when we are ready there will be folks who want to hear us and even give us a helping and generous hand."

- Samuel Sorin, 1939 Young Artist winner in piano, and whose family on the fiftieth anniversary of his winning (1989) endowed a $1,000 supplemental Young Artist Award in piano said: "I believe that the Federation, through this contest alone, has provided the serious American student of music with one of the greatest possible incentives. In addition to the Federation's cash prize, the Schubert Memorial Award (which he won also) of appearing with the Philadelphia Orchestra is something to be eagerly sought and highly valued. My musical aim consists of two parts to make the complete whole. I am desirous of learning everything that the piano... is capable of doing and to acquire the ability to exploit its every possibility. Secondly I want to develop, enrich, and deepen my own being that I may understand and recreate to an equal greatness the compositions I play... What a pleasure, and I wish to express my personal thanks for the great opportunity which has come to me through the National Federation of Music Clubs."

- Claudette Sorel, 1951 Young Artist winner, piano, also has endowed a supplemental award to the Young Artist piano winner. In expressing her gratitude to the Federation she said: "None of the other awards I had won previously were to mean as much to me as this Young Artist Award. More than anything else it was for me the beginning of a new, wonderful relationship... The Federation creates the opportunity for young artists to be heard, to develop careers, and to grow both musically and artistically... The Federation never forgets its young artists even after they have become established stars. The Federation is like a big proud family... My own sincere wish, said in all humility for my art, is to always be worthy of the honors that were bestowed upon me at the Salt Lake City Biennial in 1951."

- The 1991 winner in piano, Richard Glazier said: "Being the winner in piano is a title that I will be proud of the rest of my life... I am proud to represent the National Federation of Music Clubs with its fine history of helping, not only the young artists, but also the young stars who are just beginning their musical education. The Federation has enhanced my musical and personal life beyond my wildest dreams and I shall be indebted to the Federation always."

6

It is interesting to note that one of the finalists in the 1923 Young Artist Competition in Asheville, North Carolina was Thomas E. Dewey. Dewey, a baritone, was a twenty-one year old senior at the University of Michigan, studying with William Wheeler, and won in the Great Lakes District.

Winning the Man's Voice Competition in the finals was Cooper Lawley of Chicago, Illinois. The rest is history: Dewey served three terms as governor of New York; he was nominated for the presidency of the United State twice – in 1944 and again in 1948.

CHAPTER THREE

DUO PIANO COMPETITION

1

The National Federation of Music Clubs Ellis Competition for Duo Pianists, honoring the late Annie Lou and Edgar B. Ellis of Birmingham, Alabama, was made possible by a legacy left the National Federation by Mrs. Ellis, benefactor, whose motto throughout her life was, "Give to the World the best you have, and the best will come back to you".

The duo piano competition of the National Federation of Music Clubs was founded by Mrs. Jack C. Ward, past president, at the NFMC Fall Session in Oklahoma City, Oklahoma, Mrs. Glenn L. Brown, president.

The first biennial competition was held at Converse College, Spartanburg, South Carolina in 1991 with Hecht and Shapiro (Thomas Hecht and Sandra Shapiro), Cleveland, Ohio, winning the $10,000 first prize. Second place winners were Andrew Cooperstock and Richard Dowling, who also won the NFMC Past National President's Award honoring Mary Prudie Brown, for the best performance of American music.

Judges for the first competition were the internationally known duo piano teams: Yarbrough and Cowan (Joan Yarbrough and Robert Cowan) and Veri and Jamanis (Frances Veri and Roger Jamanis); and Gary Steigerwalt, piano winner, NFMC Young Artist Auditions.

In 1995 the number of prizes has been increased, offering five cash prizes: $10,000 first place; $3,000 second place; $1,500 third place, Fay and John Abild Award; $1,000 fourth place, Floride Smith Dean Award; and $1,500 NFMC Past National President Award, honoring Lucile Parrish Ward, for the best performance of American Music.

Judging the 1995 competition are: Yarbrough and Cowan, duo piano team; Robert Starer, outstanding composer; Allison Loebbaka, of the former Nelson and Neal duo piano team; and James Dick, noted pianist. Serving as Honorary Advisor is Van Cliburn, internationally known concert artist.

WE SALUTE...

Commissions

1

"The contribution of the National Federation of Music Clubs to the musical culture of America is immeasurable. In no area is that contribution more important than in the creative side of the art. Music stands still if each generation does not add its bit to the vast store of musical treasures. I am proud that the Federation had a part in the making of my *Concerto II*, and I hope that the Federation always will have the wisdom and vision to foster the living creators of the art we serve."
—John La Montaine, Pulitzer Prize Winner, 1958

The National Federation of Music Club's first commission was to John Powell, commissioned by Mrs. Elmer James Ottaway, in 1932, and world premiered at the Detroit Biennial Convention in 1947. The last premiere of a National Federation commission was John La Montaine's *Concerto II for Piano and Orchestra, Opus 55*, performed for the first time December 9, 1994 in Rochester, New York by the Eastman Philharmonia. *Concerto II*, commissioned by Mrs. Jack C. Ward, president in 1983, was world premiered with Barry Snyder, soloist, and David Effron conducting.

Pulitzer Prize winner John La Montaine, as a young pianist, played with the NBC Orchestra, under Arturo Toscanini, who advised and encouraged his composing efforts. After Maestro Toscanini retired, Mr. La Montaine's French teacher, Mlle. Nadia Boulanger, urged him to devote most of his time to composing, advice which he followed. Following the performance of Mr. La Montaine's first *Concerto for Piano and Orchestra* in 1958 Paul Hume wrote, "Since the concertos of Prokofieff and Bartok, we know of no other to challenge this one for size and weight." The Pulitzer Prize was awarded a few months later.

In 1972 Dr. Merle Montgomery, national president, commissioned John La Montaine to write a composition in honor of the *Diamond Jubilee* of the National Federation of Music Clubs. *Congratulations* for flute and piano was written and premiered at the Atlantic City *Diamond Jubilee* in 1973.

It was this distinguished background in 1983 that prompted Mrs. Ward to commission John La Montaine to write his second concerto – *Concerto II for Piano and Orchestra, Opus 55*, for the National Federation of Music Clubs.

2

The first commission to be offered by the National Federation of Music Clubs was in 1932 when President, Mrs. Elmer James Ottaway, commissioned John Powell of Virginia to write a symphonic work based on Anglo-Saxon folk tunes. The offer of $1,000 for a commission was new to the Federation, but a gesture which since that time has brought forth fine, typically American works of which the Federation is justly proud.

A. Walter Kramer*, editor of *Musical America*, and one of America's most able composers made this comment on the announcement of the Federation's first commission;

"The announcement of the step taken by the National Federation of Music Clubs in commissioning an orchestral work based on authentic Anglo-Saxon material seems to me to be a step in the right direction.

"That the composer commissioned is John Powell is indeed a cause for rejoicing. No composer in this country today is better equipped to undertake such a work... He has taken his place among the best composers of the day, and to which he adds the distinction of being a profound student of folklore....

"In commissioning Mr. Powell... the NFMC, which has distinguished itself in the past in offering prizes for composition in various forms, makes what is, in my opinion, an admirable departure....

"Congratulations, Mr. Powell, and congratulations to the National Federation of Music Clubs through its action, again demonstrating its right to the important place it occupies in the musical life of the United States of America."

Mr. Powell began a long and exhaustive research with the assistance of many folk musicians – an adventure which was to absorb almost fif-

184

teen years of his life. His *Symphony in A* was world premiered by the Detroit Symphony Orchestra, Dr. Karl Krueger, conducting, for the 1947 Biennial Convention in Detroit.

In an interview with the Detroit Free Press, John Powell related how his love for folk music dated back to the time he was eleven years old:

> "I always read the political articles first, even back in 1893...
> but I never read a political screed that made me as angry as the
> one about music.
> "This eminent European had the nerve to write that English
> speaking peoples had no culture because they had no folk music."

Johnny asked his mother, if they did not have folk music, what were all those songs he'd been hearing ever since he could remember.

> "Those," she replied," are just old things people have been
> singing – no one even knows who wrote them. I guess they just
> grew with the people."

John Powell felt that his mother gave him the perfect definition of folk music.

Symphony in A has been described as a cross section of lore of music and song through the centuries.

A. Walter Kramer was the husband of the National Federation of Music Clubs twenty-second president, Dr. Merle Montgomery.

3

Since 1932 many national presidents have given commissions to composers on behalf of the National Federation of Music Clubs. Others besides the John Powell and John La Montaine commissions have included:

- Mrs. Elmer James Ottaway in 1938 commissioned Annabel Morris Buchanan, acclaimed folk song collector and composer, to write a chorus of women's voices to be performed with a small orchestra. This was based on folk tunes. The completed work was *Come all Ye Fair and Tender Ladies* for which Mrs. Buchanan received $150.00.
- In 1938 Mabel Daniels was commissioned by Mrs. Julia Fuqua Ober, president, to write "an orchestral composition

to be played at the New York World's Fair, providing a performance by a major orchestra can be secured"

- Paul Creston, one of the most widely performed composers of the century and the recipient of countless awards, was commissioned by Mrs. Ada Holding Miller, president, to write his *Dance Overture* which was world premiered at the Miami Biennial Convention in 1955.
- In 1957 Mrs. Ronald A. Dougan, president, commissioned Peter Mennin, one of America's most outstanding composers, to write a work for orchestra to be performed at the 1957 convention in Columbus, Ohio. *Canto for Orchestra* was completed and performed at the opening session.
- Again in 1959 Mrs. Dougan commissioned Lucas Foss, Pulitzer Prize Winner and conductor of distinction, to write a work to be performed at the San Diego, California Biennial Convention. The orchestral work, *Variations* was not completed in time to be performed.
- The first oratorio commissioned by the Federation was commissioned by Mrs. C. Arthur Bullock, president. In 1961 *Reflections on Christmas* by Dr. Bethuel Gross was world premiered at the 1961 Biennial Convention in Kansas City, Missouri by the Chancel Choir of Community Christian Church of Kansas City.
- In 1978 Mrs. Frank A. Vought, president, commissioned a Triple Bill Opera. World premiered in New York were: *The King's Breakfast* by Joyce Barthelson, lyrics by Maurice Baring; *The Shepherdess and the Chimney Sweep* by Julia Smith, lyrics by C. D. Mackey; *The Nightingale and the Rose* by Margaret Garwood. Mrs. Vought commissioned also, *Seven Lanier Poems* by Paul Turok, and *Trio for Violin, Cello and Piano* by Marga Richter, both of which were premiered at the 1979 Biennial Convention in Portland, Oregon.
- Paul Creston received the second commission from the National Federation when he was commissioned in 1982 by Mrs. Jack C. Ward to write a piano duo. *Prelude and Dance for Two Pianos, Opus 120*, was world premiered at the Biennial Convention in Columbus, Ohio in 1983 by the duo piano team, Joan Yarbrough and Robert Cowan.
- Mrs. Dwight D. Robinson, president, commissioned the first Opera for Youth, and in 1987 it was world premiered at the Miami, Florida Biennial Convention. It was entitled *The Minion and the Three Riddles*.

THERE'S MUSIC IN THE HILLS

Summer Scholarships

1

Each year as spring bursts into summer, talented young musicians leave their homes and head for the hills and woodlands to summer music festivals or music camps. There – beside the rushing streams, in tents and rustic concert halls, National Federation of Music Clubs scholarship students enjoy a summer's study of music.

Summer music centers captured the attention of the Federation early in its history. In 1937 at the meeting of the Board of Directors of the Federation in Chattanooga, Tennessee, "Mrs. Chase moved that the National Federation form a department that will sponsor or work with music camps...." No positive action was taken. And – even though the first summer scholarship was given in 1929, it was not until 1953 that the Federation named its first Scholarship Board to obtain funds and administer summer scholarships. Dr. Merle Montgomery was named the first chairman. Some scholarships have remained through the years and increased in value; others for various reasons have been discontinued.

2

"The Summer Music Scholarship program goes back to the granting of a scholarship as a tribute to Dr. Joseph E. Maddy, founder and president of National Music Camp at Interlochen, Michigan... This camp described as 'one of the most amazing educational projects in the world,' is the granddaddy and the model for all summer music camps," said Mrs. Charles Pascoe of Tuscon, Arizona, Chairman of Summer Scholarships, 1961.

Mrs. Pascoe continued that the second summer scholarship was given to Chautauqua in New York, and the third to Transylvania Music Camp, at Brevard, North Carolina.

The Overture, the second printed yearbook of National Music Camp, printed in 1929, carries the information that in that year, the Federation gave $700 for scholarships to the Camp.

National Music Camp, or the Interlochen Center for the Arts, as it is called today, occupying a woodland campus among tall pines in northern Michigan, nestles between Lake Wahbekanetta and Lake Wahbekaness – the perfect setting selected by Dr. Joseph E. Maddy of the University of Michigan, to bring into being a music camp for talented and ambitious boys and girls who wished to spend the summer together in a beautiful environment of outdoor living – balancing enthusiasm and artistic endeavor with unlimited opportunities for developing talent in all fields of the arts. The land was purchased, the Camp was born in 1927, and then began the problem of finance. Thus began also, the close relationship between National Music Camp and the National Federation of Music Clubs, which has lasted for almost seventy years.

The booklet printed by the National Music Camp, *Joe Maddy of Interlochen* tells how Dr. Maddy first contacted the Federation in support of his most worthwhile project:

> "One day during the winter, while Joe was serving as guest conductor for the Illinois All State High School Orchestra meeting at Urbana, he learned that the National Board of the National Federation of Music Clubs was meeting in Milwaukee. This gave him an idea. Perhaps the Federation could afford to give financial assistance. He called one of the officers and was granted the opportunity to speak at the meeting.
>
> "The only way Joe could get to Milwaukee and back in the brief interval between rehearsals of his orchestra in Urbana was to fly. He engaged a private plane, operated by a University of Illinois student, to take him to Milwaukee early in the afternoon and back to Urbana right after his speech. But Joe's carefully arranged timing didn't work out as he planned. The Federation program was behind schedule and Joe had to wait until late afternoon to address the group. It grew so late that his young pilot was afraid to attempt the flight back after dark because he had no landing lights. They had no choice but to stay overnight in Milwaukee and return the next morning.
>
> "It was a cold gusty winter day. They were flying over Deerfield, Illinois, when suddenly the plane's radiator cap blew off. Steam shot out and froze over the windshield and cabin. Then the motor stopped, frozen. It was a water-cooled engine

and the pilot had neglected the anti-freeze.

"They had been flying at about two thousand feet. Below was a golf course and a plowed field. The golf course looked more inviting, but knowing about bunkers and other hazards, the pilot chose the field. They came down without injury, clipping the top of a small tree in the process. Several workmen rushed to them to find out whether anyone was injured, and Joe learned that he was on the estate of Mrs. J. Ogden Armour.

"Joe at once composed a note to Mrs. Armour, explaining that he had landed accidentally on her grounds while on a trip seeking funds for his music camp. He dispatched the note by one of the workmen. The result was an invitation to come inside for a visit, and a check for two thousand dollars. Mrs. Armour took an instant liking to Joe and a warmly sympathetic interest in his story. In addition to her own gift, she persuaded her friend Samuel Insull to duplicate the amount. In fact, Insull promised two thousand dollars a year for the next ten years –a promise he couldn't fulfill since he was bankrupt at the time. His personal check to Joe was possibly the last money Insull gave to anyone."

Note: *Samuel Insull never paid to Interlochen the $2,000 annually which he had pledged for ten years. In 1932 the $3,000,000,000 Edison Company of Chicago was forced into bankruptcy. Insull became a fugitive abroad, but was captured in Turkey and returned to the United States, where he was tried for fraud and embezzlement three times and acquitted each time. (Encyclopedia Britannica, 1960.)*

To perpetuate the Federation's scholarships to Interlochen Center for the Arts, in 1953 a scholarship lodge (at a cost of $3,000) was given by the National Federation of Music Clubs – the income from the rental to provide the annual scholarships. At the dedication ceremony on August 6, 1953, the national president, Mrs. Ada Holding Miller, presented the lodge, and it was accepted by Dr. Joseph E. Maddy, president of the Center. At the same dedication ceremony a lodge was given by the Michigan Federation of Music Clubs, Mrs. Frank A. Coolidge, president, and accepted by Dr. Maddy.

August 5-9, 1959, during the presidency of Mrs. C. Arthur Bullock, the National Federation of Music Clubs held its Fall Session at the National Music Camp with many notables in attendance, including Dr. Maddy and Dr. Howard Hanson, composer.

In 1960 the National Federation was given a grant of $1500 from the Readers Digest Foundation to be used to administer scholarships to the Music Camp; the scholarships continued for a second year.

Of interest to Federation members is the fact that the Federation's seventeenth president, Mrs. Ada Holding Miller, gave to Interlochen Music Center her violin, and for many years it was displayed in a glass case in the Giddings Concourse.

3

There are conflicting reports as to the recipient of the Federation's second summer scholarship. A report of the national historian, Mrs. Ella Lord Gilbert, in 1933 reports, "the Federation lends its aid to music camps, Interlochen, Michigan and Oakland, Maine." Yet, Mrs. Charles Pascoe reports The National Federation of Music Clubs' second summer scholarship was given to Chautauqua, New York, a revered educational institution located on 700 lake-side acres at the head of Lake Chautauqua in southwest New York. Chautauqua, both a summer resort and an educational institution, was founded in 1874 by the Methodists as an assembly for Sunday School teachers.

According to Mrs. Pascoe, who had been a summer resident of Chautauqua for many years, it was in 1945 that the Chautauqua program – including music, drama, art, religion and athletics – came to the attention of Mrs. Guy Gannett, from Portland, Maine, president of the National Federation. At the invitation of Mrs. Pascoe, Federation members were invited to Chautauqua July 27, 28, 29, 1945 to attend the first Federation Weekend, as guests of the Chautauqua Woman's Club, Mrs. Ambrose L. Cram, president.

On the scheduled date of the arrival of the national president, to the surprise of all, a seaplane landed on Lake Chautauqua, bringing to the first Federation Weekend, the national president, Mrs. Guy Gannett. Mrs. Pascoe tells how all the people on the grounds of Chautauqua were "agog" with an important person arriving in this manner.

July 28th was designated "Federation Day". The morning program at the Amphitheater featured the Chautauqua Symphony Orchestra, and two Federation Artist Winners, Eunice Podis, violin, and Paula Lenchner, dramatic soprano. The afternoon program featured the national president, Mrs. Gannett, and a forum moderated by Marian Bauer.

Mrs. Gannett quickly saw the value of the program of the summer music school, and established four scholarships, to be given by the Federation for six weeks study of voice, piano, organ and stringed instruments. These first scholarships were all named for Kate Chase of New York. There arose much confusion that the scholarships given by the Federation were called the Kate Chase Scholarships. The National Board of Directors voted to give one scholarship honoring Mrs. Charles Pascoe, founder of the first Federation Weekend. It was agreed that each state may name the scholarship honoring anyone it wished. New York chose to honor Kate Chase. Later, Mrs. Ada Holding Miller, national president, attending the Weekend persuaded the three host states, Pennsylvania, Ohio and New York to assume three of the scholarships with the fourth to be given by the National Federation. New Jersey joined, making a fifth scholarship for string ensemble players.

Through the love and generosity of Eleanor Pascoe's family and friends – in particular two nieces, Phyllis H. Evans and Elinore A. Hooper, both of Delray Beach, Florida, the "Eleanor Pascoe Scholarship Endowment for Talented Young Artists at Chautauqua, New York" was established November 19, 1979. At Federation Weekend 1980 in Chautauqua, on the thirty-fifth anniversary of that first Federation Weekend, Mrs. Jack C. Ward, national president, presented to Mrs. Evans and Mrs. Hooper, National Federation of Music Clubs Awards of Merit for their "Outstanding Participation in the Promotion of Music."

The Eleanor Pascoe Scholarship in Voice in the amount of $500, matched by the same amount from the Chautauqua Music Institute, is given annually to some worthy music student wishing a summer's study at this fine summer music camp.

In 1960 at the meeting of the NFMC Board of Directors in Louisville, Kentucky, Mrs. Warren Knox of New York, brought from Mr. and Mrs. Clayton Weber of Ithaca, New York, "owners" of the federated "Musicians' Club of Chautauqua" a proposal for the Federation to erect a practice cabin at Chautauqua to be used in conjunction with the club. The proposal was accepted and Mrs. Gilbert Burrell, NFMC vice president in charge of the Northeastern Region was named chairman. On July 14, 1962, 200 Federation members and friends gathered to dedicate the one story, 24' x 48' cabin, consisting of six practice rooms – three on each side of the Charles Wakefield Cadman Recital Hall. The cabin was built at a cost of $6,975 by the states of the Northeastern Region with an amount of $3,890 borrowed by the Region from the Federation's Foundation for the Advancement of the Musical Arts – "to be repaid within three years at 5% interest."

The amount available from the cabin for scholarships varies each year; $3,000 was given in 1993 to scholarship recipients in the North-eastern Region.

4

The Federation's third summer scholarship was given to the Transylvania Music Camp at Brevard, North Carolina according to Mrs. Charles Pascoe.

Dr. Joseph E. Maddy passed away in 1966, but the legacy left by him lives on, not only at Interlochen Center for the Arts, but also at the Brevard Music Center, nestled deep in the shadows of the Blue Ridge Mountains of western North Carolina. In 1929 James Christian Pfohl, a sixteen year old scholarship student attended Dr. Maddy's National Music Camp at Interlochen, Michigan, and it was there that he gained the inspiration, which sixteen years later would lead to his founding the Transylvania Music Camp – where among the foliage of the tall pines, the strains of musical instruments mix with the gurgling waters of the clear streams.

The National Federation of Music Clubs, and in particular the Southeastern Region, supported Dr. Pfohl in his effort to establish a music camp.

In 1948 – only three years after Mrs. Charles Pascoe had founded the Federation's first "Federation Weekend "at Chautauqua, Mrs. Maurice Honigman of Gastonia, North Carolina, founded "Federation Mid-Week" at Transylvania Music Camp. The exact date of the establishing of the Federation's scholarship to the Camp is not available, but it is to be assumed that it was soon after the "Mid-Week" was founded.

It was named the "National Federation of Music Clubs Scholarship honoring Hinda L. Honigman," in recognition of Mrs. Honigman's having founded the Mid-Week. The scholarship retained the name of Mrs. Honigman until 1992 when the National Board of Directors endowed and increased the scholarship to a full scholarship of $1850, from a legacy left by Rose Thomas Smith of Galax, Virginia. The name was changed to the "National Federation of Music Clubs Scholarship in Memory of Rose Thomas Smith."

States of the Southeastern Region have supported the Brevard Music Center (the name by which it became known when it was acquired by Converse College in 1965) through gifts, scholarships, a library given by the region, and many practice cabins given by the states.

In 1981, at the National Federation of Music Clubs Biennial Convention in Birmingham, Alabama, the South Carolina Federation of Music Clubs, Mrs. Bryan Blackwell, president, presented to the Brevard Music Center $10,000, in honor of Lucile Parrish Ward, national president, for the purpose of endowing the "Lucile Parrish Ward Chair in Opera".

In memory of Mrs. Maurice Honigman, NFMC president, 1967-1971, Mr. and Mrs. Ralph Sarlin, in 1986 established an endowment to be used to engage a National Federation of Music Clubs Young Artist to perform in concert at the annual Federation Weekend at the Music Center.

5

Today – annual Federation Weekends are held in each of the Federation's regions: Northeastern Region, Southeastern Region, Central Region, and Western Region.

In 1993 the National Federation of Music Clubs awarded summer scholarships of more than $15,000 to seventeen Music Centers in fourteen states. Chairmen in charge of the scholarships and auditions all are volunteers, where reward is a feeling of inner satisfaction in helping America's musically talented youth.

Betty Bennett, 16 year old violinist of Brecksville, Ohio – winner of the National Federation of Music Clubs Scholarship to Transylvania Music Camp at Brevard, North Carolina, 1954 (Brevard Music Center) – practices beside the lake at the camp.

Bearers of the Torch

ROSE FAY THOMAS

HONORARY PRESIDENT

MRS. EDWIN F. UHL

First President

Mrs. Edwin F. Uhl (Alice F.) of Grand Rapids, Michigan, a member of the St. Cecilia Music Club, was elected the first president of the January 28th, newly organized National Federation of Musical Clubs 1898, at Steinway Hall in Chicago. At the time of her election Mrs. Uhl was in Germany, where her husband was serving as Ambassador. Mrs. Blanche Ellis Starr, first vice president was "acting president" until Mrs. Uhl's return in May. The organization was incorporated February 28, 1898 under the laws of the State of Illinois.

Mrs. Uhl served for three years (1898-1901) as president, during which time the second Board meeting was held in St. Louis, October 1898. At this meeting Mrs. Theodore Thomas was named Honorary President, and the first Honorary members – Henry Krehbiel, Theodore Thomas, and Edward MacDowell were elected.

At the first Biennial Convention in St. Louis, May 3-8, 1899, four Regional Vice Presidents were appointed and the support of American music was made the keystone of the organization. The Federation emblem was adopted and sixteen pins were sold at Mrs. Uhl's second convention in Cleveland, Ohio in April 1901. The first years were devoted to organization and advancement of the aims of this new and historically important musical federation.

MRS. CURTIS WEBSTER

Second President

Mrs. Curtis Webster (Helen C.) of New York City, was elected the second president (1901-1903) at the Cleveland Biennial, having served as director of the Northern Middle States and First National Vice President.

She was a founder of the Fortnightly Musical Club of Cleveland, which was in 1901 the largest women's musical club in the United States.

She was a delegate to the Chicago Convention when the National Federation of Musical Clubs was organized and was a charter member and a signer of the Articles of Incorporation.

During her administration International Music Relations gained importance and a Canadian Club was federated. The first recorded junior club to join NFMC was sponsored by the Beethoven Club of Memphis, Tennessee and the first Course of Study was prepared and adopted for Senior Clubs.

In this new venture, Mrs. Webster's individual activities and efforts for six years helped raise the standards of the federated clubs, brought many into the federation each year, created better cooperation, and also helped establish good press relationships. There was no precedent to serve as a guide, and individual effort was the only method of inducing interest in this new Federation. At the close of Mrs. Webster's administration, she withdrew from active work in the Federation due to a prolonged absence from the country.

MRS. WINIFRED B. COLLINS

Third President

Mrs. Winifred B. Collins (Helen Storer) was elected the third president at the Biennial Convention in Rochester, New York in 1903 and served until 1905. Mrs. Collins had attended the World's Fair Congress of Music Clubs in Chicago in 1893 and also the organizational meeting in 1898, becoming a Charter Member and a Director.

During her administration great emphasis was placed on Extension and 125 clubs joined the Federation. This was an all-time high. Much educational material was distributed to the junior clubs and a comprehensive publicity program was carried out. On June 10, 1905 at the St. Louis convention, an amendment to the Certificate of Incorporation changed Article II so that men and men's organizations could be admitted to membership. Another innovation was the establishment of an Artist Bureau.

Although Mrs. Collins was the third national president, she never presided over a biennial convention, however she held three national meetings of the Board of Management. The first was immediately following her election but she was ill and could not attend the Denver Biennial in 1905. Mrs. Collins was a member of the Tuesday Musicale of Akron, Ohio, and the Fortnightly Club of Cleveland, Ohio.

MRS. RUSSELL RIPLEY DORR

Fourth President

Mrs. Russell Ripley Dorr (Louise Bryan) of New Jersey and New York City, was elected president in June, 1905 at the Denver Biennial. In June 1897 at the annual meeting of the Music Teachers National Association she acted as chairman of the first meeting called to organize the Women's Amateur Musical Clubs. She was chairman of the Nominating Committee for the permanent officers at the 1898 election in Chicago and signed the Articles of Incorporation. Two years later she was made Second Vice President, then First Vice President and President in 1905. She served as president for two months, resigning by mail ballot the last of July, nominating her successor, Mrs. J. E. Kinney in the same ballot. This was the first mail ballot ever taken in the Federation. She wished to devote her time to the Artists Bureau, in which capacity she was active for ten years.

After marriage she lived in Portland, Oregon; Burlington, Iowa; and St. Paul, Minnesota, where she was president for nine years of the Schubert Club. She served as National Board Member from New Jersey, Connecticut and Minnesota; was NFMC Auditor and Historian; and president of the New Jersey Federation of Music Clubs. She was a charter member of the Musical Art Society of Plainfield, New Jersey. She was an organist and choir director for forty years in Minnesota and New Jersey. It was out of her work with the Artist Bureau that the present plan of state action to engage National Young Artist winners has evolved, which has launched many young Americans upon successful musical careers.

MRS. JULIUS EUGENE KINNEY

Fifth and Seventh President

Mrs. Julius Eugene Kinney (Leila Bronson) of Denver, Colorado, was elected president in 1905, immediately following the resignation of Mrs. Russell Dorr. Mrs. Kinney served for two years and again was elected in 1911 in Philadelphia and re-elected in Chicago in 1913, giving her the distinction of having one of the two longest presidential services. Mrs. Kinney's administrations were outstanding for many innovations: *The Musical Monitor* was adopted as the official organ; the American Music Department was organized by Mrs. Jason Walker; the $10,000 Opera Prize was proposed and Los Angeles sponsored Horatio Parker's opera *Fairyland*; Young Artists Contests were launched; the Artists Bureau was established; and the NFMC Endowment was begun.

Outstanding leadership in Denver marked her life also, as her interest in Nursing and Medicine led to the endowment of a scholarship in that field. She and her physician husband were the donors of a pipe organ to St. John's Episcopal Cathedral Chapel. Her musical contributions in the early life of the Federation have left a legacy that endures to the present day.

MRS. CHARLES B. KELSEY

Sixth President

Mrs. Charles B. Kelsey of Grand Rapids, Michigan was elected to the presidency in May 1907 at the Convention in Memphis, Tennessee. She was a past president of the St. Cecilia Society of Grand Rapids and had shared the responsibility of building the St. Cecilia Music Club House. She served as president four years (1907-1911). She introduced a vast Extension program to carry the organization of clubs into every part of the United States with a vice president appointed in every state. Their duties were to organize and federate clubs. Her term was characterized by a doubling of the clubs. She traveled extensively promoting this work. She was the first to make international contact by attending as a guest of honor of the London Society of Musicians and the British Society of Musicians. Accomplishments during this administration include the forming of the first American Music Committee. American Music Study was initiated and a committee for Music in Schools was created.

In 1907 the Federation voted to award three prizes for American Composition in three classes – to be awarded in 1909. Winning in Class I was Henry Hadley who won $1,000 for his orchestral composition, *The Culprit Fay*. Arthur Shepherd won Class II with *The Lost Child*. He won also Class III with his *Sonata of the Turtle*. *The Culprit Fay* was performed at the 1909 Grand Rapids Biennial by the Theodore Thomas Orchestra with Henry Hadley conducting. These were the first cash prizes to be given by the Federation for Composition.

MRS. ALBERT J. OSCHNER

Eighth President

Mrs. Albert J. Oschner became the eighth president, elected at the Los Angeles Biennial Convention in 1915, and re-elected at the Birmingham convention in 1917. A native of Pennsylvania, Mrs. Oschner lived in Chicago.

During World War I the National Federation of Music Clubs contributed to the recreation of the service men in camps through musical programs, records, phonographs, community sings, and sings in industrial plants. State federations were formed with Wisconsin being the first. Twenty states followed. In 1916 the first Life Members were enrolled for the purpose of increasing the Endowment Fund. Artist and Individual memberships were endorsed as a part of the finance program also.

The Young Artists Contests were developed. High on the list of accomplishments was the formation of the MacDowell League, through which substantial sums were raised for the MacDowell Colony. In 1919 permanent amphitheatre seats were built and presented to the Colony at the Biennial Convention in Peterborough, New Hampshire.

In spite of the war and the president's illness of a year, the Federation survived and thrived. The Young Artist winners were awarded the first cash prizes of $150.00, and Mrs. Oschner volunteered the second prize, the Edward MacDowell prize in piano to be given in perpetuity.

MRS. FRANK A. SEIBERLING

Ninth President

Mrs. Frank A. Seiberling (Gertrude F. Penfield) of Akron, Ohio served the Federation as its ninth president 1919-1921, elected at the Peterborough, New Hampshire Biennial Convention at the MacDowell Colony. She had been appointed State Vice President of Ohio by the Board in 1913, thus making her a member of the Board. She organized Ohio in 1915. The Seiberling home, famed Stan Hywet Hall, was the scene of many National Board meetings over a period of two administrations. Her interest in Music Education was apparent. During her administration the Junior Department was established in 1919 and the first Junior Counselor was appointed. A guide for junior clubs was compiled and a Course of Study printed.

Refusing to accept re-election for a second term Mrs. Seiberling served as Chairman of the new Department of Finance which she founded in 1921. She raised over $11,000 to cover expenses of the Asheville convention, the residue being placed in the National Federation of Music Clubs Endowment Fund.

A committee for Public School Music was added to the Education Department. A Silver Jubilee Fund of $8,000 was raised for the MacDowell Colony. Twenty-one new state federations were added and member clubs grew from 400 to 1,000.

In the years following Mrs. Seiberling's presidency, her interest in music education resulted in the planning, preparation and publication of A STUDY COURSE IN MUSIC UNDERSTANDING, a series of four books designed for Students, the first such series ever published. She gave generously to the Federation, having given a bronze Memorial Plaque to be on the Peristyle at the MacDowell Colony.

Mrs. Seiberling wrote A Musical Ritual for the 1927 Chicago Biennial Convention, from which was culled the NFMC Collect by Mrs. Thomas J. Cole.

MRS. JOHN F. LYONS

Tenth President

Mrs. John F. Lyons of Fort Worth, Texas became the tenth president at the "Tri-cities" Biennial (Davenport, Moline and Rock Island) in 1921 and was reelected at the National Convention at Asheville, North Carolina in 1923. On June 6, 1921 amendments to the Certificate of Incorporation granted "The name of the Corporation is the NATIONAL FEDERATION OF MUSIC CLUBS." (Article I). Article II was amended revising the wording of OBJECT of the organization to its present form. In 1922 the Federation's *Official Bulletin* was first published and the first four books of the Study Course made available. A 50-50 plan was proposed for promoting American artists' concerts, following a club survey. In 1923 the *History and Outlook of the NFMC Junior Department*, by C. M. Tremaine of the National Bureau of the Advancement of Music, was published. In 1923 the first Junior pin, based on the design of the Senior pin was made. The Past Presidents' Assembly was founded at the Asheville Biennial Convention in 1923, with 123 signatures on the Charter. The PPA pledged to donate at least $1500 biennially, with donors of cash prizes in perpetuity. Two American works were produced: Carl Venth's prize work *Pan in America*, and Frank Patterson's opera *The Echo*. In 1924 the first National Music Week was endorsed and observed. An Extension Chart was introduced and the first Extension prize offered. Mrs. Lyons was an outstanding impresario in Fort Worth, Texas, her home.

MRS. EDGAR STILLMAN KELLEY

Eleventh President

Mrs. Edgar Stillman Kelley (Jessie) of Oxford, Ohio, was elected eleventh president at the Portland, Oregon Biennial Convention in 1925 and re-elected in Chicago in 1927. She devoted much energy and thought to the Junior Division. In 1926 Dr. Walter Damrosch accepted the appointment as Honorary Chairman of the Junior Division, the first *Junior Contest Bulletin* was published, and the "Children's Crusade" was organized to raise funds for the MacDowell Memorial. In 1927 the *Blue Book* of Past Presidents' Assembly was published, the National Council of District and State Presidents was organized, the *Junior Bulletin* and *Church Music Bulletin* were inaugurated, and $10,000 was raised and presented to Mrs. Edward MacDowell at the 1927 Chicago Biennial Convention. Other "firsts" were: Department Religious Education established; *A Musical Ritual* published (compiled by Mrs. Frank A. Seiberling for the Chicago Convention); and the *Federation Hymn* sung there for the first time (words by Irena Foreman Williams, hymn tune "Colone" arranged by Peter Christian Lutkin). The first *Official Junior Song* was adopted, (words by Mrs. Abbie L Snoddy, music by Mrs. A. H. Hamilton). The Hymn Playing Contest for the Juniors was begun and the first *NFMC Directories* were published. Mrs. Kelley excelled as a pianist. Her eight years of residence in European musical centers gave her a broad vision of conditions of American students abroad and the needs of America for greater artistic educational advantages.

MRS. ELMER JAMES OTTAWAY

Twelfth President

Mrs. Elmer James Ottaway of Port Huron, Michigan, became twelfth president at the 1929 Biennial convention in Boston, Massachusetts, and was re-elected at the San Francisco Convention in 1931. In 1929 the three official publications of NFMC were brought together into one, *Music Clubs Magazine*. The first complete program by Juniors was given at the 1931 San Francisco Convention, and the Junior Pledge, written by Julia Williams, National Junior Counselor, was adopted in 1932. A Virginia composer, John Powell, was commissioned to write an American symphony (which was premiered at the Detroit Biennial in 1947). Through a survey of general music courses made for NFMC by the Carnegie Foundation and the Association of American Colleges, college music was emphasized. This resulted in a book by Randall Thompson. In 1933 a booklet of American composers was compiled and edited by Annabel Morris Buchanan. Also in 1933, the first Junior organization folder was compiled by Julia Fuqua Ober, National Junior Counselor. In May, 1932 a week of George Washington Bicentennial programs was presented in Constitutional Hall, Washington D.C.

MRS. JOHN ALEXANDER JARDINE

Thirteenth President

Mrs. John Alexander Jardine (Agnes) of Fargo, North Dakota, was elected thirteenth president in May, 1933 at the Biennial Convention in Minneapolis, Minnesota. At the Philadelphia Convention in 1935 she was reelected to serve a second term. During her administration the organization's emphasis on musical youth was continued with the creation of a Student Division in 1936 and the establishment of a Young Artist Placement Bureau. Folk Music contests were conducted, furthering American music. The MacDowell Junior Fellowship Fund to finance an American artist at the Colony was begun and in 1935 proceeds from the sale of gavels made from wood off trees at the MacDowell Colony went towards funds for the care of Edward MacDowell's grave. "State Federation Opera" for the people and by the people became a special project. A new system of business administration was inaugurated and the establishment of a National Headquarters Office resulted in a systematic distribution of Federation literature. A Publicity Director was secured and a Managing Editor named for *Music Clubs Magazine*. In 1937 the first massed Youth Orchestra was heard at the Indianapolis Biennial Convention with Fabian Sevitsky conductor. After her presidency Mrs. Jardine continued her service to the Federation in the Finance Department.

MRS. VINCENT HILLES OBER

Fourteenth President

Mrs. Vincent Hilles Ober (Julia Fuqua) of Norfolk, Virginia became president at the Indianapolis Biennial Convention in 1937. At the Baltimore Convention she was re-elected for a second term in 1939. In 1937 the official title of the Junior Contests was changed to Competitive Festivals with adjudication by judges, and a rating system adopted. Roberts Rules of Order as the official authority added to the details of better organization and a new Constitution and Bylaws were written. The organization of Federations in every state completed the official roster, and regional divisions were changed to three. A professional Parliamentarian was engaged and a legal representative appointed. Other notable accomplishments were the establishment of a Junior scholarship honoring Edgar Stillman Kelley, a violin contest in the Junior Division, detailed study of music supervisors conducted, composition contests revived with premiere performances for winners, a PPA pin added to official Insignia, Young Artist winners presented at biennial conventions in 1939 and 1941, and a tour of one winner with 72 concerts scheduled. A major and lasting achievement was the formation of the National Music Council with Mrs. Ober named Vice President. The $3,000 Fellowship Fund at Peterborough was completed and $500 given to the gavel fund. A Western conference was held in Oregon with representatives from nine states. Junior and Student Collects were written, the *Junior Bulletin* changed to the *Junior Magazine*, and the *Junior Hymn* was adopted. A Federation Day was held at the World's Fair in New York City with John Warren Erb directing a 1,000 voice chorus of members of the National Federation of Music Clubs.

MRS. GUY PATTERSON GANNETT

Fifteenth President

The fifteenth president, Mrs. Guy Patterson Gannett (Anne Macomber) of Portland, Maine, was elected at the Biennial Convention in Los Angeles, California in 1941 and served three terms due to World War II because it was impossible to hold conventions in 1943 and 1945. Over $100,000 was raised and more than 2,500,000 articles of musical equipment, records and music were distributed to the American Armed Forces at home and abroad, including hospital ships and trains. "Bundles for Britain" was an important project.

To replace the 1943 convention a great "Festival of the Air" was broadcast over four major networks during National Music Week. In 1945 regional conferences were held in lieu of the national convention.

Several "firsts'" during her administration were: the first Federation Weekend founded at Chautauqua, New York; the White Breakfast and Memorial Service originated in Chicago, honoring the Federation's founder, Rose Fay Thomas; Music in Hospitals was established; the first Student Musicians Contest was held; scholarship programs were begun at summer music camps; the Foundation for the Advancement of the Musical Arts was established with the $10,000 left from the War Service Fund, with the Anne Gannett Fund designated as a basis for a scholarship for talented veterans; new bylaws were written and the dues were raised from twenty to fifty cents per capita; three NFMC regions expanded to four (dividing the Eastern Region into Northeastern and Southeastern); the restoration of Nathaniel Hawthorne's home, "Little Red House" at Tanglewood, where he wrote ***Tanglewood Tales***, became a new project; and gifts of music, orchestral parts and instruments for overseas orchestras became a national project.

After her term of office, Mrs. Gannett continued to serve as Chairman of International Relations.

MRS. ROYDEN JAMES KEITH

Sixteenth President

Mrs. Royden James Keith (Marie Morrisey) of Chicago, presided as sixteenth president from 1947 to 1951, elected in Detroit in 1947 and reelected in 1949 in Dallas. NFMC Headquarters office was moved from Ithaca, New York to New York City. In 1948 the Hymn of the Month was inaugurated and the Westminister Choir, John Finley Williamson director, recorded the first nine hymns with Mrs. Keith as Narrator. These were put on sale and sets of albums placed in Veterans Hospitals as gifts of the Federation. NFMC was accredited to the United Nations with an officially appointed Observer. A Citations Committee was established and the first NFMC Citation was given to the Standard Oil Company of California, recognizing the fine quality music programs broadcast to school children. A Poster Stamp was issued commemorating the 50th Anniversary of the founding of NFMC. The first Coordinator of Departmental Activities, Mrs. Ronald Dougan, was elected. She compiled and edited the first *State Presidents' Manual*.

The first President's Citation was given to Philip Maxwell of Chicago, in recognition of his instituting the Chicagoland Music Festival and his promotion of musically talented youth. The first Music Therapy scholarship was awarded in 1951 at Salt Lake City. The Cradle Roll was inaugurated as a membership classification. Canada formed a Federation of Music Clubs with assistance from NFMC. It was noted that 1175 new and reinstated clubs were added. The final indebtedness for the Little Red House was wiped out and it was dedicated at Tanglewood July 24, 1948. In 1951 the NFMC Handbook was compiled and edited. In 1950 the Organ category was added to the Young Artist Auditions and "Grass Roots Opera" adopted as a regular project.

Mrs. Keith served NFMC after her administration as Chairman of the Finance Committee.

MRS. ADA HOLDING MILLER

Seventeenth President

Mrs. Ada Holding Miller of Providence, Rhode Island was elected seventeenth president at the Salt Lake City Biennial in 1951 and was reelected in 1953 in New York City. She established the President's Promotion Fund through the initial $10,000 annual ASCAP gift. In 1952 a Student Division Handbook was published, edited by Mrs. Floride Cox. The honorarium for the national vice president was raised and regional vice presidents' travel allowance was established. The Marie Morrisey Keith Scholarship in the Student Division was created. First appointment of Summer Scholarship Committee; and Chautauqua, Interlochen and Transylvania were declared permanent Summer Camps for NFMC endorsement and support. In 1953 the first model yearbook was printed. In 1954 NFMC endorsed the Contemporary Music Congress at Pittsburgh and sent one young composer from each of the four regions. Summer scholarships were established for Berkshire and Aspen Music Centers. The managerial contract was added to the Young Artists Auditions Award. The PARADE OF AMERICAN MUSIC was inaugurated and the month of February chosen. The senior and junior magazines were separated, the junior becoming *Junior Keynotes*. The NFMC lodge was built at National Music Camp. In 1954 the Steinway Centennial Award for Piano was sponsored ($2,000), and in 1955 the first Parade of American Music held.

At the 1953 convention in New York City a highlight was a performance of *Carmen*, held at the Metropolitan Opera House to benefit the Young Artist Reserve Fund. There were daily programs of All-American music by leading artists. At the 1955 biennial the premiere of Paul Creston's commissioned orchestral work *Dance Overture* was heard.

After completing her term of office, Music for the Blind was endorsed and the Lauritz Melchoir performance contest administered.

MRS. RONALD ARTHUR DOUGAN

Eighteenth President

At the Biennial Convention in Miami, Florida in 1955, Mrs. Ronald Arthur Dougan (Vera Wardner) of Beloit, Wisconsin, was elected the eighteenth president of the National Federation of Music Clubs, and was reelected in 1957 at the Columbus, Ohio convention. The *Crusade for Strings* was created and she inaugurated Educational Workshops, stressing Orientation, Leadership Training and Evaluation. Young Artist Auditions were augmented to include both man's and woman's voice.

She commissioned Peter Mennin to compose *Canto for Orchestra* which premiered at the Columbus, Ohio convention; the Federation's Observer to the United Nations was given the title of Representative. The Opera Committee was made a department, including Grass Roots and Folk Opera; the Scholarship Board was created; an Artist Presentation Chairman was appointed; a Chaplain was named for the first time; Young Artist winners were presented in concert at conventions.

Mrs. Dougan was appointed to the Executive Music Committee, PEOPLE TO PEOPLE program by President Eisenhower. A new summer Federation Weekend was established at Peninsula Music Festival. The first brochure listing all National Federation scholarships was disseminated. National Music Week was co-sponsored by the Federation and the American Music Conference jointly in 1958. In 1959 the National Federation took sole responsibility with Mrs. Dougan as the national chairman.

She made many appearances before Congressional Committees for the "Juke Box Bill" and for a Charter for the National Music Council. The National Music Council was successful in securing a Congressional Charter.

MRS. C. ARTHUR BULLOCK

Nineteenth President

The nineteenth president was Mrs. C. Arthur Bullock (Dorothy Dann), elected at the Columbus, Ohio 1959 convention and reelected at the 1961 convention in Kansas City, Kansas. In January 1960 a formal opening of NFMC Headquarters Office was scheduled in Chicago, where 62 years earlier the organization was founded. Headquarters were in the Fairbanks Morse Building, 600 S. Michigan Avenue. Federation representatives were enrolled in Hawaii, Alaska and Puerto Rico. *Music Clubs Magazine* changed to *Showcase* (temporarily). Edward MacDowell was elected to the Hall of Fame. The first oratorio commissioned by NFMC was Dr. Bethuel Gross' *Reflections on Christmas*, premiered at the 1961 convention. Young Artist Awards were increased to $1,500.00 and an oratorio category added. Citations and Honorary memberships for past national presidents were established. Hymn of the Month booklets were published for the first time. NFMC gave special endorsement to the National Opera Company; NFMC Chairs at the National Cultural Center (later named the John F. Kennedy Center for the Performing Arts) and at the Lincoln Center, were endowed by Mrs. Robert W. Roberts.

Scholarships and awards honoring past national presidents were established. In 1962 a program of monetary awards to Educational Institutions in three classifications for the performance of American music was inaugurated, becoming an annual project supported by ASCAP. A composition contest for a symphonic work dedicated to the United Nations was administered by NFMC, with Ray Green, then Executive Secretary of the American Music Center, serving as chairman. The winning composition was *The Peaceful Land* by Williams Grant Still premiered in Miami, October 1962 by Miami University Symphony Orchestra. Dr. Bullock was appointed by President Nixon as a member of the U.S. delegation to the UNESCO Conference in Paris. Music for human welfare, music therapy and music service in hospitals was promoted. An annual Music Therapy Scholarship is given in her name.

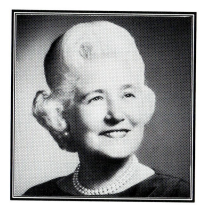

MRS. CLIFTON J. MUIR

Twentieth President

Mrs. Clifton J. Muir (Irene Steed) was elected the 20th president of the National Federation of Music Clubs in Pittsburgh in 1963 and reelected at the Miami Beach convention in 1965. Her administration emphasized "Music For All Youth" and "Music Is For Everyone." Scholarships to colleges and summer centers were increased. Official gold cups, an optional plan in the Junior Festivals, was made available at NFMC Headquarters. A Dance Department was created and new emphasis placed on all the performing arts. The 1963 Young Artists were presented in recital in the East Room of the White House during the NFMC Fall Session in Washington and a tape recording was made by the White House Communications Agency and placed in the permanent files of the historian. An Adult Non-Professional Composers' Contest was inaugurated. The title *Music Clubs Magazine* was restored as the official organ of NFMC. The Louise S. Oberne Memorial Fund for Scholarships was established through a $10,000 bequest. In 1965 a concert tour of Japan for one Young Artist winner under sponsorship of the U.S. Embassy and in cooperation with the People-to-People Music Committee of the U.S. Information Agency was given. Violinist Elaine Skorodin was chosen. Joseph Fennimore, pianist, was chosen for 1966. Four cash awards in the *Crusade for Strings* were provided by BMI in 1965. In 1965 rules, requirements and application forms for foreign memberships were adopted. The first edition of *Who's Who in the NFMC* was published as a fund-raising project. The U.S. Army Music Program joined the Parade of American Music with programs presented throughout the world. Marking the 25th anniversary of the Berkshire Music Center at Tanglewood, NFMC and the Koussevitzky Foundation jointly financed the construction of a Composer's Studio built on the Koussevitzky estate, Seranak. The first *Functional Roster of NFMC* was printed and distributed in the last year of this administration. The 34th biennial convention in New York in 1967 was saddened by the serious illness of the National President which prevented her attending. She passed away early in 1968.

214

MRS. MAURICE HONIGMAN

Twenty-first President

Mrs. Maurice Honigman (Hinda Lebo) of Gastonia, North Carolina was elected president at the 1967 Biennial Convention in New York City, New York, and re-elected in 1969 at the Albuquerque, New Mexico convention. The first International Exchange Awards program was established with each recipient receiving $2,000; Improvisation was added to the projects of the Junior Division; Special emphasis was given to composition in the Junior and Student Divisions through the "Calvacade for Creative Youth"; Eight music scholarships in the Student Division, two in each of the four regions, were established; A voice scholarship in the Student Division, honoring the late Mrs. Clifton J. Muir, national president, 1963-1967, was endowed with a gift of $10,000 from Mr. Muir; The first Summer Music Festival Award of $500 for the performance and promotion of American music was established with the cooperation and support of the American Society of Composers, Authors and Publishers.

The Official Invocation composed by Dr. Julia Smith was accepted by the Federation, and *Bless Us, O God*, composed by Glad Robinson Youse was adopted as the Official Benediction of the National Federation of Music Clubs.

During the Honigman administration the Board of Directors approved the building or purchasing of permanent headquarters for the Federation. Mrs. Honigman was named chairman, an office which she held for almost twenty years. It was during this time that the Eden-Talbott Mansion in Indianapolis, Indiana was purchased and restored. It was dedicated in 1980 and is today the official headquarters of the National Federation of Music Clubs.

MERLE MONTGOMERY, Ph.D.

Twenty-second President

Dr. Merle Montgomery of New York City became the twenty-second president at the 1971 New Orleans Biennial Convention, and was re-elected at the *Diamond Jubilee* Convention in Atlantic City, New Jersey in 1973. Her doctorate in Philosophy was earned at the Eastman School of Music, Rochester University, where she also was head of the Piano Department. Professionally she served as Educational Director of Carl Fisher, Inc. and published twenty-six songs for children and a book on musical theory.

During her administration plans for the Bicentennial Parade of American Music were completed – fifty-two concerts scheduled at the Kennedy Center for the Performing Arts in Washington, D.C., and two thirteen-week series of radio programs featuring music by state composers with 2,000 recordings sent to seventy-two radio stations. Two hundred plaques, honoring 100 American musicians were installed nationwide. The National Federation won its first Freedom Foundation Medal and helped put John Philip Sousa in the Hall of Fame.

New Scholarships were received and new commissions and supplemental awards given. Special projects included the first musical People to People trip to Belgium, England and France; the first federation group to give concerts in foreign lands (Israel, Cypress and Greece); and the first NFMC artist to tour Africa under U.S. State Department auspices.

Dr. Montgomery compiled the first edition of *Who's Who in the NFMC*. Through her efforts a subsidy was obtained to reprint *The Record*, the account of the National Federation of Music Club's initial meeting in 1893. She continued to be active in the Federation following her four years as national president; she served as the Federation's representative to the United Nations; and was responsible for the Federation giving a Steinway piano to the United Nations. She served for four years as president of the National Music Council, during which time she administered the "Bicentennial Parade of American Music."

MRS. FRANK A. VOUGHT

Twenty-third President

Mrs. Frank A. Vought (Ruby Simons) of Baton Rouge, Louisiana, assumed the presidency of the National Federation of Music Clubs at the 1975 Biennial Convention in Atlanta, Georgia, and was re-elected in 1977 in Kansas City, Missouri. Her emphasis was on "Century Three USA – A New Era for the Arts." Beginning in 1975 the "International Decade of Women" was marked by two productions in New York City at Columbia University, a concert featuring outstanding women composers, conductors, performers, and the University Orchestra; and Hunter College Playhouse presentation of three one-act operas by women composers.

Legacies and gifts to the National Federation totaled over $160,000 – Agnes Fowler of Ohio, left a legacy of $150,000. A second Irene S. Muir Scholarship making possible a $1,000 scholarship in both Man's Voice and Woman's Voice was established through a contribution from Mr. Clifton J. Muir. Two special scholarships for the blind were given – the Paul W. Benzinger Award and the Dr. Robert E. Menees Award.

The Federation voted to purchase the historic Eden-Talbott Mansion in Indianapolis for the national headquarters – a purchase not consummated until May 15, 1979.

During this administration the Federation observed and administered the "Bicentennial Parade of American Music" (1975-1976) concerts at the John F. Kennedy Center for the Performing Arts in Washington, D.C. – an innovation, founded, funded, chaired and brought to fruition by Dr. Merle Montgomery, past president, NFMC (1971-1975).

Two American composers were commissioned to create works for small ensembles – Paul Turok's *Seven Lanier Poems* and Marga Richter's *Trio for Violin, Cello and Piano*. These were premiered at the 1979 convention in Portland, Oregon.

MRS. JACK CHRISTOPHER WARD

Twenty-fourth President

Mrs. Jack Christopher Ward (Lucile Parrish) of Greenville, South Carolina, was elected in April, 1979 in Portland, Oregon, and re-elected in 1981 in Birmingham, Alabama. Her theme, "Serving Mankind Through Music" and her theme song, "When You Give of Yourself" by Stanley Adams, best portray her administration. She was the first president to have a theme song.

A permanent NFMC headquarters building was purchased May 15, 1979; restoration was begun; the headquarters was moved from Chicago to Indianapolis; and the Eden-Talbott Mansion in Indianapolis, Indiana was dedicated October 19, 1980. In 1981 a Headquarters Endowment was established for permanent maintenance.

Two compositions were commissioned of American composers: *Prelude and Dance* for two pianos, Opus 120 by Paul Creston; and *Concerto II* for piano and orchestra, Opus 55 by John La Montaine.

Scholarships and awards endowed and/or established were: Janice Cleworth Piano Award; Hazel Heffner Becchina Voice Award; Thor Johnson Strings Award; Thelma Byrum Piano Award; Ruth Robertson Music Therapy Award; Vivian Menees Nelson Handicapped Award; Gladys Coult Scholarship to Sewanee Music Center; Wendell Irish Viola Award; and Eleanor Pascoe Voice Award to Chautauqua.

On August 9, 1982, through her efforts President Ronald A. Reagan signed into law a Congressional Charter, making NFMC the third music organization to be so honored.

In 1985 Mrs. Ward wrote *Protocol at a Glance* which is today the official protocol reference of the Federation.

Following her presidency, Mrs. Ward in 1988 founded the NFMC Ellis Competition for Duo Pianists, made possible by a legacy from Annie Lou Ellis; in 1989 she founded the Rose Fay Thomas Fellows honoring the founder of the Federation.

MRS. DWIGHT DE LOSSE SMITH ROBINSON

Twenty-fifth President

Mrs. Dwight De Losse Smith Robinson (Thelma) of Athens, Ohio, was elected president of the National Federation of Music Clubs in 1983 at the Columbus, Ohio Biennial Convention, and was re-elected in 1985 in Wichita, Kansas. Her theme was "Looking to the Future – Our Talented Youth". Among the new awards and scholarships established was the Joyce Walsh Scholarship for the Handicapped in the Junior Division. Highlighting the Robinson administration was the Federation's gift of a Steinway concert grand piano to the United Nations, a project of Dr. Merle Montgomery, NFMC president, 1971-1975. The dedicatory concert was given in the Dag Hammershold Auditorium of the United Nations.

The booklet, *Protocol at a Glance*, was written for the Federation by Mrs. Jack C. Ward, NFMC past president (1979-1983), and made available to all Federation members.

A children's opera, *The Minion and the Three Riddles* by Joseph Robinette and James R. Shaw, was commissioned, with the world premiere at the 1987 biennial convention in Miami, Florida.

MRS. GLENN L. BROWN

Twenty-sixth President

At the Miami, Florida Biennial Convention in April, 1987, Mrs. Glenn L. Brown (Mary Prudie) of Stanton, Texas was elected the 26th president of the National Federation of Music Clubs. She began a second term with her re-election in Fort Worth, Texas in 1989. "Impart the Gift of Music to All Ages" was the theme of her administration, and her theme song was "Climb Every Mountain".

Under the auspices of the United States Information Agency (USIA) three and one-half tons of old music were shipped overseas to countries in need of music. One of the important innovations of the Brown administration was the founding of the Rose Fay Thomas Fellows, by the Federation's 24th president, Mrs. Jack C. Ward. Honoring the founder of the Federation, Rose Fay Thomas, to date eighty-three individuals have received the coveted Rose Fay Thomas bronze medallion. *Profiles of the National Federation of Music Clubs*, the third **Who's Who** in the Federation, was published by Mrs. William B. Millard.

Included among the many new scholarships and awards received during the Brown administration was the first Music Education Scholarship. Endowed by Miss Gretchen E. Van Roy the scholarship is known as the "Gretchen E. Van Roy Music Education Scholarship" given in the Student Division. Three awards in composition were endowed by James Schnars in memory of the late Lynn Freeman Olson.

The Federation's first competition for duo-pianists was founded in 1989 by Mrs. Jack C. Ward, made possible by a legacy from the late Mrs. Edwin B. Ellis of Birmingham, Alabama. The first competition was held in 1991 with the duo-piano team, Thomas Hecht and Sandra Shapiro declared the winners of the $10,000 first prize.

An innovation of the Brown administration was two Young Artists Concerts at the United Nations – 1988 and 1990.

MRS. D. CLIFFORD ALLISON

Twenty-seventh President

Mrs. D. Clifford Allison (Virginia) of Wichita, Kansas was elected to her first term as president of the National Federation of Music Clubs at the Biennial Convention in Philadelphia, Pennsylvania in 1991, and re-elected in Buffalo, New York in 1993. Her theme was "Promote the Opportunities of the Federation From Sea to Shining Sea", and her theme song, *The Impossible Dream.*

Special emphasis during the Allison administration has been given to Public Relations. An innovation for the Federation was the endowment of all summer scholarships, which was in part made possible by a legacy of $75,000 from the late Miss Rose Thomas Smith of Galax, Virginia. A second innovation was the securing of money management to handle investments of the assets of the Federation.

Two concerts by NFMC Young Artists were given at the United Nations in 1992 and 1994. This administration has been active in support of the National Coalition for music in the schools.

BARBARA M. IRISH, Ph.D.

Twenty-eighth President

Dr. Barbara Irish (Mrs. Wilmot Irish) of Ithaca, New York was elected to the presidency of the National Federation of Music Clubs as this book goes to press.

Dr. Irish served as president of the New York Federation of Music Clubs for five years, after which she became a director of the National Federation of Music Clubs as the representative from New York. Immediately upon her election to the National Board of Directors Dr. Irish was elected treasurer of the National Federation, an office which she held until her election to the first vice presidency in 1991. She was elected the twenty-eighth national president in April, 1995 at the Biennial Convention in Wichita, Kansas.

Dr. Irish serves as chairman of the Anniversary Committee making plans for the celebration of the 100th anniversary of the National Federation of Music Clubs, which will be observed in 1998.

MUSIC IN MOTION

The Dance

1

Although the Dance Department of the National Federation of Music Clubs was not organized until many years later, it was back as far as November 6, 1921 that "Mrs. Smith (Mrs. Ella May Smith) moved, seconded by Mrs. Foster, that the Federation prize of $1,000 be offered for the 'Lyric Dance Drama'" to be presented at the 1923 Asheville, North Carolina Biennial Convention.

The winning composition was *Pan in America*, libretto by Robert Francis Allen, Sommerville, Massachusetts (winning the $400 prize) and Carl Venth, Fort Worth, Texas, who wrote the musical setting, winning the $600 prize. The premiere performance in Asheville, conducted by Mr. Venth, was one of the highlights of the convention.

Mr. Venth, composer and educator of Fort Worth, was born in Germany, coming to the United States twenty years later. In 1912 he became conductor of the Symphony Orchestra in Dallas and later the Fort Worth Symphony.

Dance, which is said to be "music in motion" has been an integral and active program of the National Federation in its efforts to pursue every possible avenue that will lead to better dance in America. It has provided through its syllabi, an objective standard of achievement for students of the dance in ballet, modern, tap and jazz.

According to Mr. Elwood Priesing, NFMC chairman of Dance, who has been active in the promotion of dance in the Federation, "The National Dance Department was established at the Biennial Convention in St. Louis, Missouri in 1960." In the beginning it was "rather dormant". It was not until the administration of Mrs. Clifton J. Muir in 1963 that the Dance Department was "revitalized" and "reorganized" under the co-chairmen, Jane Benedict and Jeri Kettering. Immediately they contacted the dance director of the Metropolitan Opera House in New York,

Allredo Corvine, with whose help they drew up a Dance Syllabus. Thus began the Junior Dance Festivals in the Federation. In the beginning, these included only ballet and modern dance, but it was soon realized that Juniors were interested in tap, jazz and acrobatic dances. Modern dance was utilized by college teachers and the festival requirements were changed to include "Theatre Dance" rather than Modern.

Four annual dance scholarships were established "August 24, 1970 on the recommendation of the Trustees of the Foundation Fund – two in the Junior Division and two in the Student Division, each valued at $100." A gift of $800 was presented by Oliver Daniel, representative of Broadcast Music Incorporated, to fund these scholarships for two years.

"The National Federation of Music Clubs Award honoring Past National President, Thelma A. Robinson," a $1,500 ballet dance scholarship, is given in the Junior Division. It was given for the first time in 1989 under the chairmanship of Mrs. Lars Ekwurzel.

The "Giselle" dancers performed on the program of the 1979 Fall Session in Charleston, South Carolina.

PART EIGHT

Service that is Song

CHAPTER ONE

MUSIC OF THE FAITHS

Sacred Music

1

As far back as 1911 members of the "infant" Federation realized the importance and need for making Sacred Music a part of its program. They knew the deep human needs which far outreach the primary needs of food and clothing. It was in that year, at the Biennial Convention in Philadelphia, Pennsylvania, Mrs. Charles B. Kelsey, president, that the first committee on Sacred Music was appointed.

Four years later, in 1915 at the Los Angeles Biennial Convention the Sacred Music program was augmented and George Andrews was named the chairman.

A National Hymn Contest was initiated in 1924 by Mrs. Grace Widney Mabee, chairman, Church Music. Any group of ten or more persons taking up the study of eight of the twelve suggested hymns constituted one entrance, and one contest if they took the examination. Classes and departments in Sunday Schools were encouraged to enter. Any five of the hymns could be chosen for the written examination. At the time of the examination the entrants "were required to play one phrase (perhaps not the first phrase) of each of the eight hymns from the twelve, allowing the contestants to write the titles and names of the tunes first", after which they could complete "the remainder of the answers at their pleasure." A grade of 70% was required for an entrant to be declared a winner.

Among the twelve hymns selected for the 1925-1926 contest were:

- *God of Our Fathers* (Lest We Forget), 1897, Rudyard Kipling (English) and C. B. Blanchard (American) – The "Processional" was written by Kipling in honor of Queen Victoria's diamond jubilee. The opening stanzas might appropriately be called "A Prayer for all Nations."
- *Day is Dying in the West* (Chautauqua), 1877, Mary A.

Lathbury (American) and William F. Sherwin (American) –
was written by Miss Lathbury at the request of Bishop Vincent
at Chautauqua, New York, and first was used as a vesper
hymn at the summer conference there. The tune "Chautauqua" by Sherwin has a melody appropriate for the words.

- *I Would be True*, 1906, Howard Arnold Walter (American)
  and Joseph Yates Peek (American) – is of picturesque origin, having been written by Mr. Walter to his mother one
  summer when halfway around the world from her. He was
  in Japan enroute to his "chosen field of service and a Fellowship student for research abroad" when he wrote this picturesque hymn.

All of the twelve hymns from which eight were to be chosen were
just as beautiful as the above three.

An award of fifty dollars was offered to the student of any High School
music department who submitted the best musical setting to a hymn,
"the words to be chosen by a committee appointed by the Executive
Board of the National Federation of Music Clubs." The prize was to be
awarded at the 1927 Biennial Convention in Chicago, "at which time
the hymn will be sung."

Thirty thousand (30,000) circulars giving the list of hymns with the
stories were mailed to forty-eight states, Canada, India and China. Four
hundred thousand (400,000) children took the written examination and
1,000 certificates were awarded. In addition to Sunday Schools were:
Y.W.C.A.'s, Camp Fire Girls, Private and Public Schools, choirs, junior
clubs, Reform schools, orphanages, Schools for the Blind, Mission
Schools of China and India, etc.

Alabama received the $100 prize for returning the most question-
naires. Kansas won the prize of $100 for conducting the greatest num-
ber of contests. In Wichita, Kansas, forty-four Sunday Schools, fifty-
five Daily Vacation Schools, twenty-nine Week Day Schools – all num-
bering 560 pupils – received an average grade of 75%. Missouri and
Texas tied for the $100 offered for second place for the most hymn con-
tests conducted, with each receiving fifty dollars.

2

Mrs. Royden James Keith assumed the office of the national presidency in 1947 soon after World War II had ended. She believed that

music answers a deep human need, as it had through the Federation's War Service Program, and that, "it marches shoulder to shoulder with a trenchant gospel demonstrating to humanity that the universe is not an accident but through travail and sorrow we move more steadfastly forward to a triumphant goal dictated by a divine purpose...." Her administration was channeled toward a recognition "that there has been a spiritual deterioration as an inevitable aftermath of war and the Federation had a definite obligation to affect this by lending its influence to the stimulation of a spiritual revival." In 1948 the Hymn of the Month committee, a sub-committee of Church Music, was founded under the chairmanship of Mrs. Frederic Sterling of Indiana.

Mrs. Sterling's plan was to augment the Church Music program, making the keynote of the 25th Biennial Convention, "Music, the Handmaiden of Religion; Religion, the Handmaiden of Peace." All groups were asked to include in their Music Week programs Thomas Patton Mock's hymn for all denominations, *Hail Prince of Peace*, which was meant to focus attention "in every city, town and hamlet upon great music with a religious implication, and to awaken a religious impulse through the medium of song." The project met with "a success beyond our wildest dreams." Municipal carillons, among them the famous Bok Tower at Lake Wales, Florida, played the hymn. National networks cooperated, with Ted Malone, Westinghouses's Roving Reporter, making the December hymn, *Hark the Herald Angels Sing* the subject of one of his Christmas broadcasts heard over 209 stations.

Mrs. Sterling's plan was that of choosing a hymn of the month for the purpose of "bringing a tired and troubled nation the hope and courage offered by the fine hymns forgotten by many and perhaps unknown to many more." Her plans to create interest included having: all groups give the history and sing the hymn at one meeting; ministers center one sermon around the hymn; the hymn played and sung in school rooms; and local radio stations call attention to the hymn on "spot" announcements. The Mutual Network stressed religious works and the president of the National Federation, Mrs. Keith, opened the series with a message emphasizing the value of group participation through the medium of choral singing.

Albert R. Bailey, a distinguished hymnologist of Worcester, Massachusetts, inaugurated a monthly feature article in the Worcester Telegram, telling the story of each hymn as it was scheduled. The Choir Guide which reached major church groups, instituted a Hymn of the Month column which was contributed by the Federation's chairman.

The first Hymn of the Month booklet was published during the administration of Mrs. C. Arthur Bullock (1959-1963), and the first chaplain, Mrs. Bessie Whittington Pfohl, of Winston Salem, North Carolina was appointed during the administration of Mrs. Ronald A. Dougan, (1951-1955).

3

The White Breakfast Candlelighting Ceremony was compiled by Mrs. Royden James Keith for the first Illinois' White Breakfast held in 1940 at the Women's Athletic Club, Chicago, Illinois. The same ceremony was used during the four years Mrs. Keith served as Illinois' state president. Other states adopted the ceremony, and in 1944 Mrs. Guy P. Gannett, national president, was so impressed with it that the National Federation of Music Clubs adopted it. The first national White Breakfast was held that same year at the meeting of the Board of Directors in Tulsa, Oklahoma. It was revised and shortened by Mrs. Keith, national president, for the Biennial Convention in Dallas, Texas. Again in 1960 Mrs. Keith revised the ceremony in its final form for the 1961 Biennial Convention in Kansas City, Missouri.

MUSIC – AN INSTRUMENT OF MORALE

War Service

1

It ain't the guns or armaments
Nor the funds that they can pay,
But the close cooperation
That makes them win the day.
It ain't the individual
Nor the army as a whole,
But the everlasting teamwork
Of every bloomin' soul.

—Anonymous

The calendar is turned back to June 1941 – only twenty-three years since the "war to end all wars" had come to an end. The United States again was mobilizing, not for aggression, but for defense. The National Federation of Music Clubs was the first to catch the vision of supplying musical needs to the men in the armed forces in an endeavor to bring entertainment and cheer into the lives of those who were defending our democratic way of life.

That same year the Defense Committee was organized. It was under the auspices of this committee that the Federation gave a series of concerts promoting one of its chief projects, "Bundles for Britain". One of the most important of these was a concert at Carnegie Hall in New York, November 10, 1941. Heading the list of dignitaries and musical notables was the president of the National Federation of Music Clubs, Mrs. Guy Patterson Gannett. Everyone entered into the spirit and came armed with "Bundles for Britain" which were exchanged at the door for admission slips.

Artists of national and international note graciously gave their services. These included: José Iturbi and his sister, Amparo Navarro; Arthur

Carron, Metropolitan Opera tenor; Josef and Rosina Lhevinne; Eddy Duchin; and Alexander Richardson, organist at Radio City Music Hall. It was Mr. Carron's encore which he sang in honor of his native land, *There'll Always Be An England*, which most thrilled his audience.

The Lhevinnes, duo-pianists, contributed their familiar arrangement of Strauss's *Blue Danube*, and Mr. Duchin closed the program with Gershwin's *The Man I Love* and Johnny Green's *Body and Soul*. As a rousing finale Mr. Carron led the audience in *God Save the King*.

Through these concerts thousands of articles of clothing and other supplies were netted for the bombed-out people of the British Isles.

> *In music there is no East or West*
> *In song no North or South*
> *But one great fellowship of love*
> *Throughout the whole wide earth.*
> —Paraphrased by
> Augustine Smith from
> *In Christ there is no East or West.*

2

With the entry of the United States into war in 1942, and the troops beginning to go overseas, the Defense Committee became the War Service Committee, headed by Mrs. Ada Holding Miller of Providence, Rhode Island.

The Federation spearheaded efforts for the sale of War Stamps and Bonds. To emphasize the interest and leadership in this endeavor, a concert was presented in March 1942 at the Federal Treasury Building in New York City where George Washington had taken his oath of office as President of the United States. Here, an orchestra from New York University, under the direction of Dr. John Warren Erb, played the *New England Symphony* of the Federation's beloved Dr. Edgar Stillman Kelley. In attendance were ranking officers of the War Service Branch of the United States Treasury Department.

3

All of the states, of which forty-seven and the District of Columbia had War Service chairmen, supported the War Service effort enthusiastically and wholeheartedly with the purchase of war bonds, and gifts –

from cookies and cross word puzzles to band instruments, phonographs, pianos – all sent to army bases, naval bases, out-going ships, and hospital ships - scores of which were outfitted with instrument kits and records.

The ships first were serviced exclusively from New York, and Staff Sergeant Eugene List (the husband of the Federation's own Young Artist winner, Carroll Glenn), later to become famous as the GI who played for the "Big Three" at Potsdam, was the liaison officer assigned to the work. It was Carlos Mosely who was in charge of shipments to the Asiatic areas.

The Chaplains kits were considered most valuable, providing suitable music for any type of church service, so often held under virtually impossible conditions. Many letters were received from chaplains expressing their deep appreciation to the Federation:

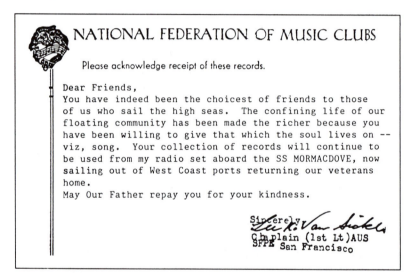

NATIONAL FEDERATION OF MUSIC CLUBS

Please acknowledge receipt of these records.

Dear Friends,
You have indeed been the choicest of friends to those of us who sail the high seas. The confining life of our floating community has been made the richer because you have been willing to give that which the soul lives on -- viz, song. Your collection of records will continue to be used from my radio set aboard the SS MORMACDOVE, now sailing out of West Coast ports returning our veterans home.
May Our Father repay you for your kindness.

Sincerely,
Chaplain (1st Lt)AUS
SFPE San Francisco

- Florida was the first state to place a music kit on a hospital ship in 1944.
- North Carolina originated Tag Day, the first Tag Day held in Elizabeth City. Winston Salem reported grossing $5,021.20 in a single day.
- Texas represented the high point in the number of Tag Days with 70 towns participating, and a total gross of $13,136.32 early in the campaign.
- The Illinois Federation of Music Clubs gave an ambulance. This great "challenge, took on added proportions in the face of the gesture of the state president, Mrs. Royden James

Keith, who not only collected $200 toward the purchase, contributed one of her prized rings" which made possible, "slightly more that one-half of the necessary $2,150.00".

"February 12, 1943 was an exceedingly cold, blustery day, but the thermometer's reading of two degrees above in no way chilled the warmth and pride of the little group gathered around the ambulance on Chicago's lake front." The light gray ambulance, provided with four stretcher carriers, was formally presented to the U.S. Naval Hospital, Great Lakes, Illinois, and carried a bronze plate, inscribed, "Contributed by the Illinois Federation of Music Clubs, February 11, 1943." Mrs. Julia Fuqua Ober, who had originated the Defense Committee, wrote, "It is fitting that the state which gave birth to the National Federation of Music Clubs, and in which it is chartered should have placed a concrete humanitarian form, a unique war service which will aid in emergencies, aid the broken bodies of American men, and wondrously bless them."

- Maine was the first to send money for purchasing materials for ports of embarkation – $588.50.
- Port Huron, Michigan club raised and gave $1,000 to the War Service.
- Virginia, among its many contributions gave a phonograph and records to the English airplane carrier, *Illustrious*, which was in the naval yard for repairs. This, with a Victory Vaudeville presented by men in the service was sponsored by the music clubs of Norfolk and Portsmouth. Virginia also adopted two nurses in foreign countries.
- Rhode Island offered musical aid to five ports and a naval base – the plan calling for the gift of a phonograph and radio to each port, together with a set of dance records, ten dollars worth of popular music, song books, hymn books, and assistance in securing orchestral instruments and pianos where necessary. This small state sent 15,000 pieces of musical equipment overseas.
- In California, the San Francisco clubs presented an ambulance to the War Service effort.
- Alabama's gifts included nine pianos sent overseas and one complete orchestra sent to the South Pacific.

These are only a few of the contributions, but there was no limit to the patriotism and enthusiasm of the clubs and states in support of the men in the service.

General George Marshall said, "I wish to express my personal appreciation to you (Mrs. Miller) and your co-workers who are contributing diversion through music on Army transports. This is most worthwhile, and will be a definite contribution to the morale of the men."

Pictures show men receiving the Federation's phonographs just before leaving this country – their last minutes on American soil, and as the major said, "only another step in their cradle on the deep."

Each state answered the "call" with the same loyal support feeling that members of the Federation could not sail ships, join the army, or run machines – but each could produce, in the words of Mrs. Ober,

"a unified, glorified spirit of patriotism which inspires our fellowmen to a loyalty to God, country and mankind. We must remember that an aggressor nation placed its bands on conquered soil by the time its army of occupation arrived to woo the captives... We must remember that it is as much the duty... of every individual... to work... at defense as it is that of the soldiers and sailors. A man, woman or child without a country is a miserable outcast. May God give us strength to carry on, vision to see the need, the will to conquer evil, hearts to save culture and spiritual values that souls of men may be free though bodies die. Keep 'em singing a triumphant song!"

- Federation members sold war bonds amounting to $1,602,537.95.
- More than $106,000 was raised for War Service.
- 2,500,000 articles of musical equipment were shipped to our men at home and overseas.
- Materials donated to camps within this country and ports of embarkation during the first two years 1941-1943 amounted to:

| 3,566 phonographs | 1,125 pianos |
| 1,735 radios | 17 organs |

3,229 miscellaneous instruments

Those places to which the Federation's gifts were sent, included Alaska, Australia, Iceland, Greenland, Newfoundland, Ireland, England, Africa, Burma, Gibraltar, Malta, Bermuda, Nassau, New Caledonia, Arctic Circle, outposts of Cuba, the Aleutians, and islands of the Pacific.

4

Many letters as from Private Joseph E. Sodam to Mrs. Ada Holding Miller were received.

Jan. 3-44.

Mrs. A. H. Miller.
28 Sventh Ave.
Providence R.I.

Dear Mrs. Miller:

Today Col. Lewis Mott gave me a letter from you to answer that he received today. I was indeed happy to find out that there was a Harmonica availble for me. There sure arent any down this part of the country. The 2# double reed Hohner that you mentioned in your letter will be satisfactory with me.

236

*Thank you very
kindly for your trouble.*

Yours truly,

*Pvt. Jos. C. Sodam.
36695739.
Co. A-216th Eng. Bn.
16th Armd Div.
A. P. O. # 412.
Camp Chaffee, Ark.*

*P.S. I forgot to tell you
I'd like to have that
in the Key of "C"*

In the fall of 1943, Donald Voorhees, conductor of the Telephone Hour and Cavalcade of America, offered $1,000 in War Savings Bonds as awards to the federated groups who sponsored most significantly serving the war effort. Seventeen states participated, and twenty-nine awards were given for programs presented by clubs or states.

CHAPTER THREE

NO EAST, NO WEST – NO NORTH, NO SOUTH

Music in Hospitals

1

"To care for him who shall have borne the battle and for his
widow and his orphan."

After the Civil War, it was with these words that President Abraham
Lincoln stated this nation's moral obligation to its veterans, when he
called for legislative action.

It was this same feeling during World War II which inspired Mrs.
Guy Patterson Gannett to initiate a nationwide Music in Hospitals pro-
gram in the spring of 1943 – a program which was to grow out of the
War Service Committee. Again, a first for the National Federation of
Music Clubs – the first organization to sponsor Music in Hospitals dur-
ing World War II.

The Menningers had launched something akin to this, stressing the
value of music in therapy, but they did not have a large volunteer organization to promote it. The Washington Federation of Music Clubs began this work by organizing programs for the entertainment of the men
sent from Alaska to Seattle for treatment. Mrs. Gannett, president of the
Federation was so impressed with the work which she observed on a
visit to Seattle, that she immediately took steps to have a worker trained
and put at the head of the Music in Hospitals Committee. Miss Ruth
Bradley of New York was named the first chairman.

The Music in Hospitals program of the National Federation of Music
Clubs was authorized by the Surgeon Generals's office for both Army and
Navy Hospitals. Official recognition of the Federation's activities in the
Music in Hospitals field through its appointment to membership in the
Veterans Voluntary Service National Advisory, by General F. R. Kerr, chair-
man of the Committee, also gave impetus to its work. This appointment
was followed by words of high commendation from Ray Green, chief of

the Music Recreation Service for the Veterans Administration. Regarding the organization Mr. Green wrote: "In addition to generous assistance through donations of musical supplies and equipment, active participation in the music program as instructors, leaders and performers is a most helpful aspect of participation by members of the Federation... It is recognized that the Federation is most willing and eager to be of service in all phases of the music program in our hospitals...."

Mrs. Gannett, who was affectionately known as "the great war president" expressed her belief in the Music in Hospitals program when she said in 1944;

> "What made our coming together memorable was the warm and quick response of our membership to every suggestion that looked toward a nobler future for the organization we love.
> "If the successful carrying forward of such projects as Music in Hospitals... meant a somewhat greater financial burden on the individual member, we were ready to meet the challenge.
> "If the Federation's role in the nationwide rehabilitation program involved a continuance of long hours of grueling toil that have fallen to our War Service Chairmen... they were prepared to give ungrudgingly. If to fulfill our destiny as America's largest musical organization demanded unremitting zeal and sacrifice, all were content to expend every human effort. It was as if the war had taught us that culture and religion, the two great outpourings of the human spirit, are closely akin, and that in guarding the one we are contributing vitally and generously to the other."

The new Music in Hospitals committee involved ward music in the Army, Navy and Air Corp hospitals; instruction to disabled servicemen wishing to learn to play instruments; and entertainment programs in those sections of the country too remote to be serviced by world famous artists who gave of their talents so liberally during the war.

Much of the equipment which was left over from the War Service work was reallocated. Of interest is the disposition of twelve left-over phonographs. On the day that the disastrous Bar Harbor fire broke out, these were packed, ready for shipment to Maine, on the little ship named the *Sunbeam* which visited isolated islands during the cold winter months. Shipment was delayed but a letter was sent offering the phonographs. The heartwarming reply from the Maine Sea Coast Missioner, Mr. Neal Bousfield, was indication of the enthusiasm with which the offer was received:

"Your letter comes like a drink of water to a thirsty man. Miss Drury, who for two years is a teacher in one of our island schools, has taken on the job of visiting as many of the small schools in our out of the way places along the Maine coast as we can care for... So many (of the teachers) have very little equipment and feel that they are at the ends of the earth."

He goes on to say that she "visits these schools, twenty-seven in number... many without electricity and most without phonographs, so a gift of these machines would be most welcome."

In a letter received by Mrs. Gannett from General Dwight D. Eisenhower, Chief of Staff of the War Department, he wrote:

"It is the policy of the War Department to assist the Veterans Administration in every way possible, and it is most gratifying to observe the great continued interest shown by you and your splendid organization in the welfare of our veterans."

Since World War II, the work has continued in the hospitals where there is a need for volunteers in both Music Therapy and Recreation Departments.

A group from the Excelsior Springs, Missouri Hospital is entertained by members of the National Federation of Music Clubs. Right is Mrs. Hart Dierks, chairman, Music in Hospitals, Missouri.

"... like water on parched tongues"

International Music Relations

1

In 1925 the National Federation of Music Clubs sponsored what was known as International Reciprocity. The main purpose of the committee was to work for the presentation of American music abroad because European publishers carried very little of any native American music. This work included the exchange of programs with the other countries.

At the close of World War II the work changed completely. As an outgrowth of the successful War Service Committee, the International Music Relations Committee was born, with Mrs. Guy Patterson Gannett as the national chairman and Mrs. Ada Holding Miller, the first vice president and former War Service Chairman as one of the staunchest supporters. It was the feeling of members of the Federation that the music needs of all peoples of the world must be met – Yugoslav and Filipino musicians have much the same wants as the Americans.

What was once upon a time the two room playhouse for the children of Ada Holding Miller and her husband, Dr. Miller – in the rear of the Miller home – became the storage rooms for shipments of music, instruments, and replacement parts. It became known as "The Little House".

The Little House had been the playhouse of the three daughters of the Millers, after which it became a children's theatre for the presentation of home-written melodramas. When Mrs. Miller succeeded Mrs. Ober as chairman of the War Service Committee, The Little House was immediately mobilized and became the center of the collection of music and its distribution to American and Allied troops in every part of the world.

Tables were set on stilt legs, shelves were repaired, and a committee of stalwart Providence Federation members pitched in. Out of The Little House, from 1941 until the close of the war went vast shipments of music and instruments and records. Service men in every corner of the globe learned of The Little House as headquarters for the shipments of music which "enlivened their rest hours and made them remember a better life, far from machine guns and foxholes. In two years, through the generosity of federated clubs more than 26,000 pieces of music were received at The Little House and shipped out in immediate response to the plea from a foreign embassy or consulate." Daily the music came in – and daily the music went out.

"The Little House has never had a chance to rest," said Mrs. Miller. "The floor sags and the walls need a coat of paint. But we've been too busy to attend to such details... If The Little House could speak, it would say that out of its doors has gone more joy by giving material than out of any house in the world."

The story of the change from the War Service Committee to the International Music Relations Committee is one that Federation members never tire of hearing. An article by Virgil Thompson appeared in a Sunday *Herald Tribune* in New York, telling of the plight of the Athens Symphony, whose members had refused to play for the Nazi invaders and had concealed all of their instruments in caves. When the instruments were taken out at the end of the war it was found that strings had rusted and that in every way the instruments were completely unplayable. The article pleaded for some philanthropically inclined organization to purchase replacement parts, at a cost of about $1,500, and deliver them to the Greek Minister of Information for shipment. This article appeared on Sunday morning. The Federation's president was contacted, and by Wednesday morning the replacement parts were delivered by the president and the War Service chairman, who were in New York to make the presentation.

Thousands of dollars and thousands of gifts followed: a grand piano to the Athens Symphony; electromagnets (which were available only in the United States) for the organs of two Paris churches which had been damaged by American bombing; a tuba, cello, and two violins to the Tokyo Symphony; an organ, accordion and xylophone to the Institute for Crippled Children in Tokyo; a complete set of instruments for a Boy Scout Band in Manila and clarinets for the Manila Symphony; musical needs for Institutes for the Blind in Naples and Bandung, Indonesia; a phonograph and needed instruments for a Teachers' Training School in Tripoli; replacement parts for an orchestra in Bolivia; and forty harmonicas ("mouth organs") to a Boys Catholic Orphanage in Brazil. The list is endless. By 1949 more than 26,000 pieces of music had passed through "The Little House" to be sent to "all parts of the globe".

There was one gift which pleased Federation members very much. On the march across Normandy, the American soldiers bombed three churches. The organs were damaged. "We knew how badly the boys felt at having to bomb the churches. We knew how much the people needed their organs," explained Mrs. Miller, "so we raised the money for electric magnets for the organs," and they were shipped to Normandy.

The Germans sought subscriptions to music magazines and most of the requests were for orchestrations and piano. Favorite American pieces sought were Negro spirituals, hillbilly music, Victor Herbert, Cole Porter, Gershwin and Stephen Foster. A gift of $500 was made to the Aachen Orchestra, the oldest music orchestra in the world, to enable it to make a good will tour of Austria.

In 1956 it became necessary to find a new home for the International Music Relations Library, as "The Little House" at the rear of the Miller home had become inadequate for the storage and shipping of music. A room in the Music Mansion in Providence, the former home of one of the Federation's most esteemed members, Mrs. George Hail, was given for the purpose – rent free. This offer was gratefully accepted by the chairman of Music Distribution, Miss Irma Howe.

On each piece of music that was mailed, was stamped "Gift of the National Federation of Music Clubs of America" as a constant reminder to young recipients of the good will of America. People from other countries also earnestly desired better international understanding as is evidenced by a quote from a letter from "Mr. Melgar" of Madrid, Spain:

> "Will you please send me some popular songs, folklore, carols, national songs, national hymn and Wisconsin hymn, even though useless and discarded, to study and better know and understand the American people."

In the words of Mrs. Hazel Post Gillette, "few of us realize the enormity of this project as it has been carried on through the years from the Music Mansion in Providence, Rhode Island... music to Finland, Africa, the West Indies, Egypt, South Vietnam, Madras, El Salvador, Spain, Indonesia, Morocco, Hong Kong, Turkey, Lebanon, Australia, Austria, France, Japan, Korea, Holland, Formosa, and the Philippine Islands... Can we ever begin to estimate the effect of such human relationships on brotherhood and world peace?"

A further activity of the International Relations Committee, was the sending of "Musical Packages," containing replacement parts for orchestral instruments damaged or worn out during the war. These were something like the "Care Food Packages". A "Musical Package" might contain accessories for brass instruments, for woodwinds and for violins; another, accessories for viola and cello; another, for flute, oboe and bassoon. Packages for the youth groups contained simple instruments and books for instruction, greatly needed by schools, orphanages and children's villages.

The packages cost $10 and the need was great. Through a generous gift of Miss Mary Howe there were several shipments of musical packages. The first shipment went to the Aachen, Germany Orchestra whose plight inspired the creation of the packages. The conductor wrote that his orchestra was so hard up for materials that five of his musicians were sharing a single piece of rosin. There was an ample supply of rosin in each package.

UNESCO wrote expressing gratitude for the "music boxes" which "help peoples speak to peoples."

In 1989 during the presidency of Mrs. Glenn L. Brown, Stanton, Texas, it again became necessary to make a third move from the Music Mansion in Providence. Through the help of Mrs. Brown's son, Dr. Guy Story Brown, and the courtesy of the United States Information Agency (USIA), the music was shipped overseas – approximately 100 boxes to seventy-five countries – again at no charge to the Federation. In response to the Music Mansion collection being shipped to many different countries around the world, the USIA has received "thank you" cables from many including: Santiago, Chile; Bamako; Manila; Istanbul; San Salvador and others. Antonarive, Madagascar received four boxes because the request not only showed great need, but contained a bit of poetry,

"… the music will be received like water on parched tongues."

We quote Mrs. Guy Patterson Gannett, national president:

"We live in an age when all the world has become our neighbor. Only as we share with the peoples of lands less fortunate than ours, our cultural riches, our cultural opportunities, and our spiritual concepts, can we live in the spirit of the Prince of Peace... The secret of richer and fuller living is found in the words of a man who walked the sands of Galilee two thousand years ago, and who said to his disciples, 'Thou shalt love thy neighbor as thyself.'"

2

The International Music Relations committee has worked very closely with the United Nations. Numerous films have been promoted in the hopes of better understanding among the nations. One of particular interest was "The United Nations as a Peace Bell". This was described vividly by the chairman, Mrs. Kathleen Davison, in 1954:

"One of the most interesting ceremonies that has recently taken place at the United Nations was the presentation of a 'Peace Bell' to the UN on June 8 by the United Nations Association of Japan. The presentation was made by Ambassador Renzo Sawado, Japanese Observer to the United Nations, and the gift was accepted by Benjamin Cohen, Assistant Secretary General. The Bell, housed in a structure of Japanese Cypress Wood, reminiscent of a Shinto Shrine, is three feet three inches high, two feet in diameter at the base, and weight 256 pounds. It was cast from old coins of Japan, badges and medals; a plaque of Christ and His mother, which had been blessed by Pope Pius XII; a medal of Pope Pius, and coins of 60 nations. The majority of the latter were donated at the 13th General Conference of the United Nations Association held in Paris in June 1951, and the Bell was cast on United Nations Day, October 24, 1952. On one side, inscribed in Japanese characters, are the words 'Long Live Absolute World Peace'; on the reverse side the date and circumstances of the casting of the Bell. In making the presentation Ambassador Sawado said: 'It is said in this country that the bells of temples all over the country are rung 108 times on New Year's Eve, each peal purges away one on the 108 afflictions of mankind, thus ushering in the New Year of Hope. I believe the peal of this Bell symbolizes the advent of the day when the world will be cleared of all the afflictions which are now besetting it, and I earnestly pray for the earliest advent of this day.' In accepting the Bell Mr. Cohen stated that the United Nations is confident that the Japanese people want peace; that the very fact that their post-war constitution provided for national disarmament is a token of their specific intentions. In concluding his address he said: 'May this Bell stand through the years undisturbed by the voices of controversy and disputation in buildings nearby, or the din of traffic in this great metropolis. Let it toll not for those who died at war, but for those who live in peace.'"

"Brighten the corner..."

Music in Industry

1

"Brighten the corner where you are" became the stirring slogan of industrial plants as war clouds gathered over Europe in the early 1940's Maintaining the morale of workers through Music in Industry became a valued patriotic service rendered by the National Federation of Music Clubs. Many industrial plants supplied musical programs in workrooms to relieve the fatigue of mechanical work. Not only was music a morale builder but plants felt it relaxed the employees and speeded up production.

Some of the highlights of the program for Music in Industry were:

- At the Republic Aviation Corporation plant in Farmingdale, Long Island, when the Nassau-Suffolk Little Symphony Orchestra serenaded aircraft workers during their noon lunch hour – a change from the clash of metal fabricating machines – it was found the music was good relaxation from the tension of rapid production.
- Grumman Aircraft Engineering Corporation had a 45-piece symphony orchestra and a 45-piece band made up of employees at its Long Island plant.
- The Sperry Gyroscope Company, Inc. of Brooklyn had an orchestra of 60 and a band of 55 organized by Miss Marguerite Ruth, chairman of Music in Industry in New York. They rehearsed once a week after working hours, and gave concerts once a month at Central YMCA in Brooklyn.
- The J. A. Jones Construction Company of Brunswick, Georgia maintained the Brunswick Little Symphony Orchestra which followed a monthly schedule: a "Pop" Concert each Sunday, a subscription concert the last Thursday, and two "complimentary" concerts for students. Rehearsals took place five times a week from one to four p.m. on company time.

Shipyard workers constituted the major membership of the Brunswick Choral Society – working on the first and third shifts so that they were free to rehearse. Musical events of the two groups included the opera, *Carmen*, *the Messiah*, *Pirates of Penzance* and *The Seven Last Words of Christ*.

Big industry's contribution to the development of choral singing was demonstrated for members of the National Federation at the 1947 Biennial Convention in Detroit. To open the second day of the convention a Glee Club came from the Chevrolet plant to sing a program of five songs under David B. Redwood's direction. The Dow Chemical Company sent its male chorus from Midland.

These programs brought federation members to the realization that music has been a part of the recreational program in Detroit areas for many years. And – it was their belief that "Music in Industry is not only a wartime morale builder, but a peacetime cultural influence which is here to stay."

PEOPLES TO PEOPLES

Philanthropic Music

1

The records reveal that dating back as far as 1927, Philanthropic Music played an important part in the programs of the Federation, and the majority of the states and clubs. And – in 1937 most of the states had Philanthropic chairmen.

Among some of the philanthropic projects which were typical, and which are worthy of mention were:

- In Wyoming a Federation member gave free lessons to children for twenty years, sometimes having eight pupils a week.
- The Atlanta, Georgia Music Club allowed the state chairman sufficient funds to develop talent in community houses and homes for the underprivileged children.
- In 1937, through the cooperation of the Detroit Community Fund and the Michigan Federation, an allocation of $5,000 for cultural activities was made, thus providing means of maintenance for nine settlement schools.
- The Oregon Federation of Music Clubs sponsored two settlement schools in Portland. They also gave assistance to blind musical students.
- Gifts of violins, a cello, a viola and pianos were made by the Rhode Island Federation. A piano was given to the Crawford Allen Hospital for Crippled Children to replace one lost in a hurricane.
- The Maine Federation contributed annually toward musical training for underprivileged children, and tickets for symphony concerts were given worthy students.
- In Virginia during the years 1927-1937, ten music students were helped financially to the extent of $3,347, the money being contributed by the clubs of the Virginia Federation.

The above are only a few of the contributions reported.

Ground breaking ceremonies for the John F. Kennedy Center for the Performing Arts was attended by Mrs. Clifton J. Muir, national president, and the National Federation pledged more than $7,000.00 toward the Center. In 1961 the Federation passed a resolution requesting that the National Federation of Music Clubs, at every level, give tangible support to this project and that the Federation urge the establishment of an Educational Television Station whereby chosen performing groups could be heard from coast to coast.

Mrs. Robert W. Roberts of St. Petersburg, Florida gave $1,000 to endow a seat in the Kennedy Center in the name of the National Federation of Music Clubs, "to be inscribed on it permanently." Mrs. Muir presented the $1,000 check to the trustees on October 18, 1962.

The Pennsylvania Federation of Music Clubs was the first state organization to respond to the appeal for seats in the National Cultural Center, voiced by Roger Stevens, Chairman of the Center's Board of Trustees.

The pledge of the Federation was surpassed by more than $6,000. The amount contributed by 1967 was $13,030.

TOGETHER IN MUSIC

Audio-Visual

1
If we could hear God,
He would speak to us in Music.

"Music", according to the late Dr. Joseph Maddy, "represents a big percentage of all the programs we hear broadcast – music is used too, in many ways in radio beyond presentation for its own sake to create mood – a theme for a program – it is used as a means of breaking the action in dramatic script like an audible curtain... it is a background to speech, played softly to fasten words in our memories." It is radio's most useful commodity.

It was for this reason that radio was instituted a project of the Federation in 1932, in the Department of Education. The program stressed the importance of Federation member's responsibility for the development of programs of high musical standards through maintaining close contacts with the broadcasting companies and local radio stations, with the desire of being helpful to them. Federation members were urged repeatedly to send favorable comments and constructive criticism to the broadcasting companies. "Write, write, write" was the "cry".

A brochure entitled "How to Listen to Music Over the Radio" by George R. Marek, was sent to all state radio chairmen; CBS and NBC received the names of all state presidents for inclusion on their mailing lists.

As a result of a poll conducted, 1935-1937, by WNRC, the Federation presented awards of illuminated parchment scrolls for the best programs in six classifications. These were awarded to:

1. Serious Music – Ford Sunday Evening Hour
2. Variety – Rudy Vallee
3. Children's Program – Dorothy Gordon in Children's Corner

4. Educational – Chicago University Round Table
5. News Commentator – Booke Carter
6. Drama – Lux Theatre of the Air

In those early years when radio was "new", amazing results were reported by almost all of the states as:

- Massachusetts – "with 90 broadcasts to their credit"
- Rhode Island – "Sixty-five programs have been given this year and last."
- Connecticut – "... choirs, Senior and Junior clubs have been granted 88 'spots' over 5 stations."
- Oregon – "... has changed its continuity in 30 weekly broadcasts by telling events – history and accomplishments of the Federation."
- West Virginia – "secured nearly 50 'spots' in 18 hours on 3 stations."

In 1943 as the biennium drew to a close in a world of martial music, marching soldiers, whirring planes, rationed food and lessened travel, there could be no biennial convention. Four major networks NBC, CBS, Blue Network, and Mutual Broadcasting Company guaranteed a period of one week – this to replace the biennial convention. In the words of Mrs. Guy Patterson Gannett, president, "I shall not feel that our Federation family is outside the range of our voices, even though the miles which separate us are many, since we have our 'Festival of the Air' to bring the Federation into the homes and hearts of all our members.... That we may truly share the riches of our Federation, I urge you all to tune in and through the magic of the radio dial, bring the Festival into your home."

Sunday, May 2, 1943 the first day of National Music Week, at 12:30 noon, the voice of the national president, Mrs. Guy Patterson Gannett reached millions of listeners through a brief broadcast on all four major networks. Her topic was "Stars from the Blue".

Four new prize-winning works chosen in Federation contests were premiered that week; the first announcement of the winners of the Young Artist Auditions, selected the previous Thursday evening, but which were not announced until the Victory Concert on Friday evening, May 7, when they were presented their $1,000 prizes; on Youth Day, May 3, the principal Federation event under Federation auspices was the presentation of Carroll Glenn, 1941 Young Artist winner. There was the Community Sing under the auspices of the Illinois Federation of Music Clubs, originating on the campus of Chicago University on May 3, and many, many others.

The National Federation in cooperation with NBC sponsored a national contest for the best patriotic song submitted. Mrs. Gannett felt assured there would be a winner since hundreds of entries were received with the identity of each composer concealed under a nom de plume. No winner was declared.

One of the Federation's most valued and esteemed members in the field of Audio-Visual Activities was Mrs. Naomi Reynolds of Los Angeles, California. With her husband, Dr. Reynolds, they founded the Denver, Colorado radio station KLZ, and for years she managed it. She was well known throughout the audio-visual world. When radio was new in the Federation Mrs. Reynolds had a radio series in Los Angeles called, "Let's Talk Music". Interviews on the air with well-known musicians and Federation members were conducted in which Federation projects from the earliest years were discussed. A great compliment was paid Mrs. Reynolds by CBS when the Publicity Department included this program on its weekly releases to the entire mailing list.

In 1939 at the New York World's Fair, Naomi Reynolds presented to the broadcasting industries an impressive plaque symbolizing freedom. On it were inscribed the words of Walt Whitman, "I say there can be no safety for these states without free tongues, and ears willing to hear the tongues."

Walter E. Koons of the National Broadcasting Company, speaking to the Federation in 1937 on what the radio – then in its infancy – had accomplished in the last ten years, to stimulate the amazing development of musical culture in America, said:

> "... these seeds were planted long before the National Broadcasting Company came into existence, long before Marconi first thought of his wireless invention – these seeds were carefully planted and tenderly nourished first by music loving individuals, and then by groups who formed themselves into music clubs, and then decided to unite in a Federation of Music Clubs – a National Federation of Music Clubs. We (of NBC) have been able to bring to a rich flowering and fruition, seeds you planted, and plants you nourished. And here we find ourselves in the same garden... Thank you for all you have done in making it possible for us to accomplish what we have accomplished in promoting musical culture...."

2

"Operation Zero Hour" was a campaign by the National Federation of Music Clubs, inaugurated in 1952 by Mrs. Ada Holding Miller, to encourage the broadcasting of light music, interspersed with a psalm, a prayer, or words of encouragement and hope, during the hours between midnight and dawn, when vitality is at its lowest ebb and many – ill, worried, or in despair – are doomed to sleepless nights.

This became a great concern to President Ada Holding Miller, who had been instrumental in the Federation's War Service Program and Music in Hospitals – both recently organized. She learned that 104 radio stations were on the air after midnight or before 6 a.m. for an hour or two. Those on until 1 a.m. programed primarily popular recordings, hillbilly, folk music, jazz, dance band and western. For three years Mrs. Miller made it a practice purposely to lie awake after midnight turning the radio dial in search for sounds other than live recordings and commercial announcements. It was this that led her to suggest "Operation Zero Hour".

Working toward this end Mrs. Miller held many interviews with radio executives. Six thousand pieces of material were distributed regarding "Operation Zero Hour" by the NFMC chairman, Mrs. Ronald A. Dougan, including questionnaires, the national presidents article, and two strong letters of endorsement from officers of the National Association of Music Therapy. Eleven radio stations incorporated all or part of the plan, including WNBC in New York and WLW in Cincinnati. WBAL in Baltimore offered a post-midnight program with excellent music played without commercials, with occasional reading of poetry and words of courage and cheer.

A second station to carry the innovation was WNBC, New York, key station of the NBC networks. Its program, "Music Through the Night" presented the finest concert music, midnight until morning. Mrs. Miller quoted the manager of the National Broadcasting Co. to the effect that in the first two weeks of "Operation Zero Hour," 4,122 letters of appreciation were received by the network.

From the hundreds of letters received by the Federation, one said:

> "May I express my congratulations to the NFMC for the time and effort which it has expended on behalf of many people who look forward now to the hours between midnight and dawn as something other than a long, dark road which they must travel alone."

3

Virgil Thompson best explained the purpose of music in Motion Pictures when he said, "the score of a motion picture supplies a sort of human warmth to the figures of the screen. The quickest way to a person's brain is through his eyes, but even in the movies, the quickest way to his heart and feelings is through the ear."

The Federation, believing it could best serve, in the early 1930's became interested and active in working for the sponsorship of the best in motion pictures. The first step was the appointment of chairmen in the states, to which thirty-seven states responded. A National Federation committee was formed to preview films before recommending them. This committee reviewed from four to six pictures weekly and their unbiased opinions were published. The committee requested the cooperation of the membership in attending the pictures recommended, and sending in their reactions. Through the work of this committee the Universal Picture Corporation planned to have judges at the Federation's final contest for concert and opera voices offering the winners "a screen test if they seem to have screen possibilities."

Through "Musical Moods" sponsored by the Federation, previews of one reel films based on musical compositions and synchronized with beautiful visual accompaniment in color, were held. $1,000 in prizes was offered to individuals or clubs suggesting the winning composition and scenario for visual accompaniment. From the beginning, New Orleans had thirty music lovers to enter the "Musical Moods" contest. Keen interest and discriminating activities in the field of musical films came from practically every state, and doing particularly fine work were: Florida and Colorado who sponsored "One Night of Love"; Louisiana with its sponsorship of "Naughty Marietta" and "Roberta"; the Buffalo, Wyoming Music Club, who through the sponsorship of "The Great Waltz" made enough money to start a music library; the Jacksonville, Florida Music Club also sponsored "The Great Waltz" from which they made $100; and the Hattiesburg, Mississippi Music Club used "Moonlight Sonata" to pay the expenses of a ten piano recital performed during Music Week.

Other films sponsored by the National Federation of Music Clubs in 1937 included: "Maytime", "Show Boat", "Rose Marie", and others. In the 1940's one of the pictures most highly recommended was "Gone With the Wind," the review of which *Music Clubs Magazine* carried,

"... the greatest achievement in the motion picture industry has been accomplished in this production... Max Steiner, who is recognized by all studios for his original synchronizations... has woven a musical score throughout the epic, that of itself, and describes the conflict... The Tara theme is subtly used and intertwined... Scarlet, Butler, and the Negro mammy are all signified musically... This is recommended as a masterpiece of screen craftsmanship, and great credit is due the Director, Victor Fleming."

In 1940 the National Federation set up awards for the best music in films, based on "excellence of musical scoring in the different classifications applicable to motion pictures... For motion picture music is the most important musical movement now going on in America, therefore the world." The awards were to be given at the twenty-second biennial convention in Los Angeles, California in June 1941, with the winners scores presented. Outstanding composers and music educators as Rudolph Ganz, Howard Hanson, Walter Spry, Charles Wakefield Cadman, Edith Keller, Paul Weaver, and others "banded together to study this phase of music and register their reports on suggested pictures."

On Saturday evening, June 21, 1941, following supper in the Hollywood Bowl, at 8:30 under the "Auspices of Motion Picture Producers and Distributors of America, Inc." the "Festival of Motion Picture Music" was featured with the president of the National Federation of Music Clubs, Mrs. Vincent Hilles Ober presenting the awards.

On the committee representing the Studio Music Directors, were chairmen from MGM, RKO-Radio, Warner Brothers, Republic, Paramount, 20th Century Fox, Universal, and Columbia.

There are certain thrills which come to a writer when doing research, and by chance comes upon pertinent information which is unexpected. Such was the case when this writer by chance learned that Walt Disney's "Fantasia" was one of those pictures receiving the Federation Award at the Hollywood Bowl in June 1941.

On a visit to Walt Disney World in Orlando, Florida in 1984, she was waiting in the Disney Theatre to see the film on the life of Walt Disney. Seeing glass cases displaying Disney memorabilia, she "strolled" over to take a look, but never got any farther than the first one. The only memorabilia displayed in the case was a bronze metal plaque bearing the inscription:

National Federation of Music Clubs
to
Walt Disney
In recognition of his contribution
to the
Advancement of Music Recording
FANTASIA
May 1940   May 1941

Mounted on green velvet in a shadow box frame was the bronze medallion backed by a 4" x 5" wooden plaque. The only other memorabilia in the display case was the program of the Premiere Performance of "Fantasia" on November 13, 1940.

ONE GREAT FELLOWSHIP OF LOVE

Music for the Blind

1

According to Charles Reed Jones, "more blind persons have achieved eminence in music than in any of the other arts, trades or professions." Yet, until the early 1950's there had been no concentrated effort made to assist the sightless to study music or enjoy listening to good records. Mr. Jones said, "We who see are hardly aware of the difficulties of the sightless."

One of the first steps taken by the National Federation of Music Clubs to help the blind was in 1953 during the administration of Mrs. Ada Holding Miller. "Music for the Blind" Month, November 15 - December 15, was instituted by the Federation in cooperation with the Louis Braille Music Institute of America. Fifty-five member clubs of the Federation participated with benefit musicales or special radio or television programs. The hope was to acquaint more of the blind with the musical service available to them, and to encourage wider employment of blind musicians.

"Scholarships for Blind Students" was established in the Junior Division in 1968, Mrs. Maurice Honigman, president, and were offered for the first time in 1969. These included eight performance awards of $100 each – two in each of the four NFMC regions, annually. Mrs. G. Franklin Onion, of Maryland, was appointed the first chairman. It also was that same year, 1969, that the "Music for the Blind Composers Awards" were founded.

The Florence Wilkinson Award for the Blind was given annually by Mrs. Wilkinson, National parliamentarian, from 1971 until her retirement in 1991. This award of $100 went to the best of the eight regional winners.

In 1979 Mrs. Paul Benzinger endowed four regional awards in memory of her late husband. The Blind Performance Awards of $200 each are known as the "W. Paul Benzinger Memorial Awards".

The "Joyce Walsh Awards for the Handicapped" (including the blind) are given annually – $1,000 to first place winner, $500 to second place winner, and three $200 awards for each of the four NFMC regions – instrumental and vocal.

The "Vivian Menees Nelson Award" of $1,000 for the Handicapped designated for the Senior Division, also includes the blind.

One of the past national presidents designated her NFMC Scholarship Honoring Past National Presidents be given to the blind. "The Hinda Honigman Scholarship for the Blind" – $500 first place and $250 second place, is given annually in the Student Division.

PART NINE

Business A' Tempo

BUSINESS A' TEMPO

Finance

1

Since the Federation's founding in 1898 the finances have been derived from four sources: Member dues and fees; interest on investments; gifts and legacies; and projects approved by the Board of Directors.

According to the bylaws adopted in Chicago in 1898 the dues were "five cents per member on all classifications." The only source of revenue during those first years was from dues and the sale of the Federation pins – sixteen of which were sold by Mrs. Leverett at the second convention in Cleveland, Ohio, increasing the treasury by thirteen dollars and thirty-six cents.

It was not until 1919 at the Peterborough, New Hampshire convention that the dues were raised to ten cents per capita. Mrs. Seiberling "inaugurated" the Department of Finance in 1921 and served as its first chairman.

The three largest legacies given to the Federation were given by dedicated and devoted members who loved the National Federation and its work in the promotion of music: Miss Agnes Fowler of Ohio, approximately $150,000; Mrs. Edwin B. Ellis (Annie Lou), Birmingham, Alabama, an amount exceeding $100,000; and Miss Rose Thomas Smith, Galax, Virginia, $75,000 – all of which has been designated for scholarships and awards.

On October 31, 1913 at a meeting of the Board of Management at the home of Mrs. Emerson Brush in Elmhurst, Illinois, Mrs. Ella May Smith (the daughter-in-law of Carrie Jacobs Bond) moved, and it was "seconded by Mrs. Leverett, that $1046.97 from the local Biennial Board meeting be placed as the beginning of an endowment fund." This represented the balance remaining after all expenses of the Chicago Biennial Convention had been paid. Mrs. Frank A. Seiberling was appointed the first chairman of the Endowment Fund in 1916. Being an astute business woman she saw the need of "planning for the future if an organization is to have a future." According to the December 5, 1917 minutes, Mrs. Seiberling "gave an interesting report showing the need of having funds for carrying on the work of the NFMC, and reported plans for securing Life Members, the goal being a permanent endowment fund of $200,000."

It was in that same year, in 1917, that the Federation's first life members were secured for the purpose of adding $1,000 to the Endowment Fund. "Mrs. Clark (Dr. Frances Elliott Clark) announced that she would be one of ten members present to take out a Life Membership in the Federation." Thus, the Federation's first life members were: "Mrs. Clark; Mrs. Edna Thomas, Louisiana; Miss McAteer, Pennsylvania; Mrs. Russell Boggs, Pennsylvania; Mrs. Grunsfeld, New Mexico; Mrs. Blankenship, Texas; Mrs. Polk, Indiana; Mrs. Phafflin, Indiana; Mrs. Cochran, West Virginia; and Mrs. Hinckle promised to secure the tenth name." The Endowment grew by $1,000. For years dues from individual members and the "sale of securities" were deposited in the "Endowment and Special Membership Fund." By 1921 the Endowment had increased to $3,756.14, with ninety "paid" life members and twenty "unpaid".

Founders' Day was founded for the purpose of increasing the Endowment, and for many years all contributions were deposited to that fund.

Through the years the fund grew slowly. In 1953 during the administration of Mrs. Ada Holding Miller, the chairman of Finance, Mrs. Edwin Chapin Thompson, proposed a drive to raise $75,000 for the Endowment Fund, with the results to be given at the "Rainbow Luncheon" at the convention in Miami, Florida in 1955. Clubs were urged to secure Memorials of $100 each honoring members and friends of music, (this is the first record found of the beginning of the Memorial and Recognition Fund); every senior, student and junior club was urged to hold Founders' Day celebrations "to pay homage where honor is long past due," with the contributions to increase the Endowment Fund; Juniors adopted the slogan, "Keep the Pennies Rolling In" with 1,000,000 pennies as their goal... "Pennies Will Grow into Bright Shining Dollars" ($10,000).

At the "Rainbow Luncheon" on April 27, 1955 honoring the Finance Department, when the roll was called each state president gave a full account of the contributions from the state; the Student Advisor reported on the amount raised by the student clubs; and the Junior Counselor presented the amount from the million pennies campaign. Thousands of dollars were added to the Endowment as the result of this project. During the administration of Mrs. Jack C. Ward (1979-1983) approximately

$100,000 was transferred from the General Fund to the Endowment, and since 1991 all monies collected from the Rose Fay Thomas Fellows are deposited in the Endowment.

The Endowment Fund was founded with the stipulation that the interest only may be used – the principal never to be spent. In 1994 the Endowment Fund has grown to approximately $400,000.

3

The historical files reveal that as far back as 1905 when the Biennial Convention was held in Denver, Colorado, there was a special emphasis placed on honoring the founders of the Federation. Originally, Founders' Day was observed in February, when clubs throughout the land held Founders' Day teas in "Memory of those of yesterday who had the vision and courage to keep the faith that the National Federation had a real place in the educational and cultural life of America." It was the feeling of Federation members that in honoring the founders who were the pioneers, was to acknowledge a debt "long since due". The clubs were asked to give generously at these teas in order that the National Endowment Fund, begun in 1913 would be increased in their honor.

In 1995, even though Founders' Day may be observed at any time during the year, many clubs honor their founders in January, recalling the founding of the Federation in January 1898.

During the administration of Mrs. Clifton J. Muir, special emphasis was placed on Founders' Day, and club members were asked to contribute one cent for each year since the Federation was founded. These contributions have made possible many programs that the Federation would not have accomplished otherwise.

4

The Headquarters Endowment was founded in 1981, during the presidency of Mrs. Jack C. Ward, for the purpose of maintaining the headquarters building, which had been completed in 1980. It was begun with $75,000 which remained from the Headquarters Building Fund, and today, in 1994 through contributions, has grown to an amount in excess of $250,000. None of the principal may be spent, with the interest automatically deposited in the Headquarters Maintenance Fund, used for the purpose of the upkeep of the building.

5

The Foundation for the Advancement of the Musical Arts* began in 1944 with the gift of one twenty-five dollar War Savings Bond. To Mrs. John McClure Chase, National Board Member from New York, goes the credit of having founded the Fund at the meeting of the Board of Directors in Tulsa, Oklahoma in 1944. In early February, 1944, Mrs. Chase, Chairman of Special and Life Members, purchased a twenty-five dollar War Bond in the name of the Federation. This, she indicated, would help establish a Federation "backlog" so that special projects might be initiated without drafting heavily upon the running expenses of the Federation.

Mrs. Royden James Keith, chairman of the Finance Department was quick to see the value of the plan, and how "war born" enthusiasm might be utilized. She speedily subscribed a bond herself, and then the national president Mrs. Guy Patterson Gannett and several other officers did likewise, and the project was launched.

The greatest impetus was given to the newly established Foundation at the Atlanta Board Meeting in the spring of 1946 when the War Service Committee assembled a special fund from the monies remaining in the War Service Fund. To this fund individuals and clubs contributed, bringing the total to $10,000. Mrs. Ada Holding Miller, chairman of the War Service Committee presented to Mrs. Gannett a check for $10,000 with the stipulation that it go toward the Anne M. Gannett Fund, and expenditures from the fund should be used "in some way for returned veterans."

Mrs. Gannett most graciously accepted the gift given in her honor saying later, "... how surprised I was, and how grateful when our National War Service Extension Chairman, Mrs. Ada Holding Miller, presented me with the check for $10,000 which is to start the Anne M. Gannett Foundation Fund for the use of disabled veterans... Mrs. Miller literally took my breath away. I am touched beyond measure, and the memory of that moment when the presentation was made will live with me always."

In 1950 Mrs. Clarence T. Pettit, co-chairman of the Foundation launched a $25,000 goal in a Foundation Fund campaign: All royalties from the sale of the Hymn of the Month booklet were turned over to the Foundation; music name plates and phone plates were sold; there was a campaign for Reader's Digest subscriptions. During the fiftieth anniversary year a stamp of Federation colors – blue and gold adorned with music symbols – to be used on letters so that the world "at large may have its attention directed to the Federation's fiftieth anniversary, to the accomplishments and prestige of America's and the world's largest musical organization", the drive was launched. Five hundred thousand (500,000) sheets were printed in the original order. Clubs purchased sheets of stamps and the Federation "backlog" grew steadily – so steadily that the need for incorporation was realized. The Foundation for the Advancement of the Musical Arts was incorporated into the bylaws at the Detroit Biennial Convention in 1947.

In the 1950 drive conducted by Mrs. Pettit, the club contributing the largest amount was the Octave Club of Norristown, Pennsylvania with a contribution of forty dollars.

Winning the first Anne M. Gannett Award for Veterans was David Laurent, baritone, a native of Mrs. Gannett's home state of Maine, but studying at Brown University in Providence, Rhode Island. David Laurent entered the army as a private in 1941. After a year and completing his officer's training course at Fort Benning, Georgia, he was commissioned and assigned to duty with the Yankee Division. He was sent overseas in 1944 and saw action with General Patton's Third Army. He returned to the United States in January 1946 and began study at Brown University where he was a member of the Glee Club. In 1981, David Laurent, then a member of the faculty of Brown University, was the guest of the National Federation of Music Clubs at the Fall Session in Providence, Rhode Island where he was presented in concert. His praise of the Federation and its contribution to furthering his musical career was overwhelming.

* *In 1993 the name of the Foundation Fund was changed from "Foundation for the Advancement of the Musical Arts" to the "Fund for the Advancement of the Musical Arts".*

6

In 1979 the National Federation of Music Clubs found itself faced with a difficult situation. With the death of the national treasurer, Mr. J. Phillip Plank in 1977, the national president, Mrs. Frank A. Vought, did not wish to elect a treasurer to fill the unexpired term. Instead, she wished to have the treasurer's office managed by one who was neither elected nor an officer.

A special meeting of the Executive Committee was called at the Mayflower Hotel in Washington, D.C. on January 9-10, 1978 for the purpose of making a decision relative to electing a treasurer. The Executive Committee acquiesced to the wishes of the president, Mrs. Vought. The office manager was to receive and deposit all monies, and the president, Mrs. Vought, was to write all checks.

Sixteen months went by without a national treasurer until April 1979 when officers for a new administration were elected with Miss Mary Heininger of Marion, Ohio elected as the national treasurer. Never in its eighty-one year history had the finances of the Federation been in the condition faced by the new officers: it was discovered that the books had not been posted in one year; the bank's checking account was overdrawn; government FHA bonds were misplaced and never found, which necessitated taking out security bonds before the government would honor the FHA bonds; approximately $80,000 was found in checks which never had been deposited – these including a check for $30,000, the final installment of the Agnes Fowler legacy, which was found in a box of old papers in a garage.

For almost one year the Federation – after receiving notice after notice – failed to fill out the required government forms and pay the withholding, income and unemployment taxes. Because of this the Internal Revenue Service filed a lien against the Federation's bank account and "all property". To clear the lien and satisfy the Internal Revenue Service, it was necessary to secure the services of an attorney as well as pay certain accumulated interest and penalties, thereby causing unnecessary expense to the Federation.

The problems seemed endless for the newly elected officers at the beginning of the 1979 administration. However, after much added expense, long hours of hard work, and the dedication of an efficient national treasurer working with reputable accountants, the problems were solved and the finances of the Federation were once again in order by the close of the administration – all of which goes to prove the old saying that: "an organization might get along without a president for a short while, but there is no way it can function properly without a treasurer."

ROSE FAY THOMAS FELLOWS

1

The Rose Fay Thomas Fellows, honoring Mrs. Theodore Thomas, the founder of the National Federation of Music Clubs, was founded at the Fort Worth, Texas Biennial Convention on April 27, 1989 by Mrs. Jack C. Ward past national president. Established with the unanimous endorsement and support of the NFMC Board of Directors, during the presidency of Mrs. Glenn L. Brown, this distinguished award is one of the highest accolades given to both members and non-members of the Federation.

Any individual (member or non-member) in whose honor or memory is contributed $1,000 to the Fund becomes a Rose Fay Thomas Fellow, and in recognition of the honor is presented a bronze medallion and lapel pin. Engraved on the front of the medallion is a sculptured likeness of Rose Fay Thomas. The reverse side bears the emblem of NFMC. Forty-two medallions, each honoring charter "fellows" carry the inscription "charter".

The first medallions were presented to thirty-eight Rose Fay Thomas Fellows at the NFMC Fall Session in Albuquerque, New Mexico in 1990.

The eighty-three Rose Fay Thomas Fellows are named in the Appendices in the order in which they received the distinguished award – as of May 1, 1995.

> *When all of our tributes are written,*
> *And all of our praises are made,*
> *When all of our Fellows are honored,*
> *And every compliment paid,*
> *There still will be a tribute to offer,*
> *To one whom we honor today,*
> *The founder of our beloved Federation,*
> *Mrs. Theodore Thomas, who was*
> *Christened Rose Fay.*
>
> —Edith Davis,
> Charter Rose Fay Thomas Fellow
> Paraphrased from
> Rudyard Kipling's *L'Envoi*

CHAPTER THREE

PAST PRESIDENTS' ASSEMBLY

1

The Past Presidents' Assembly is an auxiliary branch of the National Federation of Music Clubs composed of those who have served as presidents of a regularly organized music club, state music federation, other music organization, or the National Federation of Music Clubs.

In the words of the founder, Mrs. William Arms Fisher (Emma R.) of Boston: "At the Peterborough Biennial in 1919, I proposed the formation of the Alumnae of all the past presidents of the music clubs. The Federation postponed the project... but the plan persisted. Therefore I again proposed it at the Nashville Board of Directors meeting in March 1922...."

The Board endorsed and conducted a statistical survey which brought surprising statistics of the number of past executives which ran "upwards of three thousand women" taken from only half the clubs. What a wonderful possibility of utilizing the talents of such experienced executives!

With the permission of the national president, a prospectus was sent to one hundred presidents, including an announcement that if the proposal met with favor, such an assembly would be formed at the Asheville Biennial. Sixty-five responses were most gratifying, for the appeal "seemed to touch every past leader from the standpoint of needed service" and a wish to "carry on". One wrote, "A valid reason for starting such an organization is to have an available list of experienced women for appointments in the ever-enlarging field of Federation work." Another wrote, "I feel that the great number of women who have shouldered the responsibility of piloting a music club through a successful presidency ought to be a powerful force in the Federation if rightly directed." These ladies expressed the committee's feeling and "sounded a note of prophecy."

The initial meeting held in Asheville, June 15, 1923 made possible a charter enrollment of 106 members. Mrs. Fisher, as the "mother" of the idea, was chosen to head the organization with these officers elected to assist her: Mrs. Frederick W. Abbott of Philadelphia, vice chairman; Mrs. W. B. Nickels of Kansas City, secretary; and Mrs. Lillian Birmingham of San Francisco, treasurer.

Mrs. Abel A. Coult of Nashville, who was to succeed Mrs. Fisher as the organization's second chairman, chartered the first chapters. Mrs. Coult's own club in Nashville was the first to receive a charter, being followed by Norristown, Pennsylvania's Octave Club.

This fraternity of past presidents was founded, "to honor and dignify the women and men who have served as music club presidents... to give a signal recognition to the pioneers whose courage and unremitting efforts, reaching back many years, are largely responsible for the widespread appreciation... of music throughout the country" today.

The major project of the Past Presidents' Assembly provides, by its small dues and voluntary contributions, $4,500 of the cash prizes of $7,500 for each of the four winners of the Young Artists Contests – piano, strings, women's voice and men's voice.

The Young Artist Awards, which originally were begun at $150 for each of the winners, today are $7,500 each.

2
America, the Beautiful

At the head of Cape Cod in Falmouth, Massachusetts stands a statue of Katherine Lee Bates, commemorating the village of Falmouth as the birthplace of the writer of *America the Beautiful*.

Katherine Lee Bates, at the conclusion of teaching a summer session at Colorado College in Colorado Springs, Colorado, joined a group for a mountain excursion up Pike's Peak. At the 14,000 foot summit, she looked down and was awed by the vast expanse of the beauty of the mountains and plains. That evening she returned to Colorado Springs with four important lines in her notebook:

> *O beautiful for spacious skies,*
> *For amber waves of grain,*
> *For purple mountain majesties*
> *Above the fruited plain!*

Back at Wellesley College, in 1895 Katherine Lee Bates finished her poem. By chance the inspired lines of the great patriotic hymn were printed in a song book with the hymn tune known as "Materna" written by Samuel A. Ward. *America the Beautiful* first appeared in print in Boston, July 4, 1985.

Over sixty attempts had been made to give *America the Beautiful* a proper musical setting. None had sung their way into universal favor. The Past Presidents' Assembly of the National Federation of Music Clubs, with the permission and hearty approval of Katherine Lee Bates announced a nation-wide contest. Plans were announced by the chairman of the Past Presidents' Assembly, Mrs. William Arms Fisher. A cash prize of $500 was offered to the American-born composer whose setting best expressed the love, loyalty and majesty its lines portrayed. The prize setting was to be presented to the nation without copyright restrictions, making it available to all.

The contest was to close March 1, 1927, and the announcement and presentation of the $500 award to be made at the Chicago Biennial Convention, Thursday evening, April 21, 1927 at the banquet of the PPA, when the hymn was to be first sung. On the following evening it was to be sung in Chicago by a 1,000 trained voice choir as a climax to the Singing Biennial of the National Federation of Music Clubs.

The project created tremendous interest among the composers, the press, and general public. Almost one thousand manuscripts were submitted in the spring of 1927. The judges – Dr. Frank Damrosch of New York, Mr. Frederick S. Converse of Boston, Dean Peter C. Lutkin of Evanston, Illinois, and Felix Borowski of Chicago – were instructed to "award the prize to only a truly noble setting." The standard set was high and in keeping with the ideals of the poem.

Governor's wives who responded were: Mrs. Alvin T. Fuller, Massachusetts; Mrs. Bibb Graves, Alabama; Mrs. W. H. Spaulding, New Hampshire; Mrs. Roland H. Hartley, Washington; Mrs. John S. Newberry, Michigan; Mrs. Albert E. Ritchey, Maryland; Mrs. Marcia Higginson, Kansas, on behalf of her state. Also responding were Past Presidents' Assemblies of Rhode Island, Missouri and Arizona.

National Organization leaders who accepted places on the Honorary Advisory Committee for the adoption of the possible "noble setting" were: Mrs. John D. Sherman, President, General Federation of Women's Clubs; Mrs. Carl Price, National Hymn Society; Mrs. Alfred J. Brosseau, Regent, National Society, Daughters of the American Revolution; and Mrs. Edgar Stillman Kelley, President, National Federation of Music Clubs.

The much anticipated evening of April 21 arrived. The Past Presidents' Assembly Midnight Frolic was scheduled for 11:30 o'clock in the Gold Ballroom of the Congress Hotel. Everyone dressed in costumes – many of the most prominent men and women took part, even to dancing the Minuet. There was great excitement in anticipation of hearing the new prize setting of *America the Beautiful.* A hushed silence fell over the room, and there was great disappointment when one of the judges, Felix Borowski announced to the group that "no setting was found to be worthy of the award."

Thus, Katherine Lee Bates' wish to write "a poem that will always be remembered" became a reality, as her words set to the tune of Samuel A. Ward's "Materna" have for 100 years rung out "from sea to shining sea."

PART TEN

Overview

A DREAM FULFILLED

Little Red House

1

Our important historical sites – the Headquarters, the Little Red House, Composer's Studio, Seranak, Amphitheatre seats, Peterborough – tell a unique story. Each place is most important in the way it relates to reason-for-being in the part it plays in the overall plan and work of the Federation.

July 24, 1948 was a perfect day – sunny, warm, with folks strolling leisurely, enjoying the beauty of the surroundings – gorgeous trees, a calm lake, the Berkshire Hills, all in the shadow of Monument Mountain. A dream had been fulfilled at Lenox, Massachusetts, when the Federation project initiated seven years before by Mrs. Guy Patterson Gannett, president of the National Federation of Music Clubs, became a reality. The restoration by the Federation, of the Little Red House, former home of Nathaniel Hawthorne at Tanglewood, opened a new chapter in its long list of philanthropies in the promotion of music.

The idea of the restoration of the house as practice studios for the Berkshire Music Center emanated in the early days of Mrs. Gannett's presidency, and was initiated in the fall of 1941. She contacted Dr. Serge Koussevitzky, conductor of the Boston Symphony Orchestra, and founder of the Music Center in the Berkshires. But – Mrs. Gannett said it was Mr. George Judd, Manager of the Boston Symphony Orchestra who first conceived the idea when she expressed the desire to make a lasting contribution to the Berkshire Music Center.

First the site was inspected by Mrs. Gannett and Dr. Koussevitzky. Then there was research into the history of the Little Red House originally called "Tanglewood" whose title is perpetuated in Hawthorne's *Tanglewood Tales*. The decision was reached to rebuild in replica the original, and to furnish it as nearly as possible as when the Hawthorne family lived there.

T. F. Wolfe's *In Literary Shrines* described the cottage as a "low-eaved, one and one-half storied structure with a lower wing at the side, red in color with wind shutters of green." The house had eight rooms. The entrance hall adjoined the drawing room, and here Mrs. Hawthorne "sewed at her stand and read to the children about Christ." The drawing room accommodated a large number of heirlooms – Julian's rocking horse, toy boats, his sister's doll furniture, a blackboard for instruction. A little staircase led to the upstairs study, which was sacred to the master of the house. This was cramped for Hawthorne, but afforded a magnificent view of the lake and mountains.

To this home, during Hawthorne's residency, came many of the literary figures of America; James Russell Lowell, Oliver Wendell Holmes, Henry Wadsworth Longfellow, Henry Ward Beecher, with others too numerous to mention. The master of the house, a shy, reserved person, almost regretted that he ever had made his home in such a populous literary center. Yet their frequent presence lent further romance to the Federation's decision to rebuild the Little Red House to be used as practice studios for the Berkshire Music Center, as well as a literary shrine to the greatest of the early American novelists.

With the entry of the United States into World War II, building could not proceed. The Federation's "War Service" became uppermost in the minds and hearts of all federation members. Also, there were wartime building restrictions and a shortage of building materials. It was not until six years later – in 1947 that work could be resumed on the Little Red House.

In rebuilding, the house was reproduced in exact replica as far as the exterior is concerned, although the interior was adopted to modern studio uses. Workmen excavating on the original site uncovered bricks from the original chimney, and stones from the original fireplace, also the original firetongs with which Hawthorne probably stirred the embers while brooding over the manuscript of the *House of Seven Gables*.

Rarely has the National Federation of Music Clubs made more brilliant history than on that day of the dedication in July, 1948. The great and the near great journeyed to Tanglewood to see the Little Red House transferred from the National Federation of Music Clubs to the Berkshire Music Center.

The dedication was graced by the presence of the national president, Mrs. Royden James Keith, who brought greetings which were primarily a tribute to her predecessor, Mrs. Guy Gannett. She referred to the dedication as "an occasion of historical import and a challenge to the youth of today and tomorrow." In closing she said, "May this structure that embodies so much of our historical past, inspire the youth of Berkshire Music Center and all whose lives they touch, with a valiant sense of loyalty and patriotic devotion to America and her noble traditions."

Guests and speakers at the event were representatives of two families who had helped to write one of the most notable pages in Berkshire literary history – Manning Hawthorne, the great grandson of Nathaniel Hawthorne, and Henry Wadsworth Longfellow Dana, grandson of the poet who lived in the Berkshires before the Hawthornes came. Also in attendance was Richard Manning of Gambier, Ohio, a cousin of Hawthorne's.

In Mr. Dana's address entitled "Tanglewood Interlude" he quoted primarily from letters and manuscripts of both the Hawthornes and the Danas. He told of Hawthorne's ramblings with his children through the woods and fields.

Manning Hawthorne said that if his grandfather could know what was transpiring he would rejoice that the National Federation of Music Clubs had restored the Little Red House to further the development of one of man's greatest arts. "I cannot but believe," he added, "that there… students will be inspired to create even greater music than has yet been produced."

Mrs. Gannett's presentation was largely a tribute to those whose inspiration had made possible this accomplishment. She referred particularly to Dr. Koussevitzky, and she expressed deep gratitude to members of the Federation from forty-eight states for their gifts. In closing she said that she was confident the Little Red House would always be a living interest of the National Federation of Music Clubs.

> "It is a symbol of our aspirations for American youth and our desire to help realize those aspirations," she said – "the aspirations which Dr. Koussevitzky revealed to me six years ago, and which he has brought to rich realization through giving the young people of this and many countries the finest musical education obtainable and with this education the lofty idealism that comes only from the things of the spirit."

Dr. Koussevitzky in replying said that this was a "red letter day not only in the life of Tanglewood but in the country at large… Whether Hawthorne's fiery spirit animates Tanglewood today as of old, or muses still favor these grounds, the fact remains that Tanglewood became a place of pilgrimage, a radiating center of music, a flame with a creative spirit. The temple is now restored to serve music and the arts."

The July 31, 1948 issue of the New York Times carried an article by George F. Sokolsky, covering the dedication, which read in part:

"... This (occasion) is important because out of Tanglewood, will in time come American composers, American conductors, and American artists... No one can be in this New England long without becoming part of its rock and soil, without feeling the three centuries of America is a marrow in our bones... here Longfellow caught the lines of 'Evangeline,' and here Hawthorne came after he had written *The Scarlet Letter*... It is in these hills that one senses the manhood that produced this nation."

The two studios in the Little Red House were named the "Anne M. Gannett" and the "Robert W. Roberts," the latter honoring the husband of a National Board member from Florida, who paid off the indebtedness of the House as a "memorial gift" to her husband.

The Little Red House where Nathaniel Hawthorne wrote Tanglewood Tales, *was restored as a Composer's Studio at Tanglewood, Massachusetts by the National Federation of Music Clubs.*

SERANAK

Berkshire Music Center

1

It was at the National Convention in Miami Beach in 1965 that the National Federation of Music Clubs pledged $10,000 to assist Madame Olga Koussevitzky in building a Composer's Studio on the Koussevitzky estate, "Seranak", at Lenox, Massachusetts. To finance the project the Federation published its second copy of *Who's Who in the National Federation of Music Clubs*, dedicated to Dr. Serge Koussevitzky and the twenty-fifth anniversary of the Berkshire Music Center at Tanglewood, Massachusetts. From the book, compiled by Mrs. Ronald A. Dougan, Chairman of the Foundation for the Advancement of the Musical Arts, the Federation contributed $10,000 to the building which was dedicated in 1966.

The Northeastern Regional Conference (Dr. Merle Montgomery, vice president in charge of the region) was held at the MacDowell Colony in Peterborough, New Hampshire. The following day many went to Tanglewood to take part in the dedication services at "Seranak", the Composer's Studio and Residence Cottage built on the Koussevitzky estate, as a joint effort of the Koussevitzky Music Foundation and the National Federation of Music Clubs. Dr. Montgomery, as the originator of the *Who's Who*, expressed gratitude that through the first and second editions the Federation cleared $10,000 pledged for the project.

Madame Koussevitzky paid tribute to the Federation, which had previously given the Hawthorne cabin on the Tanglewood Festival grounds. Mrs. Ada Holding Miller, past national president made a touching dedicatory address in which she extolled the contribution to music of the late Serge Koussevitzky. Eric Leinsdorf, conductor of the Boston Symphony, and Gunther Schuller, Tanglewood faculty member, also spoke.

Dr. Serge Koussevitzky became the eighth conductor of the Boston Symphony Orchestra in 1924. Because of his combination of intellect, dramatic flair, enthusiasm and cosmopolitan taste in music he had served an unprecedented term of twenty-five years. In 1936 Dr. Koussevitzky and the Orchestra played their first summer concerts in the Berkshire Hills, and in 1938 they began their annual summer residence at the now famous estate of Tanglewood in Lenox, Massachusetts. In 1940 Dr. Koussevitzky realized his dream for many years when the Orchestra founded Berkshire Music Center at Tanglewood.

Dr. Koussevitzky retired as Music Director of the Orchestra in 1949 but continued as Director of the Berkshire Music Center until his death in the summer of 1951.

In 1967 a committee of the National Federation of Music Clubs was appointed, and they, working with Madame Koussevitzky, placed a plaque on the Composer's Studio to identify the Federation's contribution toward the building.

The first composer to use the facilities of the Koussevitzky composer's residence and studio at Seranak was a Finnish composer, Jukka Tiensuu, selected through the office of the Finnish Consul. At the time Tiensuu was chosen he was attending the Julliard School of Music. He was in residence near Tanglewood for two months during the summer of 1973.

Mme Serge Koussevitzky is pictured between Erich Leinsdorf, left, Boston Symphony Conductor, and Gunther Schuller, Tanglewood faculty member, who hold the model of the proposed composer's Studio at Serenak, on the Koussevitzky estate. The National Federation of Music Clubs co-sponsored jointly with the Koussevitzky Foundation the building of the studio.

A SYMBOL OF A CENTURY

National Federation of Music Clubs Headquarters

1

The first headquarters office of the National Federation of Music Clubs was established in 1931 at Wait Avenue in Ithaca, New York, under the national presidency of Mrs. Elmer James Ottaway. In 1951 during the administration of Mrs. Royden James Keith, the headquarters office was moved to New York City "to centralize all NFMC business and services." It was at this same time the first Office Committee was appointed. The office remained in New York until 1960 when, during the administration of Dr. Dorothy Dann Bullock, it was moved to Chicago.

With the purchase and restoration of the NFMC headquarters in Indianapolis, and the hard work of the Office Committee chairman Mrs. Lynn Turner and her faithful husband, on April 1, 1980 the offices were moved to 3901 Meridian Avenue in Indianapolis, until such time as the offices at 1336 North Delaware could be completed. On September 1, 1980 the office made its final move to the Eden-Talbott Mansion – its first permanent home.

2

The historical files of the National Federation of Music Clubs reveal that in 1944 Federation leaders envisioned a permanent headquarters for the Federation. In September 1944, the national president Mrs. Guy Gannett said to the Board of Directors in session that she visualized "the establishment of a permanent national headquarters where all business of the Federation might be housed under one roof."

In 1965, at the National Fall Session in Memphis, Tennessee, Mrs. Clifton J. Muir, president, Mrs. Ronald A. Dougan moved "that the Executive Committee of the NFMC consider the idea and investigate the possibility of buying or building the Federation's own headquarters." The motion was seconded and carried.

It was three years later, on January 30, 1968, that Mr. John Edwards, president of the American Symphony Orchestra League, wrote the president of the Federation, Mrs. Maurice Honigman, inviting the Federation "to establish its permanent headquarters facilities on a five acre tract of land at Wolf Trap Farm Park (located in the suburban area of Washington D.C.) which the League is entitled to use for development of its own national headquarters under an agreement made with the U.S. Government, dated May 20, 1966... Although the U.S. Government holds title to the five acre tract, the League holds use rights in perpetuity." According to the contract presented by the League to be signed by Mrs. Honigman, there would be one building with each of the two organizations sharing in the cost of building and the occupancy.

The administration of Mrs. Honigman voted to accept the League's invitation, and a drive for funds to build permanent headquarters in Wolf Trap Farm Park went forward. Official ground-breaking ceremonies were held in October, 1970, at Wolf Trap Farm Park, Vienna, Virginia, followed by a concert by NFMC's Artist Winners in the East Room of the White House. The nation's First Lady, Mrs. Richard M. Nixon attended and was the gracious hostess at the reception in the State Dining Room following the concert.

Plans went forward to collect funds for the new headquarters. Those contributing $5,000 were known as Master Builders (Miss Elsie Sweeney of Columbus, Indiana was the first to be listed in this category, having contributed $10,000). Grand Builders were those who contributed $1,000 or more.

As time went on – everyone was not happy with the contract which had been signed by Mrs. Honigman to build in Wolf Trap Farm Park. Dr. Merle Montgomery, president 1971-1975, was adamant that it not be accepted as written, because, according to the proposed contract, the Federation had no vested rights and would be tenants at the will of the party holding the "use rights". At the Biennial Convention in Portland, Oregon the NFMC Board of Directors voted to accept the release of the contract offered by the American Symphony Orchestra League.

It was voted, also at this same meeting to purchase the Eden-Talbott house in Indianapolis, Indiana for $66,500 to be restored as the headquarters of the National Federation of Music Clubs. It was from the Junior League of Indianapolis that the Eden-Talbott house was purchased, with the understanding that restoration would be completed within one year.

Elected members of the Headquarters Committee to assume the responsibility of restoration were: Mrs. Maurice Honigman, chairman; Mrs. H. H. McHaney, vice chairman; Mrs. Frank A. Vought, secretary; Dr. Merle Montgomery, past president; and Mrs. Jack C. Ward, president.

3

According to Myrtle Barker writing for the Indianapolis News:

"Once a descendent of John and Priscilla Alden, who the poet Longfellow immortalized in his poem 'The Courtship of Miles Standish,' lived right here in Indianapolis... He was the Reverend Nathaniel Hyde, and it was fascinating to visit just before Thanksgiving, the old mansion where he lived. It was easy to envision the luxuriant living and elegant entertaining that had no doubt transpired beneath the roof of that sedate, two story, Georgian style... house at 1336 North Delaware Street."

The history of the Eden-Talbott Mansion goes back to its first owner, Charleton Eden, a lumber dealer, who built his dream house in 1878. There are conflicting historical references as to the dates of ownership and construction. One is to the effect that the "original section" of the house was built in 1871 by Aaron Kauffman, and Eden bought it from Kauffman in 1878. Mr. Eden selected the finest woods to build his "dream house" – ornate arches, carved lions heads. At the bottom of the gently-winding staircase, leading up to the third floor, is an elaborately carved newell post containing 800 cunningly fitted pieces of wood, the best available, which is said to have been displayed at the Centennial Exposition in Philadelphia in 1876.

In 1881 the house was sold to Dr. James Stevenson, who in turn sold it in 1889 to the Devay family.

Few changes were made. Delaware Street was quiet and dignified and its trees were a feature of beauty.

In 1891 the house was purchased by the Reverend Nathaniel Hyde of Stafford, Connecticut, who was invited to fill the pulpit of the Plymouth Congregational Church, recently occupied by Henry Ward Beecher.

It was the Hyde's adopted daughter, Josephine (Mrs. Herbert E. Woodbury) who sold the house in 1892 to Henry Morrison Talbott, owner of leading theatres and opera houses in Indianapolis.

It was during the occupancy of Mr. Talbott and his charming wife "that the house came into flower". Mrs. Talbott's taste and flair for decorating were enjoyed – structural changes were made, grilled balconies added, and a "profusion of plants brought life and gayety to the solemn old facade." Again the house was sold in 1927, passing through several owners before it was purchased by the Junior League of Indianapolis to prevent demolition. It was from the Junior League that the National Federation of Music Clubs purchased the old mansion on May 15, 1979.

4

Everything was not a "bed of roses" during the eighteen months of restoration. There were misunderstandings among the committee members. Some wished to have an architect and get bids on the restoration – and one who would supervise the work during the committee's absence. Others opposed. There were those who did not approve the proposed contractor, but they too, were overruled. There was never a formal contract, a policy which some members opposed – all of which proved to be disastrous.

To quote from a letter to Mr. Stephen D. Meares (lawyer) dated June 13, 1979, from Mrs. Frank A. Vought, secretary of the committee, in which she wrote regarding the National Federation securing incorporation under the laws of the State of Indiana, and dissolving the incorporate charter in Springfield, Illinois, secured by the founders in 1898 the letter read in part:

> "Mrs. Maurice Honigman agrees that there would be no practical reason for the National Federation of Music Clubs to continue under the Illinois incorporation laws, since our national business office, the only headquarters maintained by us, will be in Indianapolis. Furthermore, since we now own property at 1336 Delaware Street it is not likely that any national business would be conducted in Illinois... As the signers of the necessary papers, relative to incorporation in Indiana, Mrs. Honigman agrees that the five members of our Building Committee would be sufficient (to sign). All of us will be in Indianapolis on June 28-29 and incorporation will be on our agenda for action."

Only Mrs. Honigman received a copy of this letter. Apparently Mr. Meares was advised to proceed with plans for incorporation in the State of Indiana. The president, Mrs. Jack C. Ward, received this information only when an invoice in excess of $700 was sent to her to approve payment to Mr. Meares. Payment was withheld until approval of the Executive Committee could be secured.

At the 1979 Fall Session of the NFMC in Charleston, South Carolina, the Executive Committee, almost in disbelief, voted overwhelmingly to retain the NFMC's incorporation in Illinois, the state of its birth. Otherwise all of the history of the Federation would have been lost, and never could the Congressional Charter, which was granted two years later, have become a reality.

5

The much anticipated event – the dedication of the Eden-Talbott House as the headquarters of the National Federation of Music Clubs finally arrived on October 19, 1980. On that cool, crispy Sunday afternoon at 2:00 p.m., more than 200 excited Federation members and guests arrived at the old mansion.

In the words of Mrs. R. E. L. Freeman, Jr. "The beautifully restored Victorian house with its spectacular carved black walnut woodwork, and its 800 piece newel post (which had been exhibited at the Philadelphia Centennial in 1876) at the stairway's first floor rise, was a showplace in itself."

The Ceremony was one of solemnity, devotion and happiness, with the main address being given by Mr. John S. Edwards, Executive Vice President of the Chicago Symphony Orchestra, who stressed the fact that in the beginnings of both the Federation and the Chicago Symphony Orchestra, Mrs. Theodore Thomas was influential.

Presiding and giving the Dedication of the building as the headquarters for the National Federation of Music Clubs, was the national president, Mrs. Jack C. Ward. She closed with these words:

> "On this 19th day of October, 1980 we do dedicate this building as the:
> ### HEADQUARTERS OF
> ### THE NATIONAL FEDERATION OF MUSIC CLUBS
> Believing that the well-being of any country depends on its culture, we commend and commit this National Headquarters of the National Federation of Music Clubs to the glory of God through service to music, and to our fellow man. May it, through all ages serve as a link uniting the good, the great and the glorious of the past with the high and lofty ideals of the present and the future."

Following the solemn dedicatory ceremony, a portrait of Mrs. Maurice Honigman, national president, 1967-1971, and chairman of the Headquarters Building Committee, was presented and unveiled by her granddaughter, Janet Michele Sarlin.

Hanging in the Presidents' Parlour – the setting for this historic event – are portraits of the Founder and Honorary President, Mrs. Theodore Thomas, and the twenty-seven presidents who have served the National Federation of Music Clubs since its founding in 1898. The portraits were a gift of the Junior Division of the Federation, brought to fruition by the enthusiastic Counselor of the Juniors, Mrs. Ruth Smith, of Jackson, Mississippi.

The carpeting, wall colors, window treatments and lighting fixtures, combined with the furnishings of antiques and reproductions, all reflect the period of which the house was built in 1871.

6

Possibly the two most historical of the memorabilia and furnishings are the baton of the famous bandmaster, Patrick S. Gilmore, mounted on black velvet, in an antique goldleaf frame – a gift of Miss Anastasia Donnelly; and the museum-piece Belter-style table (circa 1850) formerly in the home of Sumner Wells, Under Secretary of State, which was a gift of the South Carolina Federation of Music Clubs, Mrs. Bryan Blackwell, Hartsville, South Carolina, president.

The white baton with three bands of gold, once owned by the "Father of the American Band", Patrick Sarsfield Gilmore, has a rich history. On June 17, 1872, at the World Peace Jubilee in Boston, Mayor Gaston presented the baton to Gilmore, and thus began the long journey into musical history which ended in the Eden-Talbott Mansion in Indianapolis, Indiana.

The baton has three bands of gold encircling it, and the center band bears the inscription, "P. S. Gilmore, 1872 and 1876." The 1876 date signifies the enormous concert, July 4 in Independence Square in Philadelphia when Gilmore shared honors at the Philadelphia Centennial with Theodore Thomas and others.

It was perhaps from a grateful and generous heart that prompted Gilmore to give the prized baton to his solo flutist, Fred Lax in 1888. Another gold band was inscribed, "P. S. G. to Fred Lax, 1888." Four years later, in 1892, Patrick Sarsfield Gilmore died.

The baton passed from Fred Lax to C. C. Donnelly of Lancaster, Pennsylvania, an admirer of Gilmore. The third band of gold reads, "Fred Lax to C. C. Donnelly, 1905."

In 1906 a Gilbert Memorial Festival was held in Madison Square Gardens in New York City on May 15. Donnelly took the baton to New York. On that memorable night the golden baton was used by John Philip Sousa, Victor Herbert, Frank Damrosch, and Walter Damrosch – all of whom had known Gilmore personally.

In 1968 a program honoring Patrick Sarsfield Gilmore was given in Lancaster, Pennsylvania, dedicated to the "Parade of American Music" sponsored by the National Federation of Music Clubs, and presented by the Lancaster Musical Art Society. At the memorial program, the Gilmore baton was presented to the club in memory of C. C. Donnelly, by his daughter Miss Anastasia M. Donnelly.

At the 1983 Biennial Convention of the National Federation of Music Clubs in Columbus, Ohio, this baton was presented to Mrs. Jack C. Ward, national president, by Mrs. Robert Humphreville, past president, Pennsylvania Federation of Music Clubs and a member of the Musical Art Society, as a gift from Miss Anastasia Donnelly and the Musical Art Society, with the specification that it be "displayed permanently in the Presidents' Parlour of the Eden-Talbott House, Headquarters of the National Federation of Music Clubs in Indianapolis, Indiana."

This story had a sad ending: Mrs. Ward had the baton framed and hung as requested. Miss Donnelly was anxious to see the headquarters and the baton after it was framed. She planned her first trip to the headquarters, but one week before the scheduled visit she died of a heart attack. Thus, after 111 years, the baton of the famous bandmaster, Patrick Sarsfield Gilmore passed to the National Federation of Music Clubs. Because of the love and generosity of Anastasia Donnelly, the historical and prized baton will continue to hang in the Presidents' Parlour, and – it will continue to bring pleasure to all who enjoy seeing it in the years to come.

7

In early December, just six weeks after the dedication – again the grand old mansion came alive with the glow of candles and the magic sounds of Christmas. Halls which too long had been silent, came alive and were the setting for a Christmas party honoring the three new members of the office staff – Barbara Bryant, Leonard Fattic and Pat Strodtman. The lighted, tinseled tree, bare of ornaments, stood in its place in the Presidents' Parlour, as each guest, seated on the floor (because there were no chairs), rose, came forward, and placed his or her small ornament on the tree. Spread underneath, like a colorful blanket, were the beautifully wrapped gifts for the kitchen – and the only music, echoing through the silent halls, the tinkling sounds of a tiny music box playing, *Here Comes Santa Claus*.

Each of the two following Christmases of the Ward administration – both in 1981 and again in 1982, the Eden-Talbott Mansion was the setting for the second and third Christmas parties – each just a bit more elaborate than the last, as the house gradually was becoming furnished – and each honoring the members of the office staff.

On December 4, 1981 the second Christmas party was held. In these thirteen short months the dining room had been completely furnished with a table and twelve chairs – the perfect place to have a seated dinner honoring the office staff of three. The *Music Clubs Magazine* carried the following poem – an account of the party as written by Miss Gretchen Van Roy.

'Twas Three Weeks Before Christmas

(With apologies to Clement Clarke Moore)

(Editor's note: On December 4 the Eden-Talbott Mansion, NFMC Headquarters in Indianapolis, was the setting for a Christmas party honoring the NFMC office staff and hosted by the Executive and Office Committees.)

'Twas three weeks before Christmas and all through the house
Ev'ry person was stirring – no chance for a mouse.
The tree had been trimmed and the packages wrapped
For a festive occasion – all plans had been mapped.
Many weeks in advance – Vera Turner and spouse
Had harkened to pleas from the head of the house.
Our Lucile from her home on the top of the mount
Had made a decree, "Send out cards! Take a count!
Let's have a big party for NFMC
At our home on Delaware Street in In. . .dy!
The price of admission nine dollars 'twill be,
Plus a gift for the kitchen, a trim for the tree."
December the fourth was the date of the feast
And many were asked from North, South, West and East.
While those who could make it were planning to go
Lucile was already ahead of the show.
With Mary, the tender of checkbook and cash,
She shopped, vowing not to do anything rash.
The purchases made were all chosen with care –
Each one must be perfect and fit in right there!
Many helpers came early and each had a task,
For all hands were needed – one just had to ask.

The silver was polished by Hinda with care,
For she knew that Saint Nicholas soon would be there.
The president's husband worked hard with a crew,
On instructions from Vera (who had planned this – and knew).
Six tables were set with a chair at each place,
It was hurry and scurry – a right jolly old race!
A pause for a sandwich, then back hard at work,
For minutes were flying with no time to shirk.
When the five o'clock magical hour did arrive
The spirit of Christmas indeed was alive.
The office staff – Barbara, Mary Ellen and Len –
Were the ones to be honored right there and right then.
The Mansion was shining with beauty and light,
As the party took shape on that December night.
President Lucile, and Jack, her dear spouse,
And Hinda, whose dream was to have this fine house;
From Ohio came Mary and Thelma and Rob
And Vera and Lynn, who'd worked hard at the job.
Veda and LeRoy and Sophie and Joe,
Glad Robinson Youse – and her daughter also;
Mildred, Mary Prudie, Cornelia, Irene,
Eloise, Erwin, Barbara Bryant and Gene,
Leonard Fattic and Carolyn, Mary Ellen and Jim;
The season's great joy filling all to the brim.
The social hour sparkled with laughter so clear,
Then the turkey and trimmings brought lots of good cheer.
Toasts given by many were beautifully done;
There were all kinds – some were serious, some fun.
When dinner was over 'twas time to repair
To the President's Parlor – there was more fun to share.
The Christmas Tree sparkled with lights all aglow –
A star on the top and the presents below.
There were cooking utensils of every kind
And towels and potholders one also could find.
The ornaments hanging in shining array
Were given by members for this special day.
Family traditions of Christmases past
Were shared by each person, and then at the last
Some carols were sung – it was just the right touch
For the end of a party that had meant so much.
The Benediction by dear Glad Robinson Youse
Climaxed the evening in National's House.

And all were agreed ere they drove out of sight
That this special occasion had been a great night.
And when December comes 'round again the next year
They all want to come back – for a party right here!
                                    —*Gretchen E. Van Roy*
                                    (Oh yes, I was there, too!)

Again – in 1990, during the administration of Mrs. Glenn L. Brown, national president, the house came alive with the magic of Christmas, as members celebrated the tenth anniversary of that first Christmas party at the Eden-Talbott Mansion in 1980.

8

AWARD

for

EXCELLENCE IN DEVELOPMENT

NATIONAL FEDERATION OF MUSIC CLUBS

---

read the plaque presented to the National Federation of Music Clubs at the banquet at the Columbia Club in Indianapolis, Indiana on October 16, 1980. The award was presented by Mr. Michael W. Boeke, president, Metropolitan Development Commission, "in recognition of its restoration of the 1978 Eden-Talbott House at 1336 North Delaware Street." Mr. Boeke continued by saying that the awards were given only to those projects determined to be of outstanding quality in terms of site planning, architecture, renovation, graphic design and conservation of natural resources.

Accepting the award were Mrs. Jack C. Ward, national president, and Mrs. Maurice Honigman, past national president and chairman of the Headquarters Building Committee.

Peristyle and Statue of the Republic, World's Columbian Exposition, 1893. To the Peristyle's right is the Music Hall, and on its left is the Casino.
Photo by C. D. Arnold – courtesy of Chicago Historical Society.

Not only was the National Federation of Music Clubs born at the World Columbian Exposition in 1893, but there the world's first Ferris Wheel was exhibited. Designed by George W. G. Ferris, an engineer of Pittsburgh, Pennsylvania, it was a "strange looking object" with its great circle of 36 pendulum cars, each 27 feet long, 13 feet wide, and 9 feet high, carrying 60 people. A ride of two revolutions was 50¢, netting the propietor $1440 an hour if all seats were filled – truly a "wheel of fortune".

The Congress Hotel, Chicago, Illinois, where the Federation was entertained at the organizational meeting in 1898. This hotel through the years was host to many national conventions, including the "Singing Biennial" in 1927.

The Famous Gold Ballroom in the Congress Hotel which was the setting for many meetings of the National Federation of Music Clubs. It was also in the ballroom from which the first coast-to-coast radio musical broadcast was made.

Theodore Thomas, husband of Rose Fay Thomas, and founder of the Chicago Symphony Orchestra in 1891.

Pictured above is the National Board of Managers of the National Federation, meeting in Los Angeles, California for the 1915 Biennial Convention. Seated left to right are: Dr. Frances Elliott Clark, charter member; Mrs. Emerson Brush, who hosted many Federation meetings in her home; Mrs. John Leverett, who designed the Federation insignia; Mrs. Julius E. Kinney, national president. Second row, left to right: Miss Carlotta Simonds; Mrs. George Hail; Mrs. Lewis E. Yager, first Chairman, Young Artists Contests; Mrs. David A. Campbell, Director, Department of Publicity; Mrs. Jameson; Mrs. William A. Hinckle. Third row, left to right: Mrs. Ella May Smith, founder NFMC Endowment; Mrs. Albert J. Oschner, to become national president, 1917-1919.

292

*Stan Hywet Hall in Akron, Ohio, the home of Mr. and Mrs. Frank A. Seiberling
– the setting of many Federation meetings during Mrs. Seiberling's presidency, 1919-1921.*

Mrs. Edwin F. Uhl, first president of the National Federation of Music Clubs, Grand Rapids, Michigan.

The Musical Monitor, 1919 -
The MacDowell Stage Coach that appeared in the pageant at Peterborough, New Hampshire, during the Biennial Convention. On top of the Stage Coach, left to right – Mrs. John F. Lyons, Recording Secretary; Ann Falkner Obendorfer, Chairman Course of Study; Mrs. Frederick W. Abbott, Second Vice-President; Lada, the American interpretative dancer. In the coach, left to right – Mrs. David Allen Campbell, Director of Publicity; Mrs. Frank A. Seiberling, President; Mrs. William A. Hinckle, First Vice-President. On the ground, left to right – Mrs. George Oberne, Chairman Library Extension; Mrs. W. D. Steele, Director of Philanthropy; Mrs. George Houston Davis, Third Vice-President; Mrs. James Hirsch, Chairman Newspaper Publicity; Mrs. William Schupp, District President; Mrs. Bessie Bartlett Frankel, District President.

294

"House of Dreams" log cabin studio of Edward MacDowell at Peterborough, New Hampshire.

Mrs. Edward MacDowell (Marian Nevin MacDowell), left, of Peterborough, New Hampshire, wife of composer, Edward MacDowell, right.

The National Federation of Music Clubs Scholarship Lodge at National Music Camp, Interlochen, Michigan.

Thomas E. Dewey, baritone, Ann Arbor, Michigan, entrant in 1923 Young Artist Auditions, Asheville, North Carolina.

Alexander Gray, baritone, a winner in the first Young Artist Contest held in 1915.

Samuel Thaviu, Young Artist winner in violin in 1931, celebrated his Golden Anniversary – 50 years – of having won that competition by performing at the 1981 Biennial Convention in Birmingham, Alabama.

David Laurent, 26 year old concert baritone, World War II veteran and student at Brown University, winner of the first Anne M. Gannett Veterans Scholarship.

Henry Hadley, composer, conductor, and winner of the Federation's first award in composition in 1909. The Culprit Fay, the winning composition was performed by the Theodore Thomas Orchestra at the 1909 Biennial Convention, Grand Rapids, Michigan, with Mr. Hadley conducting.

296

The Central of Georgia Booster Band, Savannah, Georgia, with H. J. Applewhite, leader (first row, fifth from left), 1926. This was only one of the Federation bands of which the state of Georgia was proud. A radio concert given by them was heard as far away as Canada.

The first Prison Band in America to Federate. The U. S. Disciplinary Band and Orchestra, of San Quentin, Cal. – D. G. Gallur, director, and J. F. Brennen, Drum Major (right and left, center) – which has the distinction of being the first organization of its kind to become affiliated with the NFMC. The playing of this group of 36 men, made possible by the warden, Frank G. Smith, and the Captain of the Yard, E. J. Hobbs, has bettered the entire atmosphere of the prison.

On September 24, 1945, this bronze plaque, a gift of the National Federation of Music Clubs, was dedicated at "Home Sweet Home" – the birthplace of John Howard Payne at East Hampton, Long Island – and presented to the Mayor of East Hampton, Mr. Judson L. Bannister, by Mrs. R. A. Herbruck, national chairman for Music in the Home.

Pictured at the Whitetop Folk Festival on Whitetop Mountain near Marion, Virginia. Seated center is Mrs. Annabel Morris Buchanan, NFMC Folk Music and American Music Chairman, and founder of the Folk Music Archives at the Library of Congress. Seated, left to right, are Mr. Jay Winston Johns, Mrs. Buchanan, Mr. John Powell, composer of NFMC's first commissioned work, and Mr. John Blakemore. Standing, left to right, Mr. R. W. Gordon, Dr. John P. McConnell, Mr. Richard Chase and an unidentified gentleman.

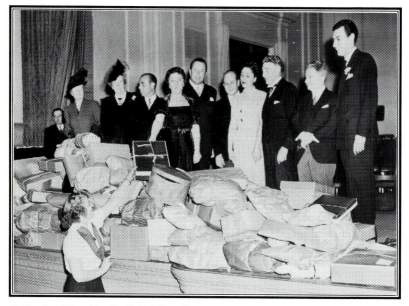

Collecting "Bundles for Britain" at Carnegie Hall in November 1941, in exchange for tickets to the concert to follow. Third from the left is Mrs. Guy P. Gannett, national president. To Mrs. Gannett's left are Josef and Rosina Lhevinne and others appearing on the concert program.

Hecht and Shapiro Duo Piano team (Thomas Hecht and Sandra Shapiro), winners of the first NFMC Ellis Duo-Piano Competition in 1991.

Mrs. Floyd D. Mehan (Myrt), National Federation of Music Clubs Chaplain (1979-1983), and Mr. Mehan at Sun Valley, Idaho Fall Session, 1980.

The ambulance presented to The United States Naval Hospital at Great Lakes by the Illinois Federation of Music Clubs, February 11, 1943.

Musical gift to the Philippines, 1958 – Two clarinets given by the Federation through the International Music Relations Department to the Manila Symphony Society of the Philippines are presented by Dr. Herbert Zipper, left, musical director of the orchestra, to its president, Mrs. Trinidad F. Legarda.

Mrs. Guy P. Gannett, president, and Mrs. Royden J. Keith attend a meeting in Ottawa, for the purpose of helping organize a Canadian Federation of Music Clubs. Left to right: Mrs. John Monty, who conceived the idea, Dr. Hazel Nohavec Morgan, Mrs. Gannett, Mrs. Keith, and Mrs. Alfreda Dorey.

The Music Room at Stan Hywet Hall. Considered by many architects and interior designers to be one of the most beautiful rooms in America, the music room, seating 250 was the setting for several national meetings during Mrs. Seiberling's presidency.

The Little Red House is dedicated. In the presence of several hundred guests, Mrs. Royden J. Keith, National President, at the microphone, pays tribute to her predecessor, Mrs. Guy P. Gannett, Chairman of the Little Red House Committee. Left to right on the speakers' stand are Mrs. Gannett; Dr. Koussevitzky; Mrs. Keith; Manning Hawthorne, great grandson of Nathaniel Hawthorne; Henry Wadsworth Longfellow Dana, grandson of the poet, Longfellow; and Richard Manning, cousin of Nathaniel Hawthorne.

Dr. Merle Montgomery, president NFMC, and Van Cliburn, following the artist's concert at the Diamond Jubilee Convention in Atlantic City, New Jersey, April 1973.

Miss Agnes Fowler of Ohio, benefactor, whose legacy to the National Federation of Music Clubs was the largest ever received by the Federation.

A gathering of celebrities at the Diamond Jubilee Convention in Atlantic City, New Jersey, 1975. Left to right are: Mr. Stanley Adams, president, ASCAP; Dr. Merle Montgomery, president, NFMC; Mr. Sol Hurok, world renowned impresario; and Mr. Henry Z. Steinway, president, Steinway and Sons. Said Mr. Hurok on this occasion: "What the National Federation of Music Clubs should do is to hire Hollywood Bowl for a week-long festival, the sole purpose of which would be to let the world know about its activities. With outstanding artists you could fill the Bowl each night, and I'll help you do it!"

302

The National Headquarters Committee at the Dedication Ceremony of the Eden-Talbott House. Left to right are: Mrs. Frank A. Vought, past president; Mrs. Hal H. McHaney, vice chairman; Mrs. Maurice Honigman, past president and chairman; Mrs. Jack C. Ward, president; and Dr. Merle Montgomery, past president.

The Old Northside Eden-Talbott House in Indianapolis, Indiana, became the headquarters of the National Federation of Music Clubs with its restoration and dedication on October 19, 1980.

The National Federation of Music Clubs celebrates a Congressional Charter for the Federation at the 1982 Baltimore, Maryland Fall Session. *"WE DID IT"* was the slogan on the pins worn by everyone in attendance.

EXTRA! EXTRA! READ ALL ABOUT IT! *The National Federation of Music Clubs receives Congressional Charter! The excited newsboy at the Charter Party, just after President Ronald A. Reagan had signed into law a Congressional Charter for the Federation, was Berniece Brown (Mrs. Rex Brown) of Marshall, Texas.*

Furnishing the music for the Congressional Charter Party were the Philadelphia Mummers in brilliant and colorful regalia. Pictured above is Mrs. Glen Weakley (Emeline), chairman, leading off the party's first dance with one of the Mummers.

304

John Powell, composer, first to receive a
National Federation Commission.

Dr. Julia Smith of Denton, Texas, composer of the National Federation of Music Clubs Official Invocation.

John La Montaine, composer, right, presents to President and Mrs. John F. Kennedy the
leatherbound copy of his overture, From Sea to Shining Sea, commissioned and performed for the Inaugural Concert in 1960. In 1972 Mr. La Montaine was commissioned
by the NFMC to write a piece for the 1973 Diamond Jubilee Convention. He was commissioned again by the NFMC in 1983 to write his second piano concerto, Concerto II,
which was premiered at Eastman School of Music, December 9, 1994.

Four national presidents stand beside the Steinway grand piano at the Dedication of the piano presented to the United Nations by the NFMC on October 18, 1985. Left to right are: Mrs. Jack C. Ward; Mrs. Dwight D. Robinson; Mrs. Maurice Honigman; and Dr. Merle Montgomery, chairman of the project.

Miss Anastasia Donnelly of Lancaster, Pennsylvania, holds the baton of Patrick Sarsfield Gilmore which she gave to the Federation in 1983 to hang in the President's Parlour of the National Headquarters. The baton was used by John Philip Sousa, Victor Herbert, Frank Damrosch and Walter Damrosch.

Mr. and Mrs. Paul Creston at the 1983 Columbus, Ohio Biennial Convention, at
which Mr. Creston's NFMC-commissioned
duo piano Prelude and Dance, was world
premiered by the duo piano artists, Joan
Yarbrough and Robert Cowan. Mr. Creston
also delivered the keynote address at the
banquet.

Mrs. Edwin B. Ellis (Annie Lou), benefactor of the NFMC, endowed the Edwin B.
Ellis Young Artist Award in memory of her
husband, the Annie Lou Ellis Piano Award
in the Student Division, and the Ellis Competition for Duo Pianists. Pictured with
Mrs. Ellis is Ruth Wood, first winner of
the Annie Lou Ellis Piano Award.

Mrs. Robert A. Dean (Floride Cox), founder of the Floride Cox Dean Endowment
which supports a $1000 prize to the fourth
place winner in the National Federation
of Music Clubs Ellis Competition for Duo
Pianists.

Seated is Glad Robinson Youse, composer
of Bless Us O God, the Official Benediction of the NFMC. Pictured with Mrs.
Youse is Onamae Ratcliff Dechert, writer, and founder of Inter-American Music
Relations.

Rose Fay Thomas Fellows pictured at the first presentation of medallions, August 1990, Albequerque, New Mexico. Center is Mrs. Glenn L. Brown, president. To Mrs. Brown's left is Mrs. Jack C. Ward, founder. Photo by Al Hancock.

Rose Fay Thomas Fellows, 1994 NFMC Fall Session, Jackson, Mississippi.
Photo by Al Hancock.

308

"Felsengarten," the summer cottage of Rose Fay and Theodore Thomas at Bethlehem, New Hampshire. It was here she spent her summers until her death in 1929.

Mrs. Jack C. Ward, NFMC president, 1979-1983, places flowers on the grave of the Federation's founder, Rose Fay Thomas, in Mount Auburn Cemetery in Cambridge, Massachusetts, 1982.

PART ELEVEN

A Rich Heritage Shared

"...food for the soul"

National Music Week

1

Mrs. Ronald Arthur Dougan, eighteenth president of the National Federation of Music Clubs (1955-1959) in addressing the National Music Week banquet at the *Diamond Jubilee* Biennial in Atlantic City in 1973, began by saying:

"A poet from the far east said, 'And if there come the singers and dancers, and the flute players – buy of their gifts also. For they are gatherers of fruit and frankincense, and that which they bring, though fashioned of dreams, is raiment and food for your soul.'

"Another kind of poet, a musician, a distinguished gentleman... the late Charles M. Tremaine, felt the need of music as 'food for the soul', and it was he, who in 1915 had the vision of a National Music Week of song.

"He said in a history of Music Week published in 1924, 'Music Week is different from other special weeks. It is a drive for music by friends of music BUT IT IS ALSO THE OCCASION OF PARTICIPATION IN, AND THE RECEIVING OF PLEASURE, thus making it independent of any Propelling Force. It is a voluntary expression of our love for music.'"

The national idea held in abeyance for over two years gradually began to take root. Its first public mention appeared in an editorial in the *Music Trade Review*, February 17, 1917 in which attention was called to Mr. Tremaine's project to inaugurate a National Music Week through the National Bureau for the Advancement of Music which he had founded.

Mr. Tremaine lists activities which led to the inauguration of the first National Music Week in 1924:

1915 – National Week of Song
1917 – First public mention of National Music Week in *Trade Review*
1917 – First city observance: Boise, Idaho
1919 – St. Louis Music Week
1919 – DeForest Music Week, Sharon, Pennsylvania
1919 – Dallas, Texas Music Week
1919 – Music Week, Navasota, Texas
1920 – Music Week, New York, at which time the Federation's connection with Music Week began, with Mrs. Julian Edwards, president, New York Federation serving on the committee
1923 – First National observance
1924 – First synchronized National Music Week

Its flowering brought fifty-one observances in 1921; forty-nine in 1922; fifty-six in 1923, culminating in the first truly National Music Week May 4-10, 1924, with 452 celebrations.

After a public survey, the first full week in May was selected and this has continued each year. Serving on the first National Music Week committee with Otto Kahn, a Patron of the Arts and Chairman of the Board of Directors of the Metropolitan Opera Company, were Dr. Walter Damrosch, Conductor of the New York Symphony Orchestra, and Mrs. John F. Lyons, president of the National Federation of Music Clubs.

The chairmanship of the Honorary Committee of Governors was accepted by Calvin Coolidge, President of the United States. Since then each President has given moral support to the annual observance. There is a national chairman from the National Federation, with each of the states and clubs appointing chairmen for the Week. Proclamations are secured from the governors and mayors throughout the United States, proclaiming the first full week of May National Music Week. Participation is encouraged by the presentation of awards to both individuals and organizations.

Mr. Tremaine wrote:

"Possibly no local contacts were responsible for more Music Weeks than those of the National Federation of Music Clubs. From the beginning of National Music Week the National Federation has given the movement its enthusiastic support by naming a national chairman and asking the state federations to appoint state chairmen to direct the work."

From 1924 until 1947 Mr. Tremaine formulated the program and made National Music Week internationally famous. From 1947 through 1957 the National Recreation Association was the sponsor. In 1957, Mrs. Dougan, president, was approached asking the Federation to sponsor the Week jointly with the American Music Conference. Mrs. Dougan expressed her concern about the enormity of the job. However, after two called meetings of the Federation's Executive Committee, and one with representatives of the American Music Conference in New York City, on December 19, 1958, at the Headquarters of the National Recreation Association, it was agreed that the two organizations would sponsor jointly National Music Week, with Mrs. Dougan designated National Chairman.

A tremendous publicity drive was carried out from both offices, making the 1958 Music Week a great success, and "seeing that the Federation could stand on its own two feet from then on." After one year the American Music Conference retired from the co-sponsorship leaving the Federation as the sole sponsor since 1959.

This writer was interested in a letter written by Mr. Tremaine to "Dear Mrs. Richter", November 30, 1954:

"... I regret to say that I do not have any Stephen Foster material of interest as we lost in a fire all of my father's records... I was a boy when my father (also Charles Milton Tremaine) died. My father who was associated with Horace Waters in the Music Publishing business... knew Stephen Foster personally. The dedication of *Why Have My Loved Ones Gone* was to the Tremaine Quartet... composed of my father, baritone, his brother, William Barnes Tremaine, tenor, and two sisters, Laura Tremaine, soprano... and Antionette Tremaine....

"I have been associated with the National Federation of Music Clubs for a great many years, going back to the days of the presidency of Mrs. John F. Lyons in 1920, and I have been an enthusiastic admirer of its accomplishments. My interest in it is still keen even though the years have lessened my own activity.

Yours very sincerely,
(signed)
C. Milton Tremaine"

In 1963 Charles M. Tremaine was to receive a Citation from the National Federation of Music Clubs, but he died a short time before the convention. It was given posthumously and received by his daughter. Thus, since 1958 the National Federation has sponsored National Music Week with great success – and since 1959 it has been the sole sponsor – bringing to countless numbers music, hoping that through listening to music one week of the year, there will be an inspiration gained to enjoy it the remaining fifty-one weeks. Music is a natural expression of the inner man, a natural means of communication, and "though fashioned of dreams, is raiment and food for your soul."

Mr. Charles M. Tremaine – Founder of National Music Week.

ONE VOICE ON MUSIC

National Music Council

1

Julia Fuqua Ober, president of the National Federation of Music Clubs, in addressing the 1941 Biennial Convention in Los Angeles, said, "The realization of the permanent organization of the National Music Council can definitely be attributed to the Federation."

And – according to Edwin Hughes, who was president of the Music Teachers National Association, "The real impetus to the forming of the National Music Council was given by Julia Fuqua Ober, then president of the National Federation of Music Clubs."

In the early 1930's there was discussed at the Music Educators National Conference a need for a representative group to act as a clearing house for all music organizations – a forum capable of speaking as one voice on music. Nothing tangible came from this, but at least a "start was made in the right direction".

Eight years later, in 1938, in an address given before the biennial convention of the Music Educators National Conference in St. Louis by Franklin Dunham, of the National Broadcasting Company, he said in surveying the growth of musical activities in America, "Yet we are not united. All of us have just begun to realize how mutually interdependent are we. Why cannot we get together? Why cannot we form a National Music Council composed of representatives of every recognized factor in the musical progress of the nation?"

Mrs. Vincent Hilles Ober answered this challenge when on December 30, 1938, at the Music Teachers National Association convention in Washington D.C., she called a meeting of twenty people representing various music organizations. Mrs. Ober presided over the meeting of composers, performers, teachers, music librarians, publishers, musicologists, etc., and the response to her proposal was "unanimous and enthusiastic". An organizational committee of nine members was appointed with Harold Spivacke, Chief of the Music Directors of the Library of Congress, as chairman. The committee met in New York on February 11, 1939 and formalized plans. A long list of musical organizations came under the scrutiny of the committee to determine just who should be invited to consider membership in the Council.

Minutes of the National Federation of Music Clubs record that on October 5, 1939, "Mrs. Ober reported on action of the National Music Council, emphasizing the Federation's lead in the formation of the organization. Mrs. (Alexander) Jardine moved that the National Federation of Music Clubs become a member of the National Music Council under classification 'B' – annual dues to be $150" a year.

After a meeting in New York on April 3rd, when the Council definitely was organized, the National Music Council was incorporated under the laws of the State of New York on April 29, 1940. Elected to serve with Edwin Hughes, president, was Julia Fuqua Ober who was elected first vice president. Since that first election, the president of the National Federation of Music Clubs has been elected consistently to the vice presidency of the Council.

In the words of Edwin Hughes, "Since the inception of the National Music Council in 1940 the National Federation of Music Clubs has been one of its strongest and most active member organizations. The Council counts strongly on the Federation for the support... for the Federation is the largest member organization in actual individual members."

The Council's Committee on Music Rehabilitation was chaired by Mrs. Anne M. Gannett, president of the National Federation, who was active in sending musical relief – printed music, musical instruments, music paper for composers, etc. – to war devastated countries.

Serving as the fifth president of the National Music Council (1975-1979) was Dr. Merle Montgomery, past president of the Federation. She succeeded to the Chairmanship of the Board, serving 1979-1983. One of the Council's most outstanding projects in the fifty-three year history, planned and executed by Dr. Montgomery during her presidency, was the Bicentennial Parade of American Music in 1976, sponsored by the Council, administered with the support of the National Federation and funded by a grant from Exxon Corporation. The following ideas were supplemented under the title "The Bicentennial Parade of American Music".

1. Featuring the District of Columbia and each state's composers and performers during fifty-two concerts at the Kennedy

Center. (This was administered entirely by the state federations within the National Federation.)

2. Recording and broadcasting music by other state composers during a thirteen week series of thirty minute programs throughout each state. (A plan that had already been tried successfully by the Ohio Federation of Music Clubs under the direction of Mrs. Eusebia Hunkins).

3. Placing bronze plaques, with suitable ceremonies at sites that have historical significance to the American musical heritage. (The Council is indebted to Mr. Leonard Feist for this idea.)

To Dr. Merle Montgomery is due all the credit of having founded the National Music Council's annual Eagle Awards Luncheon. This first benefit luncheon was held June 2, 1982 at the Plaza Hotel in New York, under the chairmanship of Dr. Montgomery. Receiving the first awards were Jule Styne and Yehudi Menuhin. It continued as an annual event until 1993.

Edwin Hughes, the first president of the Council resigned at the end of his second term (1940-1944) to become Executive Secretary. At the Kansas City Biennial Convention of the National Federation of Music Clubs in 1961, as Executive Secretary (NFMC), he presented a citation to NFMC from the Council. Standing with Mrs. Bullock in receiving the citation were Mrs. Jardine and Mrs. Dougan, past national presidents.

Today the words of the founder of the National Music Council, Julia Fuqua Ober – then president of the National Federation – are as true as they were then, "Other important work which cannot be listed here gives evidence of the important place the Council now holds in America's musical life."

HANDS ACROSS THE SEAS

United Nations

1

Twice during the memories of some of the members of the Federation there have been periods of such upheavals as in 1917 and again in 1942. The first war laid the foundation for "One World" in Geneva, Switzerland, and the second resulted in an endeavor through the establishment of the United Nations to make world citizenship no longer a dream but a reality. Toward this end, nations from throughout the world met in San Francisco in June 1945.

The National Federation of Music Clubs was one of forty-two organizations to which President Harry S. Truman invited delegates to the San Francisco meeting. Mrs. Guy Gannett, president of the Federation accepted the president's invitation and was present when the charter was signed on June 26, 1945. President Dwight D. Eisenhower said later: "The flame was lighted (which) was intended to light the path of all mankind toward the common goal of freedom and universal peace... In your dedicated efforts to keep this flame, this hope and this faith alive, burning brightly... you have my earnest wish for its success."

When the United Nations actually came into being Mrs. Marie Morrisey Keith, president of the Federation (1947-1951) had the "gifted vision" to request and receive an official accreditation to the United Nations for the National Federation of Music Clubs. In 1947 Mrs. Keith appointed Mrs. Edwin A. Sullivan of New York City as the Federation's official representative. Mrs. Sullivan was at Hunter College where the Universal Declaration of Human Rights was initiated and in Paris for the Second General Assembly of the United Nations in 1948 when the Declaration was signed, reading:

> "Everyone has the right freely to participate in the cultural
> life of the community, to enjoy the arts, and to share in scien-

tific advancements and its benefits."

Mrs. Sullivan, who had been designated originally as an observer to the United Nations, was appointed a representative, which carried much more prestige, and made the National Federation the only "strictly cultural organization represented of the Non-Governmental Organizations" (NGO) of the United Nations. The NGO was the culmination of many endeavors undertaken to keep representatives of the group up to date on United Nations activities. To obtain such a listing an organization must have a broadly based membership – national and international and the scope and resources to undertake effective informational programs.

2

For approximately twenty-five years the National Federation of Music Clubs sponsored "Hands Across the Seas" broadcasts from radio station WNYC in New York City, of which Dr. Herman Newman was the Music Director and in charge of the programming. Annually, WNYC sponsored a "Salute to the United Nations" in October, as near the October 24th United Nations Day as possible. Mrs. Sullivan was active in working with Dr. Newman on the United Nations programs which were taped and rebroadcast to nations overseas, reaching more than 200,000 people.

Featured on the programs of the "Hands Across the Seas" broadcasts were artists from the various countries of the United Nations, with distinguished diplomats from the countries as speakers. In the 1966 Salute to the United Nations, the Honorable You-Chan Yang, Ambassador at Large of the Republic of Korea, in congratulating Dr. Marion Richter, chairman of the broadcast for NFMC said:

"I congratulate members of the National Federation of Music Clubs on their salute to the United Nations through wonderful music... I am sure there will be no objections, abstentions or otherwise when good music brings thorough understanding between nations and peoples. We Koreans love music and people who enjoy its thrilling message... The common language of music is understood everywhere among all peoples even though words may not be understood and shared. It is wonderful to know your clubs throughout America are trying to bring about thorough understanding between all peoples regardless of culture or color. That is exactly what the United Nations is trying to accomplish too."

Music on these "Hands Across the Seas" programs featured musicians from China, Korea, Poland, Spain, Russia, the United States, etc.

With these words His Excellency, Don Jose de Liquerica, Ambassador from Spain to the United Nations closed his message on one of the Federation's "Hands Across the Seas" Salutes:

"Internal peace which so many of us seek during a lifetime without ever reaching it, is frequently achieved – if only for a precious moment – when we listen to music. That is why I say; Let the voice of the spirit talk the international language of music and encourage the youth of the world to follow the roads of permanent and positive understanding and, under God's guidance, form a universal orchestra which will sing the greatness of a peaceful and united world."

3

Early in the history of the United Nations there was created an agency called the United Nations International Children's Fund (UNICEF) for the purpose of trying to salvage the lives of the countless children who were left homeless, sick and starving in countries devastated by World War II. The Federation became active in the program through contributions and the Juniors supporting two projects: Trick or Treat for UNICEF at Halloween, and the sale of UNICEF greeting cards at Christmas. In 1965 UNICEF was granted the Nobel Peace Prize. The Federation continued the support of UNICEF for approximately thirty-five years.

4

In 1960 the United States Commission for the United Nations requested an American Composer's Contest for an orchestral work to be written and dedicated to the United Nations. This was on a nationwide basis. The Aeolian Foundation announced a contribution of $2,000 to cover the amount of the award and expenses of the competition – all details to be under the control of the National Federation of Music Clubs. The competition was chaired by Ray Green, Executive Secretary, American Music Center.

The announcement attracted many entrants, with more than eighty-five composers represented. Judges were: Robert Ward, David Van Vactor and Ray Green, and on August 23, 1961 Mrs. C. Arthur Bullock, NFMC president, announced the winner, "William Grant Still, winning with his orchestral composition *The Peaceful Land*."

The orchestral work was world premiered by the University of Miami Symphony Orchestra on October 22. Mr. Still's reflections on *The Peaceful Land* were taped for broadcast on the "Hands Across the Sea" program over WNYC in New York City on October 21. In part they say:

"One morning a few months ago I awoke after having 'a deep dream of peace.' In my dream, I had witnessed a land so peaceful that its beauty was almost beyond description... Because I am a composer, my feelings on any subject are usually expressed through music. Accordingly, I began to plan a work to be called *The Peaceful Land*... To my way of thinking, the first requisite of a peaceful world is brotherhood... Music in general can serve that ideal and it is my hope that my composition *The Peaceful Land* will help in some way. Help bring nearer that day when men will live together in peace, when men will at last discover that strife and hatred do not solve problems."

5

A grand instrument of music, capable of expressing that serene harmony toward which we will all strive, is a particularly apt gift to the United Nations on its Fortieth Anniversary.

We at the United Nations live in the hope that our work will help move the world closer to the beauty and joy reflected in the perfect concert of great music.

Javier Pérez de Cuéllar, Secretary General

On Friday, October 18, 1985 the Dag Hammarskjold Auditorium was "alive with the sounds of music" as Federation members and guests came together for the dedicatory ceremony and presentation of their gift to the United Nations on the occasion of its fortieth birthday – a Steinway Grand Piano.

Dr. Merle Montgomery, national president 1971-1975, the Federation's official representative to the UN, conceived the idea and spearheaded the fund campaign. Following the opening greetings by Dr. Montgomery, the black ebony Steinway Grand Piano, Model B, was unveiled and presented by Mrs. Dwight D. Robinson, national president. Accepting on behalf of the Secretary General of the United Nations, Javier Pérez de Cuéllar, was Mr. Robert Muller, Assistant Secretary General for the Fortieth Anniversary.

The United Nations Official Seal affixed to the front treble side of the piano was hand-carved and painted by Steinway and Sons. Also affixed was a brass plate reading:

Presented to
The United Nations
by
The National Federation of Music Clubs, USA
NGO Member
October 18, 1985

CHAPTER FOUR

A FITTING TRIBUTE

Citations

1

The highest award that may be given an individual or organization by the National Federation of Music Clubs for distinguished musical service is the National Citation. The Citation Committee was established in 1949 and the first citation was presented by the president, Mrs. Royden James Keith to Standard Oil Company of Southern California in recognition of its exceptionally fine quality of programs broadcasted to the school children of Southern California.

One year later, in 1950, the President's Citations were inaugurated. Again, Marie Morrisey Keith, presented the first Presidential Citation to Philip F. Maxwell, Director of Chicago's Chicagoland Music Festival, in recognition of his devotion to the youth of America through the medium of radio and music.

Citations given by the National Federation of Music Clubs and its presidents, were created to honor and give recognition to those outstanding individuals and organizations whose contributions have distinguished them in the cultural and musical life of America. It is the highest honor the Federation can bestow. Since their beginning in 1949 more that 150 individuals and organizations have received recognition for their distinguished service to music.

A "Special Citation" was inaugurated, to be awarded to past national presidents who have made outstanding contributions to music. Since the first was awarded in 1961, thirteen national presidents have received these citations.

In 1961 at the Biennial Convention in Kansas City, Missouri, Dr. Edwin Hughes, the first president of the National Music Council, and at that time executive secretary, presented a Citation to the National Federation of Music Clubs from the National Music Council.

The Citation was given "In recognition of its distinguished service to

American music and musicians, through pioneering encouragement and steadfast support of United States composers; through the discovery of and assistance to gifted young American performers in its biennial contests; through the annual 'Parade of American Music' every February; through its awards for the performance of American music overseas; through its many scholarships and its promotion of string playing among young musicians; and through the championing in general of the welfare of music and musicians in the United States."

Dr. Hughes presented the citation for Dr. Howard Hanson, President of the National Music Council. It was accepted by Mrs. Bullock.

At the Fall Session at Interlochen, Michigan in 1959, a Citation was presented to the National Federation of Music Clubs from the National Music Camp. The Citation presented by Dr. Joseph Maddy was accepted by Mrs. C. Arthur Bullock, national president.

CHAPTER FIVE

"– in the glow of freedom's light"

Bicentennial Parade of American Music

1

In anticipation of the two hundredth anniversary of the birth of our country, observed in 1976, Congress created the American Revolution Bicentennial Administration. The time had come to give recognition to the progress which had been made in the cultural arts in these two hundred years.

It was an article, written by Paul Hume, Music Critic for the Washington Post, which appeared in the Sunday, April 22, 1973 issue of the paper, that attracted the attention of Dr. Merle Montgomery, President of the National Federation of Music Clubs. He wrote:

"Why should not the Federation of Music Clubs, for example, in cooperation with the universities and colleges of each state, arrange for the outstanding representative music of the states to be heard at festivals in central locations of these states in 1976... why not send that program to the Kennedy Center where it would present the music achievements of the country in a 50 weeks series?"

Four months later, Dr. Montgomery presented the idea to the Board of Directors of the Federation. It received the full approval and an NFMC Planning Committee was appointed with Mrs. Muriel Hunkins, Chairman, and Miss Mary Heininger, Vice Chairman.

The following December, Mr. Stanley Adams, President, American Society of Composers, Authors and Publishers, called together musical leaders, and it was decided that the National Music Council would become the "umbrella" organization for the project, with Dr. Montgomery appointed the general chairman. It was to be called the Bicentennial Parade of American Music. There were to be: concerts featuring each state, with music and composers indigenous to the state; a thirteen week series of radio broadcasts featuring the state's music and composers; and historical sites of interest to music to be marked with appropriate plaques,

The National Federation was asked to be in charge of the concerts of the fifty states, and the radio series.

The concerts were scheduled in the order in which each state joined the Union, with the original thirteen states performing in the beginning. It was Delaware who led the Parade because it was the first to ratify the constitution. Their's was a program of contemporary music on May 7, 1975. Pennsylvania's Day followed on May 13, featuring traditional music, with performances of early Moravian music. New Jersey Day returned to the contemporary on November 11 - and the last concert of the original thirteen states was Rhode Island on December 9, 1975. In 1976, performed were the concerts of the remaining fifty states.

On the morning preceding the last of the fifty-two concerts, at 11:00 o'clock, a dedicatory ceremony at the John F. Kennedy Center for the Performing Arts, records – photos, posters, States' Day concert programs and many other memorabilia were placed in a gleaming four foot stainless steel time capsule, to be opened in early January, 2076, at which time the ceremony will be reversed.

The bicentennial year came to a close, December 31, 1976, with an All-Sousa Program, played by the United States Marine Band. In the words of Dr. Montgomery, who had been elected to the presidency of the National Music Council in 1975: "Everyone present at this 'Stars and Stripes Forever' Day, including two of John Philip Sousa's nieces, shared with the largest audience ever assembled in the Concert Hall, a patriotic feeling that left everyone breathless as the Band played its last encore: *The Stars and Stripes Forever!*"

Many laudatory statements and congratulatory messages were uttered and written about Dr. Montgomery and her mammoth undertaking. Few words may serve a more fitting epitaph for the one hundred year resting place of the program's archives than those expressed by Dr. Otto Luening, Wisconsin's dean of American composers: "The Bicentennial Parade of American Music is the best thing that has happened to the American composer since the W.P.A.!"

The January 1, 1977 issue of the *New York Times* carried the following:

"Washington, Dec. 31 (UPI) – With a Marine bugle fanfare, the Bicentennial Parade of American Music concluded a year-long salute to the nation's composers today, and placed in a 100 year time capsule a sampling of two centuries of their music.

"A New Year's Eve concert of John Philip Sousa marches, by the Marine Band at the Kennedy Center for the Performing Arts, was the 52nd and last of the Bicentennial series commemorating music from all the states.

"Earlier in the day, a stainless-steel time capsule was filled with pamphlets, tape recordings, clippings, photographs 'and musical scores to be held until the year 2076. Speakers told of the contributions of American musicians from Sousa to Jelly Roll Morton, and Marine buglers performed.

"A tape recorder was included, in case the Americans a century from now have nothing on which to play the tapes of today."

The Time Capsule, containing the records of the Bicentennial observance in 1976 will be opened in January 2076, America's Tricentennial year. The 1976 observance was under the chairmanship of Dr. Merle Montgomery, NFMC past president. Pictured are Frank Spagnoletti, left, and Thomas Faath, right, executives of the American Can Company, who made the Time Capsule.

MAKING MUSIC – MAKING HISTORY

Congressional Charter

1

Napoleon said, "Music of all the liberal arts has the greatest influence over the passions, and it is that to which the legislator ought to give the greatest encouragement." This was the same feeling of members of the National Federation of Music Clubs and Miss Marie Hurley, Washington D.C., chairman of Legislation in 1963 when they met in Pittsburgh, Pennsylvania for the biennial convention during the administration of Dr. Dorothy Dann Bullock. The Board of Directors voted unanimously to petition Congress by "Resolution" to grant a Congressional Charter to the then sixty-five year old Federation. The resolution adopted by the Board of Directors was sent to every member of Congress. It read in part:

RESOLUTION
WHEREAS, the National Federation of Music Clubs, a nonprofit, non-partisan organization was organized in the City of Chicago in 1898, and granted an Illinois Charter under which it still operates years later, the largest single musical organization in the world, with more than 5,000 clubs and a total membership of more than 600,000 consisting of musicians, teachers, composers, concert artists, students, choral and symphonic societies; and
WHEREAS, the purpose of the National Federation of Music Clubs is to aid and encourage musical education and to develop and maintain high musical standards throughout America, and to that end, and without limiting such general purpose, to encourage the composition and performance of music; to aid performing and creative musical artists; to assist in the establishment of musical education; to promote musical education; to increase public knowledge and appreciation of music; to promote musical

activities in the armed forces; to aid veterans in commencing or resuming musical careers; and to keep music and the arts on a par with the current emphasis on science and technology, and

WHEREAS, the National Federation of Music Clubs has supported consistently through the years, legislative proposals furthering music, the arts and education..., and

WHEREAS, In the words of Clifford V. Buttleman, Executive Secretary Emeritus, Music Educators National Conference... in July 1957 while testifying before the House Committee on Education and Labor for the establishment of a Federal Advisory Council on the Arts, the power of the National Federation of Music Clubs "is far reaching and has been used for good in so many ways, not exclusively in the field of one art, MUSIC"; and

WHEREAS, the granting to the National Federation of Music Clubs of a Congressional Charter would give the Federation the prestige it deserves, and would be further recognition of MUSIC...

NOW THEREFORE BE IT RESOLVED; that the National Federation of Music Clubs... in Biennial convention assembled at Pittsburgh, Pennsylvania, April 19-23, 1963, strongly urges the United States Senate and the United States House of Representatives to grant the National Federation of Music Clubs a congressional Charter during the current session of the 88th Congress; and

BE IT FURTHER RESOLVED; that a copy of this Resolution be forwarded to each member of the United States Senate and to each member of the United States House of Representatives.

Miss Hurley moved the adoption of the Resolution. It was carried unanimously.

The 88th Congress failed to take action on the "Resolution" and it was not until seven years later, in 1970 that Mrs. Maurice Honigman, president, requested Senator Sam J. Ervin, Jr. of North Carolina to introduce the Bill to incorporate the Federation. Again in 1975, it was introduced by Senator Hugh Scott of Pennsylvania, and again by Senator Herman Talmadge of Georgia. Each time it was referred to the Senate Judiciary Committee, only to "die" a natural death.

With the election of Mrs. Jack C. Ward to the presidency of the National Federation of Music Clubs in 1979, top priority was given to completing the work begun by Miss Marie Hurley in 1963 – that of securing a Congressional Charter for the Federation. The Honorable Senators Thad Cochran of Mississippi and Robert A. Dole of Kansas, and Congressman Carroll A. Campbell of South Carolina, graciously agreed to introduce the legislation in their respective Houses of Congress.

Every member of the Federation worked unselfishly and untiringly toward getting the legislation passed – lobbying their congressmen through every committee to which it was referred. Not always was the "going" smooth. Congressman Toby Moffett of Connecticut wrote: "Congress does not often approve charter proposals... hundreds of charter proposals will be introduced, so Congress makes very sure it only moves on those which it finds of exceptional merit."

But – on June 3, 1982 a letter was sent from the president, Mrs. Ward to all members of the National Federation stating, "Today a call was received from Senator Cochran – Both the Senate Judiciary Committee and the Senate have approved Senate Bill #1634 granting a Congressional Charter to the National Federation of Music Clubs."

It was only a short time before a like call came from Congressman Campbell giving the same happy news, and in which he said,

"I am delighted by the charter. Music club members did an incredible lobbying job. They deserve the full measure of credit for the bill's passage. The NFMC has worked for America's musical heritage for eighty-four years. They have made a major contribution through hard work and dedication without federal assistance. This charter serves as a commendation that the Federation richly deserves."

And – thus, Public Law 97-231 passed by the 97th Congress, was signed into law by the Honorable Ronald A. Reagan, President, on August 9, 1982, making the National Federation of Music Clubs only the third musical organization to be incorporated by the Congress of the United States of America.

The following were authorized by the charter as incorporators of the federal corporation:

Mrs. Jack C. Ward, President, South Carolina
Mrs. Dwight D. Robinson, Ohio
Mrs. Clifford Allison, Kansas
Mrs. William B. Millard, Pennsylvania
Mrs. Robert E. L. Freeman, South Carolina
Mrs. Alan W. Trorey, California
Mrs. Joe Ince, Texas
Miss Mary Heininger, Ohio
Mrs. Maurice Honigman, North Carolina

The original charter as signed by President Reagan is on file in The Library of Congress. The following letter was delivered to Mrs. Ward, NFMC President, by Special Courier of President Reagan, Mr. Kenneth Cribb, Assistant Counsellor to the President, at the final banquet of the Baltimore Fall Session, August, 1982, at which time it was read to Federation members in attendance.

THE WHITE HOUSE

WASHINGTON

August 20, 1982

It gives me great pleasure to extend my warm greetings to members and guests of the National Federation of Music Clubs as you meet in your 1982 Fall Session.

On August 9 I had the privilege of signing into law an act granting a congressional charter to the Federation. This charter signifies official recognition by the government of the United States of the important work you are doing.

The Federation is the largest philanthropic organization in the world. Its effectiveness over the past 84 years is well known, and its support of music education and promotion of live performances have enhanced an appreciation and knowledge of the arts on the part of the American public.

The Federation's extensive program of scholarships and awards has made it a premier force in support of the American composer and performer. In a time of budgetary constraints, it is particularly significant that your 600,000 members remain a bulwark of support for the performing arts in our nation.

You have my best wishes for a most successful conference.

Ronald Reagan

Highlighting the celebration of the announcement by the president that the work for a charter begun nineteen years ago by Miss Marie Hurley, had now become a reality, was the Baltimore Charter Party. As described by Onamae Ratcliff it was:

"Unscheduled and with only a few hints here and there that 'something might be going on,' the Baltimore Charter Party burst upon the scene, 'an affair to be remembered in the history of the Federation as the Boston Tea Party is in the history of the United States,' the National President remarked! With much advance and secretive planning, Mrs. Ward had enlisted the help of Mrs. Glen M. Weakley of Philadelphia, in arranging an outstanding celebration. As members moved toward another ballroom on invitation of the President, at the end of the Gary Lakes concert, the doors opened on a gala scene. Red, white and blue streamers fluttered, several members dressed in traditional street newsboy clothes, hawked, 'extra, extra' papers, giving each guest a copy of the Congressional Record for the time of the passage of the Bill providing for the Charter, along with a badge which read 'WE DID IT – NFMC Congressional Charter, 1982.' A table stacked with party hats and noisemakers of various sorts helped diminish any dignified reserve remaining! And then came the surprise, the Philadelphia Mummers – in full regalia! What a celebration... Before the evening ended, it was... like being at a college football-victory party – congo lines, snake dance lines, round dancing, square dancing, contemporary and traditional ballroom steps... Who will ever forget the Baltimore Charter Party and fail to appreciate the plans that served to bring back the enthusiasm of youth!"

And who will ever forget the thrill of hearing that on August 9, 1982, President Ronald A. Reagan had signed a Bill granting a Federal Charter to the NATIONAL FEDERATION OF MUSIC CLUBS!

DIAMOND JUBILEE

1

The National Federation of Music Clubs' *Diamond Jubilee* Convention in Atlantic City, New Jersey, April 1973, celebrating seventy-five years of working toward a more musical America, was one of the most beautiful and elaborate in the Federation's 100 year history. From the time the national president, Dr. Merle Montgomery, tapped the gavel to announce the seventy-five year celebration, until the curtain was lowered five days later with the final *Diamond Jubilee* Banquet – with the beautifully gowned ladies in their "diamond" tiaras, and the concert by Shirley Verrett of the Metropolitan Opera, an NFMC Young Artist winner – the days were filled to overflowing with outstanding artists and speakers. Each presented a perfect picture of the past, the present, and the future in the history of the Federation.

The Past Presidents' Assembly dinner was dedicated to Mrs. John F. Lyons, past national president, in whose administration the PPA was founded. A nostalgic enactment of a "typical turn of the century" music club meeting was presented in costume, directed by Mrs. Whayne Priest, with historical connotations by the Kentucky Federation of Music Clubs, and dedicated to the Past Presidents' Assembly.

Youth Day was a "veritable explosion" of music and dance billed as a *Musical Festival Marathon*; The Atlantic City Convention Hall on the Board Walk was the impressive setting for a full concert of American music by the United States Continental Army Band; The afternoon program featured the dance from the most primitive of tribal dances – in a sequence which began with the *Tribes* and portrayed the story of an African village romance – to the sophisticated movements of the ballet, dedicated to Mrs. Jane Kettering, former dance chairman.

Two Federation organ winners, Keith Warner of Ohio and Diane Bish of Florida, were presented; Choral groups from as far away as Orem, Utah composed the *Festival Marathon*.

Climaxing Saturday's *Musical Festival Marathon* in the Atlantic City Convention Hall was the thrilling and "electrifying" concert performed by Van Cliburn, world renowned pianist.

It was at the Celebrity Luncheon that the host, Stanley Adams, distinguished president of American Society of Composers, Authors and Publishers, announced the inauguration of the "'Victor Herbert Composers Award' to be given in the Student Division of the Federation, with a first prize of $1,000 and second and third prizes of $500 each."

Highlighting the afternoon American Music program was the presentation of the commissioned work of John La Montaine, who was commissioned to write a composition for the NFMC *Diamond Jubilee*. His *Conversations* for clarinet and piano was given its premiere by David Glick, 1972 winner of the National Federation's Anne M. Gannett Award for Veterans.

Additional artists and celebrities were included among others: Lawerence Foster, 1967 Stillman Kelley winner; Claudette Sorel, Joseph Fennimore, Henry Criz, Melvin Brown, Carolyne James – former Young Artist winners; Sol Hurok, world renowned impresario; Mrs. Jouett Shouse, benefactor; Oliver Daniel, Broadcast Music Incorporated; Madame Serge Koussevitzky; Leonard Feist, president, National Music Council; Amyas Ames, chairman, Board of Directors, New York Philharmonic Orchestra; and Iain Hamilton, British composer.

Guests and dignitaries alike enjoyed a five day panorama of seventy-five years of history filled to overflowing with a constellation of outstanding artists and speakers.

MUSICAL POTPOURRI

1

1902 – The first Course of Study Program was written by Mrs. Frank S. Wardwell.

1905 – The first "Sectional Conferences" were held during the administration of Mrs. Winifred B. Collins – the Eastern Section was hosted by the Treble Clef Club, of Philadelphia, Pennsylvania, one of the charter members of the National Federation. A prominent part of the "festival" was on the closing evening when the host club "bade goodbye" to its guests with a long remembered concert chosen from its own ranks."

The Central Region (then called the Middle Section) met in St. Louis, Missouri, with the meetings held "in the handsome library of Washington University, given over at that time to the St. Louis Exposition and known as the Hall of Congress."

1913 – "$300.00 was voted as an allowance for the president."

1913 – The eighth Biennial Convention of the National Federation of Music Clubs met at the Congress Hotel in Chicago, April 21-26, 1913.

A Chicago newspaper carried an article entitled, "Fight to Bar Suggestive Ragtime to Be Started by Musical Clubs." The article read:

"Suggestive ragtime and the objectionable syncopated melody of the dance hall and the cabaret will be condemned today by the National Federation of Musical Clubs at the symposium of American music, in charge of Mrs. Jason P. Walker... Miss Nellie Strong Stevenson of New York will attack modern music in an animated address 'General Plans for the Advancement of American Art'. Mrs. Walker will lead the discussion in what promises to be one of the most interesting sessions of the convention...

"Madame Anna E. Zeigler of New York City advocated the production of American operas... declaring that cabarets were a detriment to musical culture and that the foreign musical trust was dwarfing American musicians.

"Americans are running more and more to ragtime. One hears *Row, Row, Row* and *In My Harem* in American homes where among the same class in Europe one hears opera. In Italy little street urchins are familiar with the Italian operas and sing them at their play. But in New York on Broadway we are forced to listen to the ear-splitting strains of some player in a music house or cafe or to the tones of a hurdy gurdy...."

At the closing session at the Congress Hotel the Board of Management passed "Resolutions seeking the suppression of 'smut' songs."

1914 – "The secretary was instructed to write Mr. Charles Wakefield Cadman expressing the disapproval of the Board of having Walter Spry appear on the Biennial program owing to his opposition to Women's Musical organizations."

1917 – The December 4th meeting of the Board at Stan Hywet stated in the minutes, "that eighty dollars had been sent to Madame Paderewski as a contribution from the National Federation of Music Clubs toward the fund she is now raising to build homes in Poland for the destitute Polish mothers and children."

1917 – At the same meeting, the "clubs are asked to observe Theodore Thomas' birthday – October 11 – as Federation Day, Mrs. Thomas having been the promulgator of the National Federation of Music Clubs; to also celebrate MacDowell's birthday – December 18 – as American Music Day; to observe Thanksgiving Day as International Song Day."

1919 – The first State President's Day was held at the Biennial Convention in Peterborough, New Hampshire with the entire day devoted to state presidents reports on "various assigned subjects".

1919 – At the meeting of the Board at Stan Hywet, the home of the national president, Mrs. Frank A. Seiberling, she called attention "to the beautiful gavel of ivory and gold, presented to the Federation by the Fortnightly Musical Club of Cleveland, Ohio, in honor of three national presidents that club had furnished the Federation, Mrs. Seiberling being the third."

1920 – Mrs. David Campbell prepared and presented to Mrs. Frank Seiberling the "Compact of Loyalty", following the form of the "Compact" signed by the Pilgrim Fathers on the Mayflower, three hundred years before – November 11, 1620. This was presented in appreciation of Mrs. Seiberling's having entertained the Board.

1921 – February 6, the Federation discussed the possibility of applying for a "national charter".

1921 – "The president, Mrs. Seiberling... asked for a report of the committee on Resolutions. Mrs. Frances E. Clark, chairman, reported as follows: '... that we rejoice in the action of the Senate in eliminating the tax on musical instruments. We now most earnestly urge the Conference Committee to strike out all tax on musical instruments from the final bill. Music is no longer a luxury but a necessity and a vital force in education. Any obstacle placed in the way of service of music to our people and children is a blow to our home and school life, and a menace to the development of music in America.'"

1921 – June 6, The Articles of Certificate of Incorporation were amended changing the organization's name from National Federation of Musical Clubs to National Federation of Music Clubs.

1921 – It was moved by Mrs. Frank A. Seiberling, that a vote of thanks be sent to the Harmony Club of Fort Worth, Texas for placing $1,000 in the bank for the use of Mrs. Lyons, president of the Federation, and signifying their intent of still further supporting her if she needed further financial assistance in carrying on her duties as president.

1922 – March 28, the Board voted to send a note of thanks to Mrs. F. F. Abbott and Mrs. Frances E. Clark for "having secured the publishing of a special Federation number of *Etude Magazine*, and that a note of appreciation be sent to Mr. James Francis Cooke, editor, for his generous publicity."

1923 – At the Asheville Biennial Convention Mrs. Seiberling suggested a plan for club rating to be studied and presented at the next Fall Session.

1927 – The District and State President's Council was founded.

1928 – October, the Indiana Federation of Music Clubs "formally passed a resolution making Thomas A. Edison the first Honorary Member of the state." Mr. Edison graciously accepted this honor.

    The National Federation of Music Clubs, Mrs. James Ottaway, president, was later to pay tribute to Mr. Edison for his outstanding contributions, in particular to music. Mrs. Edison was gracious in her reply:

GLENMONT
LLEWELLYN PARK, ORANGE
NEW JERSEY

Dear Mrs. Ottaway and members of the National Federation of Music Clubs —

Of all the arts with Mr. Edison his love for music came first and his great aim and thought was to reach out to all. His effort was unlimited in trying to perfect his instrument in order that the best of music might be made available. It is most gratifying to realize that he has such appreciation of his arduous labors by the musical clubs of his own country in the tribute paid by you. If he were with us he would do all in his power to advance the fine work of this most powerful organization and help to spread the beautiful influence of music.

Yours sincerely,

Mina M. Edison

1930 – The Federation worked for the appointment of a Secretary of Fine Arts for the President's Cabinet.

1933-1935 – Clubs in the Federation contributed $2,000 to the Stephen Foster Memorial in Pittsburgh, Pennsylvania.

1939 – It was during the administration of Mrs. Julia Fuqua Ober that the services of a professional parliamentarian were secured for the first time.

1939 – May 14, 1939 was declared National Federation of Music Clubs Day at the World's Fair in New York. One of the most important events of the day was the Massed Chorus of 1,000 singing under the direction of John Warren Erb. The New York Federation of Music Clubs was host for the day.

1941 – The four regions of NFMC were founded by dividing the Eastern Region into the Northeastern and Southeastern.

1951 – Otto Harbach, president of American Society of Composers, Authors and Publishers attended the Biennial Convention in Salt Lake

City, Utah, and was so impressed with the work of the Federation that he gave $10,000 to establish the first President's Promotion Fund for the advancement of American Composition.

1959 – At the NFMC meeting in Chicago, Mrs. Robert W. Roberts of Florida moved that the Federation pledge $500 to the Howard Hanson Memorial Chapel at Eastman School of Music. The last installment was paid in 1961.

1963 – Six national affiliate organizations joined as Associate Members – Austria, Israel, Jordan, Lebanon, Scotland and Turkey.

1965 – On August 30th Mrs. Sullivan, U.S. representative to the United Nations presented to Mrs. Ada Holding Miller a letter written by eminent composer, Jean Sibelius, thanking the Federation for instruments (including a piano) supplied to his country, Finland, when it was in desperate need following World War II. Mrs. Miller "made the appropriate presentation to President Muir, recommending that it be framed and occupy a prominent place among Federation treasures."

THE AFTERGLOW

"And then the sun goes down
and long the afterglow gives light."
—Thoreau

The last meeting of the National Federation of Music Clubs attended by Rose Fay Thomas was the Chicago Biennial Convention in 1927. She was honored as the Honorary President and gave an address at the luncheon. It was only by chance that the Federation acquired the address given by Mrs. Thomas on that occasion.

On April 14, 1934 Mr. Clarence Gustlin wrote from Santa Ana, California, and attached to the address:

"To Whom it May Concern: It is my wish that this address shall be presented to the proper officer of the National Federation of Music Clubs to be retained by that organization among its historical works and documents in case of my demise."

The address, after having been misplaced for thirty-five years, on August 19, 1962, was sent by Mr. Gustlin to Mrs. C. Arthur Bullock, president of the National Federation, with the information that he had been seated beside Mrs. Thomas at the luncheon in Chicago in 1927, at which time it was delivered. Upon his complimenting her on the address, "she very graciously presented to me the original typewritten copy annotated in her own handwriting." He said of Mrs. Thomas, "She was a dynamic New Englander whose dream had been realized far beyond her fondest expectations."

Following is a copy of her address:

Madame President & Ladies & Gentlemen:

Chicago 1927

Chicago promised *to give* us a good time and when Chicago
sets out to give anything, she gives it royally, and we
have all enjoyed a perfectly splendid week in this Western
Metropolis,— *even tho a trifle hectic!*

At our opening meeting on Tuesday evening, when
I contemplated the great gathering of delegates in shining
costumes, bearing silken banners, which thronged every
inch of this large hall, I felt as if I were in a dream.
In 1893 when I called the first Convention of Musical Clubs
(which might be named the cradle in which the Federation
was rocked) I managed to get a fair representation.from the
eastern, western, northern and central sections of America
but none from the States of the Far South. Not one, South
of Tennessee, sent me a single delegate to that Convention,
because, either I could not discover any Clubs there, or
if I did, they would not come. How different is the case
today! At this meeting not only all the northern but all
the Southern States as well, are represented by large
Delegations. This rejoices my heart and I hope that if we
are fortunate enough to entertain the Biennal in my home
town of Boston two years from now, that we may welcome still
larger delegations of our Southern and far-Western Sisters.
You all need to come to good old Boston, and good old Boston
needs to have you come to her even more.

I stress especially my wish for the cooperation
of our Southern Clubs because I believe the Federation has a

mission which is even greater and more important than
creating a propaganda for good music- it is that of creating a nation-wide propaganda of love, sympathy, good
fellowship and unity among American women.

In the last Century, because there was then no
such restraining influence among the women, our foolish
grandfathers of the North and South got into a family
quarrel, and like all family feuds it, became fierce and
bitter and left behind it wounds that still smart and rankle.

But now things are happily changed in America-
Those mistaken old fighters have long since made up their
differences and shaken hands in Heaven. Methinks I even
hear a Northern soldier in genial conversation with a
Southern soldier under the trees of Paradise saying,
"We fooled you nicely that day you brought your bunch over
Green Hill- We were hiding in the woods all the time." -
"That's so" says the other, "how in the dickens did you
get there? But don't forget that we took it out of you
good and plenty next day!" - and they both laugh at at-
some good old joke.
And now even here on earth we grandchildren
have no quarrel with each other. In the World War our
Northern boys sang "Dixie", and Southern boys heard themselves called "Yanks" without a protest. And a Southern
gentleman reigned 8 years in the White House. That is as it
should be- the time has come to forget the struggle of
1860, but there is one thing about it that we all need to

remember. Before the Northern States fought to preserve the Union, they had given the Southern States what they believed a just cause for breaking it.

It is the grave and solemn duty now of the women of America to see to it that hereafter no section of our country shall ever give cause to any other to leave the Union. Fighting to bring back seceded States is not at all the same thing; as preventing them from wishing to secede, and it is my firm conviction that the National Federation of Musical Clubs can do this better than any other agency, because it draws together the women from every State and section of our great country, bringing them now to California, again to New Hampshire- to Chicago- to Boston- teaching us all to know each other in our own home sections, opening our hearts as hostesses and guests, uniting us through Song and Symphony and holding us together in one great sisterhood, which is neither of the east or the west, the north or the south, but of America. So long as this continues among our women, our men will never draw the sword against each other again.

Oh, my dear friends - I pray you take with you to your distant homes this message from your old Federation Foster Mother, and this Resolution; that however deep and tender be your love for your own city, state or section, you will hold in still deeper reverence as the

immediate jewel   of your souls America- America the
Beautiful- our Own America, every part of which belongs
to each and all of us, and that you will use our splendid
Federation not only to carry a knowledge of the most
beautiful of the arts to all our people, but to make it
the evangelist of the gospel of the Brotherhood of
Man and the Sisterhood of Woman from Ocean to Ocean -
from the Great Lakes to the Gulf- So that the Star
Spangled Banner may wave - not in triumph, but in unity
of heart and spirit, over a country which shall be in
every truth the land of the Free and the Home of the
Brave forever.   I thank you.

Two years after Rose Fay Thomas addressed the 1927 convention in Chicago, on April 19, 1929, the light by which she had been reading the pages of life, flickered, grew dim and went out. The "Soldiers and Sailors" Club gave her a military funeral; a guard of soldiers and sailors carrying her casket at Christ Church. The Brass Choir from the Boston Symphony Orchestra played (as the Brass of the Chicago Symphony Orchestra had played at her husband's funeral) the Magnificent Chorale from an orchestration of Bach's *Suite*; and the Beethoven Hymn from the *9th Symphony*.

At Mount Auburn Cemetery in Cambridge, Massachusetts, an old family resting place, the soldiers and sailors lowered "her form into the grave; cast in their gloves, military fashion; sounded *Taps* on the bugles; and left her there heaped with flowers." In Mount Auburn, one of the world's most beautiful cemeteries, praised by poets for its immortal beauty, Mrs. Thomas had reproduced years earlier, over Mr. Thomas's grave, an exact replica of perhaps the most famous of the antique Celtic Crosses – standing on a gentle slope facing the Charles River. And – in the words of Charles Norman Fay, "There she lies beside him with her name on the reverse base of the stone – a fitting resting place for two lovers of beauty and makers of it... Each Memorial Day the Soldier's and Sailor's Club decorates her grave, as a good soldier, with flag and blooms."

Possibly Rose Fay Thomas felt something akin to what Charles O'Donnell expressed when he wrote:

When I go otherwhere, on my unreturning journey,
I will leave a whisper of a song in these old oaks,
A footfall, lingering 'til in some distant summer,
Another stranger down these paths may stray,
And may remember that I passed this way.

A life that touches others leaves an afterglow that continues to give light long after the sun goes down.

During this writer's presidency of the National Federation of Music Clubs, it was her pleasure to visit in 1982, beautiful Mount Auburn Cemetery in Cambridge, Massachusetts, and place roses on the grave of Rose Fay Thomas, on behalf of the hundreds of thousands of members of the Federation.

EPILOGUE

I must conclude now the task I began thousands of words ago. To paraphrase Emily Dickinson who said, "I'll tell you how the sun rose – a ribbon at a time," this writer has endeavored, through these pages to tell you how the Federation began "a ribbon at a time" A century now has passed into a happy and beautiful memory.

The *Centennial Hymn* written by John Knowles Payne for the American Centennial in Philadelphia, 1876, and conducted by Theodore Thomas, is as applicable for the Centennial celebration of the National Federation of Music Clubs today as it was for that Centennial celebration in 1876:

> *Our Father's God, from out whose hand,*
> *The centuries fall like grains of sand,*
> *We meet today, united, free,*
> *And loyal to our land and Thee,*
> *To thank Thee for the era done,*
> *And trust Thee for the opening one.*

The National Federation of Music Clubs might be likened to the ancient God Janus, who had two faces. One looked backward, the other forward. Looking back through the one hundred years we see the Federation's achievements emblazoned on the sands of time. They have more than justified the faith of our founders, whose spirits have had a way of gently touching our lives.

Looking forward – the next century is at hand. When it arrives Federation members will be ready. Although this birthday is three years away – in 1998, a committee, including the four living past national presidents, Mrs. C. Arthur Bullock, Mrs. Jack C. Ward, Mrs. Glenn L. Brown, Mrs. D. Clifford Allison, Honorary Chairmen, with Dr. Barbara Irish, national president, chairman, is already looking ahead to plans involving many Federation members. The plans call for major celebrations throughout the United States, but in particular: a Fall Session in the city of the Federation's birth – Chicago – in 1998; followed by a Biennial Convention in 1999 in the city where the first Biennial Convention was held in 1899 – St. Louis, Missouri.

No matter how far ahead we look we must not forget those brave women who met in Chicago at the invitation of Rose Fay Thomas in 1893, and again in 1898 – our founders. It is their dream which made today a reality.

We close with a quote with which the late Stanley Adams, then president of American Society of Composers, Authors and Publishers concluded his "ASCAP Story" on the occasion of its fiftieth Anniversary in 1964, and which is applicable to the National Federation of Music Clubs on this 100th Anniversary:

> *We are singing in a full voice now*
> *Because they sang in a small voice then.*
> *We gaze from the roof of a shining tower*
> *Because they labored to build a firm*
> *foundation.*
> *We are – because they were.*

APPENDICES

348

ROSE FAY THOMAS FELLOWS
* Denotes Charter Member

*1. Mrs. Jack C. Ward (Lucile)
*2. Mrs. Edward P. Nelson (Vivian Menees)
*3. Mrs. Wilmot W. Irish (Barbara)
*4. Mrs. Hal H. McHaney (Beulah Hale)
*5. Mrs. Dallas Goss (Rowena)
*6. Mrs. Joseph H. Albrecht (Sophie)
*7. Mrs. Norman A. Johnson, Jr. (Mary Grace)
*8. Dr. Ruth Halle Rowen
*9. Mrs. Charles Rasmussen (Ruth)
*10. Mrs. William B. Millard (Lucy)
*11. Mrs. Bruce Howar (Florence Esmay)
*12. Mrs. Claude Kirkpatrick (Edith)
*13. Mrs. Harry Gillig (Ann)
*14. Mrs. C. E. Christmann (Francis)
*15. Mrs. Leroy W. Kranert (Veda) (Deceased)
*16. Mrs. Rex Brown (Bernice) (Deceased)
*17. Mrs. Norman H. Hanson (Lydia)
*18. Miss Gretchen E. Van Roy
*19. Mrs. Robert A. Dean (Floride)
*20. Mrs. Glenn L. Brown (Mary Prudie)
*21. Mrs. George Deen (Frances)
*22. Miss Ann McClure
*23. Mr. Kenneth Self
*24. Mrs. Eleanor Lieber Ray (Deceased)
*25. Mrs. Lamoine M. Hall, Jr. (Betty)
*26. Mrs. Clifton Bond (Marjorie)
*27. Mrs. Robert E. L. Freeman (Cornelia)
*28. Mrs. William B. Wilson (Irma)
*29. Mrs. Charles J. Davis (Edith) (Deceased)
*30. Mrs. Glen M. Weakley (Emeline)
*31. Mrs. Dwight D. Robinson (Thelma) (Deceased – given posthumously)
*32. Mrs. Wayne D. Williams (Marion)
*33. Mrs. Sylvio Russo (Madeleine)
*34. Dr. Bruce Howar (Deceased)
*35. Mrs. Ralph Reed (Marguerette)
*36. Mrs. Fred C. Boyce (Elizabeth)
*37. Mrs. H. E. Miller (Mabry)
*38. Mrs. Arthur E. Reynolds (Ruby)
*39. Mrs. J. H. Kerns (Hazel)
*40. Mrs. Margaret E. Holan
*41. Mrs. Lynn Turner (Vera) (Deceased)

*42. Dr. Isabella Laude
43. Mrs. Harold Walters (Dolores)
44. Mrs. Ralph Kinsman (Viola) (Deceased)
45. Mrs. John H. Rhoades (Evelyn)
46. Mrs. Ruth Smith
47. Dr. Joseph Albrecht (Joe)
48. Dr. Edward P. Nelson (Ed)
49. Mr. Stillman Kelly
50. Mrs. Lee Rinker (Delores)
51. Mrs. Clayton B. Smith (Jenene)
52. Miss Marilyn Hardy
53. Judge Clifton Bond
54. Mrs. Ben K. Wright (Nelly)
55. Mrs. Clifford Allison (Virginia)
56. Mrs. Frank H. Walker (Jo)
57. Mrs. Rose Zygmanski
58. Mrs. Benjamin M. Thompson (Mildred)
59. Mrs. Franklin D. Moore (Eleanor)
60. Mrs. R. Keith Newton (Myrleann)
61. Mrs. W. Burke Neville (Marjorie)
62. Mrs. Gilbert Stephenson (Margaret)
63. Mrs. Kenneth Cribb (Dicksie)
64. Miss Rose Thomas Smith (Deceased – given posthumously)
65. Maestro Theodore Thomas (Deceased – given posthumously)
66. Dr. Katherine H. Mahan
67. Mrs. Gordon Howle (Patricia)
68. Onamae Ratcliff (Mrs. H. V. Dechert)
69. Mrs. Violet M. Clark
70. Mrs. Mark D. Paul (Doris)
71. Mrs. Stephen L. Johnston (Eva)
72. Mr. William Byrne Paullin (Bill)
73. Mrs. Gerald J. Rowan (Anne)
74. Dr. Jean Little
75. Mrs. Emil Beyer (Ruth)
76. Mrs. Ernest Grilk (Gloria)
77. Mrs. George Heimrich (Lucille)
78. Mrs. George Ecklund (Shirley)
79. Mrs. James Milne (Nancy)
80. Mrs. Ralph Suggs (Rose)
81. Ms. Mary Helen Rowan
82. Miss Carla Johnson
83. Ms. Kathleen Fitzgerald

YOUNG ARTIST AUDITIONS WINNERS
1915-1995

1915   LOS ANGELES, CALIFORNIA

No national contest. Winners of District contests performed at the Biennial Convention.

VOICE: Kathryn Meisle, New York, NY
Alexander Gray, Evanston, IL
Mildred Shaughnessy, El Reno, OK
Julia Jack, Portland, OR

VIOLIN: Wallace Grieves, Lacon, IL
Winston Wilkinson, Lynchburg, VA
May Anderson, Salt Lake City, UT
Helen Boyle, Ithaca, NY

PIANO: Aurora LaCroix, Boston, MA
Carol Robinson, Chicago, IL
Prudence Neff, Birmingham, AL
Julia Kitchen, Fresno, CA

1917   BIRMINGHAM, ALABAMA

VOICE: Marie Loughney, Schroon Lake, NY
VIOLIN: Graham Harris, Detroit, MI
PIANO: Selon Robinson, Northampton, MA

1919   PETERBOROUGH, NEW HAMPSHIRE

VOICE: Ruth Hutchinson, Los Angeles, CA
VIOLIN: Terry Ferrell, Fort Worth, TX
PIANO: Arthur Klein, New York, NY

1921   TRI-CITIES (Davenport, Iowa; Moline and Rock Island, Illinois)

VOICE: Devora Nadworney, Bayonne, NJ
George B. Smith, Chicago, IL
VIOLIN: Herman Rosen, Cleveland, OH
PIANO: Enrique Ross, New York, NY

1923   ASHEVILLE, NORTH CAROLINA

VOICE: Gladys Burns, Newark, NJ
Cooper Lawley, Chicago, IL
VIOLIN: Alma Berneman, Columbus, OH
PIANO: Nellie Miller, Oklahoma City, OK

1925   PORTLAND, OREGON

VOICE: Kathryn Noll, Cornwall, PA
VIOLIN: Catherine Wade-Smith, New York, NY
PIANO: William Beller, New York, NY

1927   CHICAGO, ILLINOIS

VOICE: Kathryn Witwer, Chicago, IL
James R. Houghton, Sommerville, MA
(2nd) Robert Wiedefeld (Weede), Baltimore, MD

(2nd) Hilda Burke, Baltimore, MD
VIOLIN: William Levitt, Chicago, IL
(2nd) Helen Berlin, Philadelphia, PA
PIANO: Hazel Hallett, Boston, MA
(2nd) Ethel Plentye, Chicago, IL

1929   BOSTON, MASSACHUSETTS

VOICE:
Soprano: Elsie Craft Hurley, Baltimore, MD
(2nd) Marie Herron Truitt, Milwaukee, WI
Contralto: Virginia Kendrick, Pittsburgh, PA
(2nd) Vera F. Keane, Roxbury, MA
Tenor: William Hain, Brooklyn, NY
(2nd) Norman Price, Denver, CO
Baritone: Raymond E. Eaton, Danvers, MA
(2nd) Paul Jers, Chicago, IL
VIOLIN: Philip Frank, New York, NY
(2nd) Phyllis Feingold, Chicago, IL
PIANO: Florence Frantz, Philadelphia, PA
(2nd) Annabel Hess, Cleveland, OH

1931   SAN FRANCISCO, CALIFORNIA

VOICE (WOMEN):
High: Helen Stokes, Baltimore, MD (Civic Concert Service Award)
(2nd) Martha E. Dwyer, Dayton, OH
Low: Louise Bernhardt, Melrose, MA
(2nd) Kathleen Sauerwald, Milwaukee, WI
Operatic, High: Helen Stokes, Baltimore, MD
(2nd) Martha E. Dwyer, Dayton, OH
Operatic, Low: Mary Gordon Ledgerwood, New York, NY
(2nd) Louise Bernhardt, Melrose, MA
VOICE (MEN):
High: George Tinker, Providence, RI
(2nd) John Barr, Brooklyn, NY
Low: Earl Lippy, Baltimore, MD
(2nd) John Wilson Crosby, Cincinnati, OH
Operatic, High: George Tinker, Providence, RI
(2nd) Nick Economo, Montezuma, GA
VIOLIN: Samuel Thaviu, Wilmette, IL
(2nd) Isler Solomon, East Lansing, MI
CELLO: Lillian Rehberg, Chicago, IL
(2nd) Elizabeth Reeves, Seattle, WA
ORGAN: Ruth Spindler, Lawrence, KS
(2nd) Henry D. Herried, Madison, WI

1933   MINNEAPOLIS, MINNESOTA
VOICE:
Mezzo-
Soprano: Genevieve Rowe, Wooster, OH
Tenor: Edward Austin Kane, New York, NY
Operatic: Lucille Fletcher Hart, Minneota, MN
VIOLIN: Byrd Elliott, Seattle, WA
CELLO: Louise Essex, Indianapolis, IN
    (Shubert Memorial Award, orchestra
    appearance)
ORGAN: Marion Clayton, Brooklyn, NY
PIANO: Dalies Frantz, Ann Arbor, MI
    (Shubert, orchestra appearance)

**1935   PHILADELPHIA,
    PENNSYLVANIA**
VOICE:
Contralto: Margaret Harshaw, Narberth, PA
Operatic: Leonard Treash, Philadelphia, PA
    (Best in classification)
VIOLIN: Joseph Knitzer, New York, NY (Tied
    with Miss Tureck for Schubert)
PIANO: Rosalyn Tureck, New York, NY
    (Tied with Mr. Knitzer for Schubert)

1937   INDIANAPOLIS, INDIANA
VOICE:
Lyric
Soprano: Mary Lida Bowen, Baltimore, MD
    (Best in classification)
VIOLIN: Eudice Shapiro, New York, NY
PIANO: Ida Krehm, Chicago, IL
    Jacques Abram, Houston, TX
    (Tied for Federation Award; both
    received Schubert)

1939   BALTIMORE, MARYLAND
VOICE:
Contralto: Martha Lipton, New York, NY
    (Firestone Award, radio appearance
    with orchestra)
VIOLIN: Marion Head, Upper Darby, PA
    Bernard Kundell, New York, NY
    (Tie, best in classification)
PIANO: Samuel Sorin, Detroit, MI (Schubert)

**1941   LOS ANGELES,
    CALIFORNIA**
VOICE:
Contralto: Mary Louise Beltz, Belton, TX
    Eula Beal, Los Angeles, CA (Tie)
VIOLIN: Elizabeth Carroll Glenn, Greenville, SC
PIANO: Sylvia Heimowitz, Winter Park, FL
    (Best in classification)

1943   WORLD WAR II
No national convention. "Festival of the Air" over
four major networks.
VOICE: Nan Merriman, Cincinnati, OH

VIOLIN: Fredell Lack, Houston, TX (Best in
    classification)
PIANO: Gladys Gladstone, Whipple, AZ
    Zadel Skolovsky, Boston, VA (Tie,
    best in classification)

1945   WORLD WAR II
Regional Conferences held and "Festival of the Air".
VOICE: Paula Lenchner, Cincinnati, OH
VIOLIN: Marian Burroughs, CT
    Robert Rudio, Oklahoma City, OK
    (Tie, best in classification)
PIANO: Eunice Podis, Cleveland Heights, OH

1947   DETROIT, MICHIGAN
VOICE: Joan Brainderd, Hamden, CT
PIANO: William Masselos, New York, NY

1949   DALLAS, TEXAS
VOICE: Jean Geis, New York, NY (NBC
    Symphony appearance)
ORGAN: William Watkins, VA (Dallas
    Symphony appearance)

1951   SALT LAKE CITY, UTAH
VOICE: Carol Smith, Chicago, IL
VIOLIN: Stanley Plummer, Pasadena, CA
PIANO: Claudette Sorel, New York, NY
    (N.C.A.C. contract)

1953   NEW YORK, NEW YORK
VOICE: Naomi Farr, Salt Lake City, UT
    (N.C.A.C. contract, NBC Symphony
    appearance, Metropolitan audition)
PIANO: Richard Cass, Greenville, SC

1955   MIAMI, FLORIDA
VOICE:
Baritone: Miles Nekolny, Chicago, IL
    (Metropolitan audition)
PIANO: Ivan Davis, Jr., Hobbs, NM (Boston
    "Pops" appearance)
CHAMBER
MUSIC: Alard String Quartet, Austin, TX
    (N.C.A.C. contract, Cincinnati
    Symphony appearance)

1957   COLUMBUS, OHIO
VOICE:
Mezzo-
Soprano: Evelyn McGarity, Indiana
    University, Bloomington, IN
Lyric
Soprano: Martha Deatherage, Chicago, IL
Baritone: McHenry Boatwright, Boston, MA
    (N.C.A.C. contract)
VIOLIN: Sylvia Rosenberg, NY
PIANO: Tana Bawden, NY and Portland, OR
    (Boston "Pops" appearance)

1959   SAN DIEGO, CALIFORNIA
VOICE:
Lyric
Soprano: Patricia Lou MacDonald, Portland, OR (N.C.A.C. contract)
Bass-
Baritone: James Standard, San Francisco, CA
VIOLIN: Diana Steiner, Philadelphia, PA
PIANO: Robert Brownlee, Provo, UT

1961   KANSAS CITY, MISSOURI
VOICE:
Mezzo-
Soprano: Shirley Verrett-Carter, New York, NY
Contralto: (Finalist runner-up) Elizabeth Fischer, Milwaukee, WI (Harry Salter Award)
VIOLIN: Tiberius Klausner, Kansas City, MO (Detroit Symphony Orchestra appearance in Summer Series)
PIANO: William Alton, Greensboro, NC (Brevard Symphony, Boston "Pops", Chautauqua Symphony appearances) (Finalist runner-up) James Mathis, New York, NY (Van Cliburn-Theodore Steinway Award) (Semi-finalist) Lois Pachucki, New York, NY (Harry Salter Award)

1963   PITTSBURGH, PENNSYLVANIA
VOICE:
Soprano: Lee Dougherty, New York, NY
Mezzo-
Soprano: Elizabeth Fischer, Dubuque, IA
Elizabeth Mannion, NY
Lyric
Tenor: Alan Rogers, Chicago, IL
Baritone: James Tippey, CA
ORATORIO: Dale Moore, OH - Baritone
VIOLIN: Elaine Skorodin, Chicago, IL

1965   MIAMI BEACH, FLORIDA
VOICE:
Mezzo-
Soprano: Claudine Carlson, San Francisco, CA
Lyric
Tenor: Melvin Brown, CA
ORATORIO: Jeanne Grealish, Albuquerque, NM - Mezzo-Soprano
PIANO: Joseph Fennimore, NY

1967   NEW YORK, NEW YORK
VOICE:
Soprano: Esther Hinds, New York, NY
ORATORIO: Carol Stuart, Hopkins, MN - Soprano
PIANO: Louis Nagel, NY

1969   ALBUQUERQUE, NEW MEXICO
VOICE:
Baritone: Benjamin Middaugh, Montevallo, AL
ORATORIO: David Doig, Buffalo, NY - Tenor
VIOLIN: Henry Criz, Chicago, IL
PIANO: Voytek Matushevski, Baltimore, MD

1971   NEW ORLEANS, LOUISIANA
VOICE:
Baritone: Stanley Norsworthy, New York, NY
ORATORIO: Carolyne James, Ames, IA - Mezzo-Soprano
PIANO: William Phemister, Baltimore, MD

1973   ATLANTIC CITY, NEW JERSEY
VOICE:
Soprano: Mary Elizabeth Poor, MI
Bass: Gary K. Kendall, Philadelphia, PA
ORATORIO: Mary Ann Busching, SC - Mezzo-Soprano
PIANO: Virginia Laico, MD

1975   ATLANTA, GEORGIA
VOICE:
Mezzo-
Soprano: Sharon Kay Edgemon, AZ
Lyric
Soprano: Kathleen Battle, OH
Lyrico
Spinto: Jeanine Kelley, MA
Tenor: Lionel Stubblefield, CO
VIOLIN: David Ehrlich, IL
PIANO: Lauren David Gayle, CA

1977   KANSAS CITY, MISSOURI
VOICE:
Soprano: Kris Elaine Reed, FL
Baritone: Randie Blooding, OH
ORATORIO: Vonna Miller, MO - Soprano
VIOLIN: Peter Zazofsky, FL
PIANO: Gary Steigerwalt, NY

1979   PORTLAND, OREGON
WOMAN'S VOICE:
Soprano: Jmel Wilson, TX (Chaminade Club Award)
MAN'S VOICE:
Tenor: Jonathan Mack, CA (Merle Montgomery Opera Award)
ORATORIO: Margaret Donnell, KS - Soprano
CELLO: Christopher Rex, PA
PIANO: Robert James McDonald, NY

1981 BIRMINGHAM, ALABAMA
WOMAN'S VOICE:
Soprano: Brenda Rucker-Smith, OH
MAN'S VOICE:
Tenor: Gary Lakes, WA
ORATORIO: Judith Malafronte, CT (Merle
Montgomery Opera Award)
VIOLIN: Ralph Evans, NY

1983 COLUMBUS, OHIO
ORATORIO: Richard Lalli, CT - Lyric Baritone
VIOLIN: Ming Feng Hsin, PA
PIANO: David Allen Wehr, CA

1985 WICHITA, KANSAS
WOMAN'S VOICE:
Soprano: Donna Zapola, PA
ORATORIO: William Doyle Riley, NJ - Baritone
PIANO: Jody Gelbogis, CT

1987 MIAMI, FLORIDA
WOMAN'S VOICE:
Mezzo
Soprano: Kitt Reuter-Foss, WI
MAN'S VOICE:
Baritone: John M. Koch, Cincinnati, OH
VIOLIN: Michael Ludwig, Philadelphia, PA
PIANO: Thomas Otten, CA

1989 FORT WORTH, TEXAS
WOMAN'S VOICE:
Lynda Keith, Cincinnati, OH
VIOLIN: Alexander Kerr, Alexandria, VA
PIANO: Andrew Cooperstock, Magnolia, AR

1991 PHILADELPHIA, PENNSYLVANIA
MAN'S VOICE:
Baritone: Stephen Rushing, Baton Rouge, LA
CELLO: Zuill Bailey, Woodbridge, VA
PIANO: Richard Glazier, Indianapolis, IN

1993 BUFFALO, NEW YORK
WOMAN'S VOICE:
Mezzo-
Soprano: Lorie Gratis, West Chester, PA
MAN'S VOICE:
Baritone: Anthony Turner, Cincinnati, OH
VIOLIN: Emil Israel Chudnovsky, New York, NY
PIANO: Andrew Armstrong, New Canaan, CT

1995 WICHITA, KANSAS
WOMAN'S VOICE:
Soprano: Jane L. Ohmes, Kansas City, MO
MAN'S VOICE:
Baritone: Allen Henderson, TN
PIANO: Mia Kim, Rochester, NY

BIENNIAL CONVENTIONS

1898 – Organization, Chicago, Illinois
1899 – Saint Louis, Missouri
1901 – Cleveland, Ohio
1903 – Rochester, New York
1905 – Denver, Colorado
1907 – Memphis, Tennessee
1909 – Grand Rapids, Michigan
1911 – Philadelphia, Pennsylvania
1913 – Chicago, Illinois
1915 – Los Angeles, California
1917 – Birmingham, Alabama
1919 – Peterborough, New Hampshire
1921 – Tri-Cities: Davenport, Iowa; Moline and Rock Island, Illinois
1923 – Asheville, North Carolina
1925 – Portland, Oregon
1927 – Chicago, Illinois
1929 – Boston, Massachusetts
1931 – San Francisco, California
1933 – Minneapolis, Minnesota
1935 – Philadelphia, Pennsylvania
1937 – Indianapolis, Indiana
1939 – Baltimore, Maryland
1941 – Los Angeles, California
1943 – World War II; "Festival of the Air" over four major networks and Business Meeting – no elections
1945 – World War II; "Festival of the Air" and Regional Conferences

1947 – Detroit, Michigan
1949 – Dallas, Texas
1951 – Salt Lake City, Utah
1953 – New York, New York
1955 – Miami, Florida
1957 – Columbus, Ohio
1959 – San Diego, California
1961 – Kansas City, Missouri
1963 – Pittsburgh, Pennsylvania
1965 – Miami, Florida
1967 – New York, New York
1969 – Albuquerque, New Mexico
1971 – New Orlean, Louisiana
1973 – Diamond Jubilee – Atlantic City, New Jersey
1975 – Atlanta, Georgia
1977 – Kansas City, Missouri
1979 – Portland, Oregon
1981 – Birmingham, Alabama
1983 – Columbus, Ohio
1985 – Wichita, Kansas
1987 – Miami, Florida
1989 – Fort Worth, Texas
1991 – Piliadelpina, Pennsylvania
1993 – Buffalo, New York
1995 – Wichita, Kansas
1997 –
1999 – St. Louis, Missouri

NATIONAL BOARD MEETINGS
(This list does not include Board Meetings held at Biennial Conventions)
* Denotes Executive Committee Meetings

October 17-18, 1898	St. Louis, MO
1900-1913	Places and dates missing
October 30-31, 1913	Elmhurst, IL
November 22, 1914	Chicago, IL
July 9, 1915	Chicago, IL
November 18-26, 1915	Chicago, IL
December 4-7, 1917	Stan Hywet Hall, Akron, OH
December 3-7, 1918	Chicago, IL
October 25-31, 1919	Stan Hywet Hall, Akron, OH
May 27-31, 1920	New York, NY
* July 6, 1920	New York, NY
* September 2-3, 1920	New York, NY
*September 26-27, 1920	New York, NY
November 10-16, 1920	Stan Hywet Hall, Akron, OH
* January 22, 1921	New York, NY
* February 5, 1921	New York, NY
November 7-11, 1921	St. Louis, MO
March 25-28, 1922	Nashville, TN
November 14-17, 1922	Philadelphia, PA
November 15-18, 1923	New York, NY
November 17-21, 1924	Pittsburg, PA
September 26-27, 1925	Stan Hywet Hall, Akron, OH
November 17-21, 1925	Philadelphia, PA
1926	Memphis, TN
December 4-12, 1927	New York, NY
August 26-30, 1928	Keystone Heights, FL
November 18-20, 1929	Milwaukee, WI
April 6-11, 1930	Charleston, SC
October 25-31, 1931	Hot Springs, AR
May 9-15, 1932	Washington, DC
October 16-21, 1932	New Orleans, LA
October 22-26, 1933	St. Louis, MO
September 6-9, 1934	Chicago, IL
September 10-13, 1935	Denver, CO
October 15-18, 1936	Dallas, TX
September 8-11, 1937	Lookout Mountain, Chattanooga, TN
September 6-10, 1938	Chicago, IL
October 4-7, 1939	Salt Lake City, UT
September 11-14, 1940	Milwaukee, WI
September 10-13, 1941	Cincinnati, OH
August 30-September 3, 1942	Providence, RI
September 16-19, 1943	Minneapolis, MN
September 11-14, 1944	Tulsa, OK
1945	World War II – only regional meetings
April 7-11, 1946	Atlanta, GA
September 19-22, 1947	Des Moines, IA
September 7-10, 1948	Chicago, IL
September 25-29, 1950	Raleigh, NC
September 16-19, 1951	Hot Springs, AR
September 14-17, 1952	Duluth, MN
August 19-23, 1953	Evanston, IL
July 8-12, 1954	Denver, CO
September 19-23, 1955	Odessa, TX
August 23-26, 1956	Chicago, IL
August 21-26, 1957	Albuquerque, NM
September 7-12, 1958	Green Lake, WI
August 5-9, 1959	Interlochen, MI
August 27-31, 1960	Louisville, KY
August 18-23, 1961	Asheville, NC
September 11-14, 1962	Boise, ID
September 6-9, 1963	Washington, DC
August 28-30, 1964	Oklahoma City, OK
August 27-30, 1965	Memphis, TN
August 26-29, 1966	Minneapolis, MN
August 24-28, 1967	St. Louis, MO
August 22-27, 1968	Cleveland, OH
August 22-25, 1969	Charlotte, NC
August 19-23, 1970	Detroit, MI
August 28-31, 1971	Cheyenne, WY
August 12-15, 1972	Hot Springs, AR
August 16-20, 1973	Green Bay, WI
August 21-26, 1974	Fargo, ND
August 14-18, 1975	Los Angeles, CA
August 25-30, 1976	San Antonio, TX
August 24-29, 1977	Denver, CO
August 4-7, 1978	Indianapolis, IN
August 8-13, 1979	Charleston, SC
August 20-25, 1980	Sun Valley, ID
August 19-24, 1981	Providence, RI
August 18-23, 1982	Baltimore, MD
August 10-15, 1983	Grand Rapids, MI
August 15-20, 1984	Lexington, KY
August 14-19, 1985	Indianapolis, IN
August 20-25, 1986	Williamsburg, VA
August 11-17, 1987	Long Beach, CA
August 17-22, 1988	Oklahoma City, OK
August 9-15, 1989	Minneapolis, MN
August 8-14, 1990	Albuquerque, NM
August 14-20, 1991	Greensboro, NC
August 7-10, 1992	Cheyenne, WY
August 20-23, 1993	Indianapolis, IN
August 9-16, 1994	Jackson, MS
August 23-29, 1995	Hilton Head, SC

CITATIONS
1949-1995

NFMC CITATIONS:

1949 – Standard Oil Company of California
1950 – The Philharmonic Orchestra, New York
 Wanda Landowsky, New York
1951 – The Texas Company
1953 – Opera Workshop of Indiana University
 National Broadcasting Company,
 Chicago
1955 – Johnny Green, Metro-Goldwyn Mayer
 Thor Johnson
1957 – Firestone Tire and Rubber Company
 Dr. Rudolph Ganz
 Dr. Joseph E. Maddy
 Robert Whitney
1959 – Boris Goldovsky
 Julius Rudel
 Van Cliburn
 Julia Fuqua Ober
1961 – Leonard Bernstein
 The Orchestra of America, Richard
 Korn, Musical Director
 Mme. Rosina Lhevinne
 Dr. Kermit Hunter and Dr. Jack
 Kilpatrick
 Meredith Willson
 Mr. and Mrs. Henry Drinker
1963 – Marjorie Merriweather Post May
 Isaac Stern
 Pablo Casals
 Eugene Ormandy
 WGN Radio and Television, Chicago
 Columbia Broadcasting System,
 New York
1965 – The Ford Foundation, Henry T. Heald,
 President
 The University of Texas, Dr. Henry
 Ranson, Chancellor
 Dr. Bertha Foster, Founder, Musicians
 Club of America
 Dr. Erich Leinsdorf, Boston Symphony
 Orchestra
1967 – American Society of Composers,
 Authors and Publishers (ASCAP)
 Dr. John Jacob Niles
 Dr. William Schuman
 Dr. Leopold Stokowski
1969 – American Symphony Orchestra League
 American Airlines ("Music Till Dawn")
 American Telephone and Telegraph Co.
 ("Bell Telephone Hour")
1971 – Irving Berlin
 Fred Waring
 Milton Cross
 Nancy Hanks

1973 – Marjorie Lawrence
 Rosa Ponselle
 Gunnar Johansen
1975 – Nelson A. Rockefeller
 William Steinberg
 Robert Shaw
1977 – Maurice Abravanel
 Sarah Caldwell
 Exxon
1979 – Public Broadcasting Service
 Beverly Sills
 Rosalyn Tureck
1981 – Community Concert, Inc.
 Margaret Hillis
1983 – Carlisle Floyd
 Paul Creston
 Dorothy Delay
 Vincent Persichetti
1985 – Dave Brubeck
 John De Lancie
1987 – Marta Istomin
 Josef Gingold
1989 – Martina Arroyo
 Diane Bish
 Joseph Silverstein
1991 – Carlos Dupré Moseley
 Catherine Comet
 Barry Shelley Brook
1993 – Dr. Paul Lehman, School of Music,
 University of Michigan
 Dr. Karl Husa, 1969 Pulitzer Prize
 winner, Music
 Dr. Eunice Boardman, Professor, Music
 Education, University of Illinois,
1995 – Dr. Karl Hass
 Joan Peyser

NFMC PRESIDENTIAL CITATIONS:

1950 – Philip Maxwell, Founder, Chicago Music
 Festival
1951 – The Salt Lake City Tabernacle Choir
1955 – Otto Harbach, retiring President, ASCAP
 James Fassett, NY Philharmonic
 Symphony Broadcast, Commentator
 Ted Scott, WNBC, New York
 Archdale Jones, WBAL, Baltimore
1955 – WNCY, New York
 American Airlines
 James Christian Pfohl, Brevard Music
 Center
 Florida Symphony Orchestra
 Dr. Sigmund Spaeth

1957 – John Tasker Howard
A. J. Fletcher
Dr. Howard Hanson
"Woolworth Hour"
1959 – Pierre Monteux
Dr. Guy Fraser Harrison
Dr. E. Thayer Gaston
Southwest Symposium of Contemporary Music
1961 – Ray Green
Edwin Hughes
Stanley Adams, President, ASCAP
1963 – Charles Tremaine
Louis Sudler
Herman Neuman
Dr. Benjamin Swalin
1965 – Dr. Ted Shawn, University of Dance, Jacob Pillow, MA
Dr. Henry Robert, Founder, Inspiration Point Fine Arts Colony, AR
Dr. Arturo de Filippi, Miami Opera Company
1967 – Dr. Hazel Post Gillette
Mr. Thomas Schippers
Sigma Alpha Iota
1969 – Dr. Janet Schenck
Dr. Jan Philip Schinhan
Dr. Grace H. Spofford
Broadcast Music Incorporated
1971 – Archie Jones
Dr. Henry Janiec
Harold Boxer
Leonard Feist, National Music Publishers, Inc.
Elsie Sweeney
1973 – Lynn Rohrbrough and Katherine Rohrbrough (Given posthumously)
1975 – Lily Peter
Alice Tully
F. Warren O'Reilly
Albert Schweitzer (Given posthumously)
1977 – Isaac van Grove
Dr. George C. Wilson
Prof. Howard Shanet
Antonia Brico
1979 – Robert Sherman
James Dick
Lawrence Welk

1981 – Glad Robinson Youse
Florence Golson Bateman
Dr. Roger Jacobi
1983 – Van Cliburn
Delta Omicron International Music Fraternity
1985 – Martin Bookspan
John S. Edwards (Given posthumously)
1987 – Morton Gould
John La Montaine
Stanley F. Nosal
Carleen Maley Hutchins
Wiley L. Housewright
1989 – Rildia Bee O'Bryan Cliburn
Martin E. Segal
Mu Phi Epsilon Music Fraternity
1991 – Ezra Laderman
Robert Page
1993 – Dr. Merton Utgaard, Founder, International Music Camp at Peace Gardens
Founders for the National Coalition for Music Education:
Music Education, National Conference
National Association of Music Werchants
National Academy of Recording Arts and Sciences
1995 – Texaco

SPECIAL CITATIONS TO PAST PRESIDENTS:
1961 – Agnes Bishop Jardine
Marie Morrisey Keith
Ada Holding Miller
Vera Wardner Dougan
1963 – Dorothy Dann Bullock
1967 – Dr. Irene Steed Muir
1971 – Mrs. Maurice Honigman
1979 – Dr. Merle Montgomery
Mrs. Frank A. Vought
1983 – Mrs. Jack C. Ward
1987 – Mrs. Dwight D. Robinson
1991 – Mrs. Glenn L. Brown
1995 – Mrs. D. Clifford Allison

JUNIOR AND JUVENILE PLEDGES
JUNIOR COLLECT
JUNIOR HYMN

The Pledge

I ACKNOWLEDGE my indebtedness to good music; I know that the music of a nation inspires or degrades; I realize that acquaintance with great music instills a love of that which brings courage and lofty ideals and tends toward clean, noble living; I promise to do all in my power to make America truly musical.

The Hymn

LORD OF ALL LIFE, our God and King,
Hear Thou the hymn thy children sing,
Alleluia, Alleluia!
Rich in our heritage we stand,
Forward we press at thy command,
Alleluia, Alleluia!

WE WOULD seek beauty, search for truth,
Inspired by Thee through all our youth,
Alleluia!
Bless Thou our effort, guide our will,
Thy love our inspiration still.
Alleluia!

BIRD, TREE, and flower acknowledge
Thee,
We learn from them Thy melody,
Alleluia!
From Thee all harmony derives,
Thine be the power that guides our lives,
Alleluia!

WITH STEADY singleness of heart
May we discern the better part,
Alleluia!
Thy presence near will keep us strong,
Praise, glory, love, to Thee belong,
Alleluia!

The Collect

WE THANK Thee, our Father,
For all things beautiful.

OPEN OUR minds to the beauty
That is music
And teach us to remember it
As part of Thy great goodness
To us.

HELP US to grow each day
Unto the stature of Thy grace
And keep our hearts so tuned
With Thy heart
That our lives may re-sound
Thy very music
In the melody of lovely living
And in service that is song.

Juvenile Pledge

I KNOW that by learning
To make beautiful Music
I am helping to make
America TRULY MUSICAL.

I PROMISE with all my heart
To give beautiful Music
To my country.

BIBLIOGRAPHY

The Artistic Guide to Chicago and the World's Columbian Exposition, 1982, Columbian Art Company, R. S. Peale Company, Chicago, Illinois.

Schepps' World's Fair Photographed, 1893, James W. Shepp and Daniel B. Shepp, Globe Bible Publishing Company, Chicago, Illinois.

Historical Fine Art Series, 1894, H. S. Smith and C. R. Gresham, Historical Publishing Company, Philadelphia, Pennsylvania.

Portfolio of World's Columbian Exposition, 1893, C. Graham, The Winters Art Lithographing Company, Chicago, Illinois.

Etude Magazines, 1898 and 1922, James Francis Cooke, editor, Theodore Presser Publishing Company, Philadelphia, Pennsylvania.

Archives of the National Federation of Music Clubs in the Library of Congress, Washington, D.C. and the Headquarters Office, Indianapolis, Indiana, including: old letters; Federation minutes of official meetings; convention programs; Books of Proceedings; official magazines – *The Musical Monitor, Official Bulletin, Music Clubs Magazine, Showcase, Junior Bulletin, Junior Keynotes*; old newspaper clippings – *NewYork Tribune, Chicago Tribune, Chicago Record Herald*; constitutions and bylaws; and miscellaneous notes and records.

INDEX

360

A Beacon in the Darkness 170
A Memorial Sing 152
A Musical Ritual 116-118, 154, 202, 204
Abbott, Mae Ruth 12
Abbott, Mrs. Frederick W. 267
Abild, John and Fay 181
Adams, Mr. and Mrs. Stanley 149
Adams, Mrs. Crosby 98, 124, 130
Adams, Stanley 149, 163, 217, 324, 333, 346
Adult Non-Professional Composers' Contest 170, 213
Aeolian Foundation 319
After Dinner Opera Company 137
Agnes Jardine Scholarship 171
Alden, John and Priscilla 280
Alexander, Mrs. Hadden 65, 73
Alexander, Mrs. J. A. 150
Allen, Barbara 140, 141
Allison, Mrs. D. Clifford 220, 329, 345
Alpha Corinne Mayfield Opera Award 150
Amateur Musical Club
    Chicago, Illinois 26, 44, 53, 57-59, 68, 81, 92
    Ottawa, Illinois 28
America the Beautiful 152, 268-270
America United 170
American Composers 70, 132-134, 136, 138, 152, 166, 205, 216, 217, 275, 325
American Composer's Contest 319
American Music 6, 31, 60, 74, 86, 92, 94, 132-136, 138, 141-143, 150, 166, 168, 171, 172, 181, 195, 199, 200, 206, 210, 212, 214, 215, 240, 323, 332-335
American Music Conference 211, 312
American Music Department 86, 133, 135, 139, 145, 199
American Music Festival Chorus 154
American Music Month 135
American National Orchestra 134
American Opera Association 145
American Revolution Bicentennial Administration 324
American Society of Composers, Authors and Publishers 110, 137, 138, 146, 149, 151, 163, 167, 210, 212, 214, 324, 333, 337, 346
American Symphony Orchestra League 279
Americans All 170
Ames, Amyas 333
Andelin, Julie Dawn 12
Anderson, Marian 88

Anderson, Wallace G. 170
Andrews, George 226
Angell, Mary 59
Anne M. Gannett Award for Veterans 171, 264, 333
Anne M. Gannett Fund 263
Apollo Club, Chicago, Illinois 153
Armed Forces Song Folio 136
Armour, Mrs. J. Ogden 188
Army-NFMC Parade Composers Contest 137
Artists Foreign Goodwill Tours 177, 242
Audio-Visual 249, 251

B Sharp Club 130
Badge 73
Bailey, Albert R. 228
Baker, George P. 101
Baltimore Charter Party 331
Bands and Orchestras 158, 159, 161
Baring, Maurice 148, 185
Barthelson, Joyce 146, 148, 185
Bates, Katherine Lee 268-270
Battle, Kathleen 174
Beecher, Henry Ward 273, 280
Beethoven Club
    Memphis, Tennessee 76, 85, 96, 196
    Moline, Illinois 28
Benedict, Jane 223
Benzinger, Mrs. Paul 256
Benzinger, Paul W. 216
Bergman, Marilyn 163
Berkshire Music Center 155, 210, 213, 272-274, 276, 277
Bethlehem, New Hampshire 32, 37
Bicentennial Parade of American Music 215, 216, 315, 324, 325
Biennial Competition 86, 133, 181
Birmingham, Lillian 267
Bish, Diane 332
Bishop, Genevra Johnstone 53
Bitkner, Arthur J. 173
Black, Dr. Frank 169
Blackwell, Martha Ann 11, 191, 283
Blair, Mrs. James L. 59, 74, 78
Blanchard, F. W. 145
Blankenship, Mrs. 261
Bless Us O God 125
Blitzstein, Marc 150, 151
Bloomfield-Zeisler, Fanny 54, 83
Boeke, Michael W. 287
Boggs, Mrs. Russell 261

Bolz, Harriett 170
Bond, Carrie Jacobs 108, 143, 260
Bond, Elizabeth 33
Bond, Victoria 148
Borowski, Felix 269, 270
Boston Symphony Orchestra 272, 276, 344
Bousfield, Neal 238
Bradley, Ruth 120, 237
Branscombe, Gena 106, 120
Brennan, J. F. 161
Brevard Music Center 10, 149, 191
Bridge, Dr. Norman 102
Broadcast Music Incorporated 157, 213, 224, 333
Broido, Arnold 11
Bronson, Lt. Colonel Howard 169
Brooks, Miss Marie 52
Brosseau, Mrs. Alfred J. 269
Brown, Mrs. Glenn L. 11, 146, 172, 181, 219, 243, 266, 287, 345
Brown, Dr. Guy Story 243
Brown, Melvin 333
Brown, Suzanna 12
Browning, John 173
Brunswick Choral Society 154, 246
Brush, Mrs. Emerson H. 86, 108, 133, 260
Bryan, Josephine 154
Bryant, Barbara 284, 286
Buchanan, Annabel Morris 139, 140, 142, 184, 205
Bullock, Mrs. C. Arthur 111, 119, 136, 147, 150, 171, 185, 188, 212, 229, 278, 316, 319, 323, 327, 339, 345
Bundles for Britain 208, 230
Burnham, Daniel H. 22
Burrell, Mrs. Gilbert 190
Burritt, Mrs. Nelson 59

Cadman, Charles Wakefield 106, 134, 190, 254, 335
Cale, Mrs. Charles Allen 48, 71
Cambridge, Massachusetts 12, 31-34, 344
Campbell, Congressman Carroll A. 328, 329
Campbell, Mrs. David Allen 65, 70, 74, 86, 88, 116, 126, 127, 133, 335
Carpenter, Mrs. George H. 53, 72, 74
Carron, Arthur 230, 231
Carty, Sergeant William, A.A.F. 170
Centennial Exposition 280
Central of Georgia Railroad 159, 160
Central Prison for Men, Raleigh, NC 161
Certificate of Incorporation 71, 84, 197, 203,

336
Chadwick, George 134
Chanticleer 146
Charter 10, 56, 71, 76, 126, 203, 217, 282, 317, 327-331, 336
Chase, Mrs. John McClure 186, 190, 263
Chasins, Abram 148
Chautauqua Music Institute / New York 186, 189-191, 208, 210, 217, 226, 227
Chicago Symphony Orchestra 30, 35, 94, 133, 154, 158, 282, 344
Chicago Tribune 31, 63, 67, 94
Chicagoland Music Festival 209, 322
Child of Promise 147
Children's Crusade 99, 104, 204
Choral Music 152
Church Music Bulletin 128, 204
Cibber, Colley 149
Citations 209, 212, 322
Clara Schumann Club 77
Clark, Dr. Frances Elliott 29-31, 90, 97, 127, 166, 261, 336
Clark, Mrs. John M. 54
Clark, Tim 105
Claudette Sorel Piano Award 175
Cleveland, President Grover 23, 38, 64
Cliburn, Rildia Bee O'Bryan, 13
Cliburn, Van 13, 173, 176, 181, 333
Club Rating 156, 336
Cochran, Mrs. 261
Cochran, Senator Thad 328, 329
Cole, Mrs. Thomas Jefferson 98, 116-119, 154, 202
Cole, Mrs. Jirah 59
Collins, Mrs. Winifred B. 84, 197, 334
Columbus, Christopher 22, 24
Columbus Quadriga 24
Commissions 158, 159, 182, 184, 215
Community Chorus, Beloit, Wisconsin 153
Compact of Loyalty 335
Competitive Festivals 97, 207
Composer's Studio 213, 272, 276, 277
Concert Goer 126
Confucius 26
Congressional Charter 10, 211, 217, 282, 327-329, 331
Converse, Frederick S. 269
Conway, Olive F. 98, 119
Cooke, James Francis 18, 336
Coolidge, Mrs. F. S. 53
Coolidge, Mrs. Frank A. 188
Coolidge, President Calvin 311

Cooper, Mrs. A. Deane 73
Cooperstock, Andrew 181
Copland, Aaron 99, 100
Coult, Mrs. Abel A. 268
Course of Study Program 97, 196, 202, 334
Cowan, Robert 181, 185
Cram, Mrs. Ambrose L. 189
Creston, Paul 185, 210, 217
Cribb, Dixie 12
Cribb, Kenneth, Jr. 12, 330
Criz, Henry 333
Crowell, Grace Noll 125
Crusade for Strings 155, 156, 158, 211, 213
Cunningham, Paul 163
Curran, Mrs. John F. 73
Cushamm, Ralph Spaulding 125

D/Angelo Bergh School of Singing 83, 172
Daisy 149
Damrosch, Dr. Frank 269, 284
Damrosch, Dr. Walter 152, 204, 284, 311
Dana, Edith Longfellow 32, 33
Dana, Henry Wadsworth Longfellow 274
Dance 223, 224, 332, 334
Dance Department 213, 223
Daniel, Oliver 224, 333
Daniels, Mabel 120, 184
Darracott, Virginia 12
David, Hal 163
Davis, Agnes 173
Davis, Lulu Emerson 15
Davis, Professor I. C. 160
Day is Dying in the West 226
De Cuéllar, Javier Pérez 321
De Liquerica, Don Jose 319
Dean, Floride Smith 181
Dean, Professor W. C. 160
Dearing, SPC James C. 137
Dedication of the Eden-Talbott House 282
Defense Committee 230, 231, 233
Department of Finance 202
Devora Nadwomey Award 110, 178
Dewey, Thomas E. 180
Diamond Jubilee / Convention 183, 215, 310, 332, 333
Dickinson, Emily 345
Dingus, Mrs. Leonidas R. 104
Disney, Walt 254, 255
Dock Street Theatre 149
Dole, Senator Robert A. 328
Donald Voorhees Contest 109, 173, 236
Donnelly, Anastasia M. 283, 284

Donnelly, C. C. 283, 284
Dorothy Dann Bullock Music Therapy Award 171
Dorr, Mrs. Russell Ripley 40-43, 46-48, 51-53, 56-58, 62, 63, 65, 66, 68-70, 81, 84-86, 90-92, 127, 198, 199
Dougan, Mrs. Ronald Arthur 136, 150, 155-159, 171, 173, 175, 176, 185, 209, 211, 229, 252, 276, 278, 310, 312, 316
Douglas, Ada B. 65, 71
Dow Chemical Company 246
Dowling, Richard 181
Duchin, Eddy 231
Duncan, Ligon 11
Duncan, Mel 11
Duncan, Shirley 11
Dungan, Olive 120
Dunham, Franklin 314
Duo Piano Competition 181
Dusenberry, Mrs. 141

Eagle Awards Luncheon 316
Eakin, Vera 120
Eastman Philharmonia 159, 182
Eastman School of Music 159, 173, 215, 338
Eddy, Clarence 23
Eddy, Mrs. Clarence 54
Eden, Charleton 280
Eden-Talbott House / Mansion 99, 129, 214, 216, 217, 278-280, 282-285, 287
Edison, Thomas A. 336
Editorial Board 129
Edwards, George 102
Edwards, John S. 279, 282
Edwin B. Ellis Award 175
Effron, David 159, 182
Eisenhower, General / President Dwight D. 211, 239, 317
Ekwurzel, Mrs. Lars 224
Eleanor Pascoe Scholarship 190
Ellis, Mrs. Edwin B. 181, 217, 219, 260
Ellis Competition for Duo Pianists 171, 181, 217
Ellison, Mrs. Thomas E. 65, 80, 81
Emblem 74, 114, 115, 122, 195, 266
Endowment Fund 107, 199, 201, 202, 260-262
Erb, Dr. John Warren 154, 207, 231, 337
Erb, Lawerence 42, 90
Ervin, Senator Sam J., Jr. 328
Etude Magazine 11, 18, 30, 47, 71, 93, 336

Evans, Etelka 96, 105-107
Evans, Phyllis H. 190
Evans, Wilbur W. 173
Extension of NFMC 70, 108, 197, 200, 203, 263
Exxon Corporation 315
Ezell, Bill and Loretta 12

Fairhaven, Massachusetts 32, 37
Fairyland 145, 146, 199
Fantasia 254, 255
Farnum, D. G. 160
Farr, Naomi 176
Farwell, Arthur 86, 133
Fattic, Leonard 284, 286
Fay, Amy 32, 40, 41, 46, 63
Fay and John Abild Award 181
Fay, Charles Norman 31, 33-35, 37, 344
Fay, Charlotte Emily Hopkins 31
Fay, Judge S. P. P. 32
Fay, Lily 31, 32
Fay, Reverend Dr. Charles 31, 32
Federation Banner 122
Federation Collect 84, 116-119, 154, 202
Federation Hymn 123, 124, 204
Federation Insignia 83, 114, 115, 145, 174, 207
Feist, Leonard 316, 333
Felsengarten 32, 33, 37
Fennimore, Joseph 177, 213, 333
Ferrell, Ernestine 154
Festival of the Air 208, 250
Finance 187, 201, 206, 209, 260, 261, 263, 265
Finance Department 206, 261, 263
Firestone, Harvey S., Jr. 176
Firestone Tire and Rubber Company 176
First Headquarters Office 278
First Mail Ballot 86, 198
Fisher, Gladys Washburn 120
Fisher, Mrs. William Arms 267-269
Fleming, Victor 254
Fletcher, A. J. 146, 147
Flora or Hob in the Well 149
Floride Smith Dean Award 181
Folk Music 139-142, 183, 184, 206, 252
Folk Music Archives 139
Folk Songs 81, 109, 132, 133, 139
Fortnightly Musical Club 81-83, 88, 196, 197, 335
Foss, Lucas 159, 185
Foster, Lawrence 333

Foster, Stephen 171, 242, 312, 337
Foundation for the Advancement of the Musical Arts 208, 263, 264, 276
Founders' Day 261, 262
Fowler, Agnes 111, 216, 260, 265
Franko, Sam 84
Freehoff, Ruth 149
Freeman, Mrs. Robert E. L., Jr. 11, 110, 170, 282, 329
Frey, Maude 84
From a Log Cabin 105
Fuller, Mrs. Alvin T. 269
Fund for the Advancement of the Musical Arts 264

Gabrilowitsch, Ossip 176
Gallico, Paolio 144
Gallur, D. G. 161
Gannett, Mrs. Guy Patterson 114, 155, 169, 171, 177, 189, 208, 229, 230, 237-240, 243, 250, 251, 263, 264, 272, 273, 275, 278, 315, 317, 333
Ganz, Rudolph 254
Garwood, Margaret 148, 185
Genee, Edith Hope 125
General Federation of Women's Clubs 85, 151, 269
Georgia Shop Band 159
Gibby, Desta 12
Giese, Jeanne C. 12
Giesick, Carol 12
Gignilliant, Peggy Thomson 156
Gilbert, Ella Lord 189
Gillette, Dr. Hazel Post 170, 242
Gilmore, Patrick Sarsfield 283, 284
Glad Robinson Youse Adult Composers' Award 170
Glazier, Richard 180
Glenn, Carroll 232, 250
Glick, David 333
Gloyd, Marjorie 12
God of Our Fathers 226
Gold Trophy Cup Plan 97
Goldmark, Rubin 144
Gone With the Wind 253
Gould, Miss Helen 52
Gould, Morton 110, 163
Gould, Mrs. George 52
Governors Island Prison 161
Grainger, Percy 88, 98
Gramm, Donald 173
Grand Central Palace Hotel 40, 42

Grass Roots Opera 146, 147, 209
Graves, Mrs. Bibb 269
Green, Ray 212, 237, 319
Greene, President (of MTNA) 51
Greenspan, Gerri 12
Gronert, Hazel Dessery 120
Gross, Dr. Bethuel 144, 185
Grothe, Mrs. Martin E. 155
Grumman Aircraft Engineering Corporation 245
Grunsfeld, Mrs. 261
Gustlin, Clarence 339

Hadley, Henry 133, 134, 158, 169, 200
Hahn, Mrs. Alfred 106
Hail, Mary Kimball 175, 242
Hall, Mrs. William John 97
Hall, Paul 11
Hamilton, Anna Heurermann 96-98, 204
Hamilton, Iain 333
Hammarskjold, Dag 321
Hammood, Dr. Emily 147
Hands Across the Seas 317-319
Hanson, Dr. Howard 188, 254, 323, 338
Hanson, Phyllis Lations 97
Harbach, Otto 163, 337
Hardt, Mrs. J. W. 65
Harmonica Bands 98
Harmonica Department 97
Harmony Club
    Dothan, Alabama 153
    Fort Worth, Texas 336
Harris, Billy and Mary 12
Harrison, Mrs. Milton 88
Harshaw, Margaret 178
Hartley, Mrs. Roland H. 269
Hawthorne, Manning 274
Hawthorne, Nathaniel 208, 272-276
Headquarters Building Fund 125, 262
Headquarters Endowment 217, 262
Headquarters Maintenance Fund 262
Heagy, Ruth 144
Hecht and Shapiro 181
Heininger, Mary 265, 324, 329
Herbert, Victor 83, 110, 144, 242, 284, 333
Herbruck, Mrs. R. A. 106
Heyward, DuBose 140
Higginson, Marcia 269
Hill, Barre 147
Hill, Benjamin 18
Hill, Mrs. Napoleon 65, 70, 77
Hill, Robert 145

Hillcrest 100, 101
Hinckle, Mrs. 88, 261
Hinda Honigman Scholarship for the Blind 111, 171, 257
Hobart, Dr. Henry 150
Hoffman, Mrs. John A. 106
Hollywood Bowl 172, 254
Holmes, Mr. and Mrs. John D. 162
Holmes, Oliver Wendell 150, 273
Holsinger, SPC David R. 137
Honigman, Mrs. Maurice 111, 137, 171, 191, 192, 214, 256, 257, 279-281, 283, 287, 328, 329
Hooper, Brian 145
Hooper, Elinore A. 190
Hopkins, Reverend John Henry 31
Hopkins, Rt. Reverend John Henry 31
Hosmer, Reverend F. L. 78
House of Seven Gables 273
Howard, John E. 109
Howard, John Tasker 35, 139, 166
Howe, Irma 242
Howe, Mary 120, 243
Hudson, James 12
Hughes, Edwin 314-316, 322, 323
Hume, Paul 182, 324
Humphreville, Mrs. Robert 284
Humphrey, Doris Allbee 97
Hunkins, Eusebia Simpson 120, 147, 148, 316, 324
Hurley, Marie 327, 328, 331
Hurok, Sol 333
Hyde, Reverend Nathaniel 280
Hymn of the Month 209, 212, 228, 229, 263

I Would be True 227
Iler, Charles 139
Ince, Mrs. Joe 329
Incorporation in Illinois 282
Inspiration Point Fine Arts Colony 150, 172
Insull, Samuel 188
Interlochen Center for the Arts 147, 186-189, 191, 210, 323
Internal Revenue Service 265
International Music Relations 196, 208, 240-242, 244
International Music Relations Library 242
Irene Steed Muir Scholarship 171
Irish, Dr. Barbara 221, 345
Iturbi, José 158, 178, 230
Ives, Burl 142

J. A. Jones Construction Company 245
Jackson, Doris L. 170
Jackson Park 22, 23, 26
Jacobus, Dale Asher 120
James, Carolyne 333
James, Edith Fitzpatrick 139
James H. Rogers Prize 174
Janiec, Dr. Henry 149
Jardine, Mrs. John Alexander 3, 108, 109, 118, 140, 171, 206, 315, 316
John F. Kennedy Center for the Performing Arts 147, 212, 215, 216, 248, 315, 324-326
Johnson, Gwen 11
Johnson, President Lyndon B. 121
Johnson, Dr. Thor 156, 217
Johnston, Eva 12
Jones, Mrs. Conway, Jr. 115
Jones, Mrs. Conway, Sr. 115
Josefly, Rafael 84
Judd, George 272
Julliard School of Music 155, 178, 277
Junior Bulletin 97, 98, 128, 130, 204, 207
Junior Collect 98, 119, 356
Junior Division 76, 96-99, 101, 104, 106, 108, 117-119, 171, 204, 207, 214, 218, 224, 256, 283
Junior Festivals 97, 213
Junior Hymn 98, 207, 356
Junior Keynotes 128, 130, 210
Junior League of Indianapolis 279, 281
Junior Pledge 98, 205

Kahn, Otto 311
Kaiser, Carl 140
Kate Chase Scholarships 190
Kauffman, Aaron 280
Keith, Mrs. Royden James 30, 110, 111, 163, 171, 209, 210, 227-229, 233, 263, 273, 278, 317, 322, 332
Keller, Edith 254
Kelly, Stillman 11, 144
Kelsey, Mrs. Charles B. 29, 83, 84, 114, 200, 226
Kent, Atwater 172, 173
Kern, Mildred E. 12
Kettering, Jane 332
Kettering, Jeri 223
Kindler, Hans 178
King, Lori J. 11
Kinney 84-86, 133, 198, 199
Kirby, Paul 170

Kneisel Quartet 81
Knerr, Mrs. Walter 108
Knox, Mrs. Warren 190
Koons, Mrs. H. H. 161
Koons, Walter E. 251
Korn, Clara A. 58, 59, 63-65, 67, 80
Koussevitzky, Dr. Serge 155, 213, 272, 274, 276, 277
Koussevitzky, Olga 276, 277, 333
Kramer, Walter A. 120, 183, 184
Krehbiel, Henry E. 41-43, 74, 81, 132, 195
Kreisler, Fritz 177
Krueger, Dr. Karl 184
Kruger, Paul 158

La Montaine, John 159, 182-184, 217, 333
Ladies Matinee Musicale 15
Ladies Musical Club 81
Ladies Musical Society 28
Lake Michigan 22, 24, 25
Lakes, Gary 174, 331
Lancaster, Mrs. Reid 108
Lancaster Musical Art Society 284
LaPrade, Ernest 169
Laurent, David 264
Lavalle, Paul 173
Lawley, Cooper 180
Lax, Fred 283
Leinsdorf, Eric 276
Lenchner, Paula 189
Leverett, Mrs. John 73, 74, 81, 114, 115, 260
Lewis, Dr. Merrills 110
Lhevinne, Josef and Rosina 231
Library of Congress 11, 18, 71, 126, 139, 145-147, 169, 315, 330
Life Members 201, 261, 263
Lily Peter String Award 175
Lincoln, President Abraham 237
Lind, Jenny 34
Lipton, Martha 176, 179
List, Eugene 137, 232
Little Red House 155, 208, 209, 272, 273-275
Lockwood, Margaret 106, 107
Longfellow, Henry Wadsworth 27, 273, 275, 280
Los Angeles Rose Bowl 33
Low, Juliette Gordon 149
Lowell, James Russell 273
Lucile Parrish Ward Award for American Music Performance 171

Lucile Parrish Ward Chair in Opera 10, 192
Luening, Dr. Otto 325
Lutkin, Dean Peter Christian 123, 124, 204, 269
Lyons, Mrs. John F. 127, 203, 311, 312, 332, 336
Lyric Dance Drama 223

Mabee, Grace Widney 128, 226
MacArthur, Pauline Arnoux 88, 143, 144
MacDowell, Edward 41, 74, 99-106, 175, 195, 201, 206, 212, 335
MacDowell Colony 99-101, 105, 106, 201, 202, 206, 276
MacDowell Festival 104
MacDowell Junior Fellowship Fund 104, 105, 206, 207
MacDowell League 101, 104, 201
MacDowell, Marian 100-105, 204
Mackey, C. D. 148, 185
Maddy, Dr. Joseph E. 186-188, 191, 249, 323
Magney, Ruth Taylor 120
Marie Morrisey Keith Scholarship 171
Marshall, General George 234
Mary Prudie Brown Award 172
Mathew, Gladys 147
Mathews, W. S. B. 72
Mathis, James 173, 176
Maxwell, Philip F. 209, 322
Mayfield, Alpha Corinne 12
McAteer, Miss 261
McCartney, Mrs. George 84
McCollin, Frances 120
McCrae, John Richards 149
McGehee, Thomasine 139
McHaney, Mrs. Hal H. 280
McNabb, Marian 147, 148
Meares, Stephen D. 281
Mehan, Myrt 12
Melton, James 88
Memoirs of Rose Fay Thomas 31
Memoirs of Theodore Thomas 37
Memorial and Recognition Fund 261
Mennin, Peter 158, 185, 211
Menuhin, Yehudi 316
Merle Montgomery Opera Award 171
Merrill, Robert 170
Merriman, Nan 170, 177
Metropolitan Opera Company 150, 151, 178, 210, 223, 231, 311, 332
Midgley, Pat 11
Midnight Frolic 269

Milam, Dr. Lena 156
Millard, Mrs. William B. 219, 329
Miller, Mrs. Ada Holding 120, 135, 156, 171, 185, 188-190, 210, 231, 234, 235, 240-242, 252, 256, 261, 263, 276, 338
Miller, Christine 102, 175
Miller, Lillian Anne 120
Mills, Mrs. Helen Harrison 46, 47, 92, 117, 128
Moffett, Congressman Toby 329
Mollineur 144
Montgomery, Dr. Merle 37, 120, 148, 149, 171, 175, 183-186, 215-218, 276, 279, 280, 315, 316, 321, 324, 325, 332
Moody Hospital Saxophone Players 160
Moon, F. Edson 102
Moore, Dale 175
Moore, Mrs. Philip N. 59, 65, 73, 81, 126
Mosely, Carlos 232
Motion Pictures 253, 254
Mount Auburn Cemetery 12, 344
Mount Theodore Thomas 32, 37
Mozart Club 81
Muir, Mrs. Clifton J. 105, 111, 136, 170, 171, 213-216, 223, 248, 262, 278, 338
Muller, Robert 321
Music Clubs Magazine 12, 117, 128, 129, 167, 205, 206, 212, 213, 253, 285
Music Educators National Conference 151, 314, 328
Music for the Blind 172, 210, 256
Music Hall 24, 25, 28
Music in Hospitals 208, 237, 238, 252
Music in Industry 154, 245, 246
Music in Prisons 161
Music Mansion 242, 243
Music Teachers National Association 39-42, 51, 53, 58, 61, 198, 314
Music Through the Night 252
Musical Festival Marathon 332
Musical Moods 253
Musical Package 242, 243
Musical Potpourri 334
Musicians Club of Women 12, 58

Nadworney, Devora 110
Nancy and Russell Hatz Award 110
National Association of Music Therapy 252
National Broadcasting Company 155, 169, 173, 177, 182, 249-252, 314
National Charter 336
National Citation 322

National Concert and Artist Corporation 176
National Council of Women of the United
    States 152
National Federation of Women's Amateur
    Musical Clubs 38, 41, 57, 63
National Federation of Women's Musical
    Clubs 39-47, 57, 60-63, 66, 67, 71, 73,
    74, 76, 78-86, 91-93, 102, 115, 116, 119,
    122, 126, 168, 195, 196, 334, 336
National Hymn Contest 128, 226
National Music Camp 12, 147, 186-188,
    191, 210, 323
National Music Council 151, 207, 211, 215,
    314-316, 322-325, 333
National Music Week 203, 208, 211, 228,
    250, 253, 310-313
National Opera Club of America 146
National Recreation Association 312
National Symphony Orchestra 178
Navarro, Amparo 230
Nelson, Vivian Menees 217, 257
New England Symphony 107
New York Herald Tribune 176, 241
New York Philharmonic Orchestra 169, 176,
    333
New York Tribune 41, 42, 53, 60, 61, 66, 93
New York Woodwind Quintet 137
Newberry, Mrs. John S. 269
Newman, Dr. Herman 318
NFMC Artist Presentation 70
Nickels, Mrs. W. B. 267
Niles, John Jacob 142
Nixon, Mrs. Richard M. 279
Nixon, President Richard M. 212
Nobel Peace Prize 319
Norden, Laura Howell 120

Oakland, Maine 189
Ober, Mrs. Vincent Hilles 105, 114, 117,
    118, 184, 205, 207, 233, 234, 240, 254,
    314-316, 337
Octave Club 264, 268
O'Donnell, Charles 344
Office Committee 129, 278
Official Benediction 125, 214, 286
Official Bulletin 88, 92, 104, 126, 128, 153,
    203
Official Invocation 120, 121, 214
Official Junior Song 98, 204
Old Smokey 147
O'Leary, Mother 22, 30
Olmstead, Frederick L. 22

Onion, Mrs. G. Franklin 256
Opera 53, 109, 121, 137, 143, 145-149, 151,
    166, 172, 178, 192, 199, 206, 211, 212,
    218, 246, 253, 280, 335
Opera Department 145, 149
Opera for Youth 147, 148, 185
Opera in the Ozarks 150
Operation Zero Hour 252
Oratorio 23, 89, 109, 143, 144, 154, 175,
    185, 212
Orchestra Hall 35, 153
Orr, Arthur 35
Oschner, Mrs. Albert J. 88, 96, 101, 102,
    104, 175, 201
Ottaway, Mrs. Elmer James 36, 128, 140,
    182-184, 205, 278, 336
Otten, Joseph 81
Our Mountain Garden 37
Outdoor Theatre 88, 101

Paddock, William D. 102
Paderewski, Ignace J. 36, 88, 177
Pageant Stage Seats 102
Pan in America 203, 223
Panama-Pacific Exposition 145
Parade of American Music 135, 136, 210,
    213-216, 284, 315, 323-325
Parker, Horatio 134, 145, 146, 199
Parkman, Francis 17
Parliamentarian 207, 256, 337
Parrish, Britt 12
Parrish, Emmett 12
Parrish, Mignonette Williams 12
Pascoe, Mrs. Charles 186, 189-191, 217
Past National President's Scholarship 171
Past Presidents' Assembly 12, 203, 204,
    267-269, 332
Paul, Doria A. 120
Payne, John Knowles 345
Peabody Conservatory 173
Peace Bell 244
Peck, Mrs. Clarence 54
Pedersen, Mrs. James A. 41, 44, 45, 48, 59,
    65, 69-71, 73, 80, 81, 91
Peel, Mrs. Hal Holt 139
Peirce, Mrs. Charles S. 32, 41, 46, 63
People to People Project 177, 211, 215
Peristyle 24, 25
Perry, Mrs. A. F. 65, 77
Peterborough, New Hampshire 88, 96, 100,
    101, 105, 106, 174, 201, 202, 207, 260,
    267, 272, 276, 335

Pettit, Mrs. Clarence T. 263, 264
Pfohl, Dr. James Christian 191
Pfohl, Bessie Whittington 120
Phafflin, Mrs. 261
Philadelphia Centennial 282, 283
Philadelphia Mummers 331
Philanthropic Music 26, 247
Plank, J. Phillip 264
Plato 21, 79
Podis, Eunice 189
Polk, Grace Porterfield 97, 175
Polk, Mrs. 261
Porgy and Bess 105
Powell, John 142, 158, 182-184, 205
Pratt, Dr. Waldo S. 41, 90
President's Citation 209, 322
President's Promotion Fund 210, 338
Price, Mrs. Carl 269
Prideaux, Gary 12
Prideaux, Pamela Parrish 12
Priesing, Elwood 223
Priest, Mrs. Whayne 332
Prigmore, PFC James M. 136
Princess Red Wing 140

Radcliffe College 32
Radio 135, 136, 160, 173, 176, 215, 228,
  233, 234, 249-256, 318, 322, 325
Rainbow Luncheon 261
Ralston, Frances Marion 39-42, 46, 48, 51,
  57, 58, 62, 66, 71, 90
Rand, Emily K. 27
Ratcliff, Onamae 331
Readers Digest Foundation 173, 189
Ready, Ann 12
Reagan, President Ronald A. 10, 217, 329-
  331
Reflections on Christmas 144, 185, 212
Regin-Watson, Mrs. 54
Remember the Alamo 121
Republic Aviation Corporation 245
Reynolds, Naomi 251
Rhythm Bands 159
Richardson, Alexander 231
Richter, Dr. Marion 146, 312, 318
Right Way Band 159
Riley, The Honorable Richard W. and Mrs.
  149
Ritchey, Mrs. Albert E. 269
Roberts, Mrs. Robert W. 170, 212, 248, 338
Robertson, Mrs. A. M. 65
Robinson, Mrs. Dwight D. 148, 185, 218,

224, 321, 329
Roche, Henri Pierre 143
Rodes, Mrs. J. H. 96, 97
Rogers, Will 88
Rohrer, Gertrude M. 119
Roosevelt, Mrs. Franklin D. 140
Rose Fay Thomas Fellows 217, 219, 262,
  266
Rose, James A. 71
Rossini Club 27
Rubinstein 81
Ruby S. Vought Scholarship in Organ 171
Rucker-Smith, Brenda 177
Ruth Freehoff Opera Award 149
Ruth, Marguerite 245

Sacred Music 226
St. Albans, New York 31
St. Cecilia Society 27, 29, 81, 200
Salt Lake City, Utah 31, 163, 180, 209, 210,
  337
Salute to the United Nations 318
Samuel Sorin Piano Award 175
Sandburg, Carl 142
Santa Fe Opera Program 149
Sarlin, Janet Michele 283
Sarlin, Mr. and Mrs. Ralph 192
Schade, Miss 59
Scholarships and Awards 11, 111, 166, 172,
  212, 217, 219, 260
Schubert Club 81, 198
Schubert Memorial Award 176, 179
Schuller, Gunther 276
Schumann-Heink, Ernestine 83, 88
Scott, Senator Hugh 328
Seiberling, Mrs Frank A. 87-89, 101, 102,
  115-117, 122, 127, 153, 154, 174, 202,
  204, 260, 261, 335, 336
Selden, Judge and Mrs. 32
Seranak 213, 272, 276, 277
Shannon, Ruth 11
Shepherd, Arthur 133, 200
Sherman, Mrs. John D. 269
Shouse, Mrs. Jouett 333
Showcase 129, 212
Sibelius, Jean 338
Singing Convention 153
Skorodin, Elaine 177, 213
Smith, Ella May 108, 143, 144, 223, 260
Smith, David 107
Smith, Julia 120, 121, 148, 149, 185, 214
Smith, Miss Rosalie B. 41, 48, 91

Smith, Mrs. Ruth 99, 283
Smith, Rose Thomas 191, 220, 260
Snoddy, Abbie L. 98, 128, 204
Snyder, Barry 159, 182
Sodam, Private Joseph E. 235
Sokoloff, Dr. Nikalai 176
'Soldiers and Sailors' Club 33
Sonata of the Turtle 133, 200
Sorel, Claudette 175, 176, 179, 333
Sousa, John Philip 215, 284, 325, 326
South Carolina Federation of Music Clubs
    10, 89, 156, 191, 283
Spalding, Albert 177
Special Citation 322
Sperry Gyroscope Company, Inc. 245
Spivacke, Harold 18, 315
Spry, Walter 254, 335
Stan Hywet Hall 87-89, 101, 115, 122, 128,
    143, 202, 335
Standard Oil Company 209, 322
Starr, Mrs. Chandler 40-43, 46, 53, 57, 62,
    64- 66, 70, 71, 90, 195
Starr, Mrs. Morton Hull 140
Steel, Mrs. John N. 83, 88
Steele, Mrs. W. D. 96
Steigerwalt, Gary 181
Stein, Gertrude 84
Steiner, Max 254
Steinway Hall 53, 56-58, 63-67, 195
Steinway Memorial Award 173
Steinway Piano Company 173
Steinway, Theodore 173, 176
Stephen Foster Memorial 337
Stephens, Nan 104
Sterling, Mrs. Frederic 228
Stevenson, Dr. James 280
Still, William Grant 212, 320
Stillman Kelley, Edgar 104, 106, 153, 207,
    231
Stillman Kelley, Mrs. Edgar 11, 97, 104,
    107, 128, 130, 173, 204, 269
Stock, Frederick 158
Stokowski, Leopold 88, 155, 158, 168, 169
Stokowski, Olga Samaroff 176
Storer, Helen A. 65
Strauss, Richard 34-36, 231
Strickland, William 136
Strodtman, Pat 284
Student Division 76, 108-111, 117, 118, 171,
    178, 206, 210, 214, 219, 224, 257, 333
Styne, Jule 316
Sudler, Louis 144, 175

Sullivan, Mrs. Alexander 54
Sullivan, Mrs. Edwin A. 317, 318, 338
Sutro, Mrs. Theodore S. 40-48, 51-53, 58,
    60-68, 90, 93
Sweeney, Elsie 279
Sykes, Martha 146
Symphony in A 158, 184

Tag Day 232
Talbott, Henry Morrison 280
Talmadge, Senator Herman 328
Tanglewood 208, 209, 213, 272-277
Tanglewood Tales 208, 272
Taussig, Grace 80
Taylor, Deems 134, 167, 169
Ten Thousand Times Ten Thousand 143,
    144
The Culprit Fay 133, 158, 200
The King's Breakfast 148, 185
The Little House 240-242
The Lost Child 133, 200
The Minion and the Three Riddles 148, 185,
    218
The Musical Monitor 94, 96, 97, 102, 126,
    127, 132, 199
The Musical World 126
The Nightingale and the Rose 148, 185
The Peaceful Land 212, 320
The Shepherdess and the Chimney Sweep
    148, 185
The Shoo Fly 141
The Siren Song 167-169
Thelma A. Robinson Ballet Award 171
Theodore Thomas Orchestra 35, 133, 158,
    200
Thomas, Edna 261
Thomas, Jean 140
Thomas, Rose Fay 12, 15, 17, 23, 25, 26,
    28-37, 40, 41, 43, 46-48, 53, 57, 62-64,
    66, 68, 71, 73, 79, 85, 90-94, 126, 194,
    195, 208, 217, 219, 262, 266, 282, 283,
    335, 339, 344, 346
Thomas, Theodore 12, 22, 23, 26, 28, 31-37,
    41, 57, 72, 74, 85, 90, 133, 158, 195,
    200, 283, 335, 344, 345
Thompson, Mrs. Edwin Chapin 261
Thompson, Virgil 241, 253
Tibbett, Lawerence 169
Tiensuu, Jukka 277
Tomlins, William L. 23
Toscanini, Arturo 182
Toy Orchestras 159

370

Transylvania Music Camp 186, 191, 210
Treas, Charles 12
Treble Clef Club, Niagara Falls, New York
153
Tremaine, Charles Milton 203, 310-312
Trevitt, Mrs. Emily S. 65
Trorey, Mrs. Alan W. 329
Truman, President Harry S. 317
Tuesday Musicale
Akron, Ohio 197
Denver, Colorado 84
Monmouth, Illinois 30
Pittsburg, Pennsylvania 153
Rochester, New York 83
St. Louis, Missouri 39
Tureck, Rosalyn 174
Turner, Lynn 129, 278
Turner, Vera 129, 285

Uhl, Mrs. Edwin F. 27, 28, 38, 43, 53, 54,
62-68, 73, 78-82, 91-93, 132, 195
Ullman, Mrs. Frederick 59, 73
United Nations 209, 211, 212, 215, 218-220,
244, 317-319, 321, 338
United Nations Day 244, 318
United Nations International Children's
Fund 319
United States Army 136
United States Continental Army Band 332
United States Disciplinary Band and
Orchestra 161
United States Information Agency 151, 177,
219, 243
Universal Declaration of Human Rights 317

Van Cliburn-Theodore Steinway Award 176
Van Roy, Gretchen 11, 219, 285, 287
Van Vactor, David 319
Venth, Carl 203, 223
Vera Wardner Dougan Award 171
Verdery, Mrs. Eugene F. 65, 77, 80
Veri and Jamanis 181
Verrett, Shirley 174, 332
Veterans Administration 238, 239
Vick's Chemical Company 173
Victor Herbert-ASCAP Young Composers
Awards 110, 333
Virgil, Mrs. Charles S. 40, 41, 57, 71, 72,
80, 91
Vivace Junior Group 76, 96
Voice of America 151, 177
Voorhees, Donald 109, 173, 236

Vought, Mrs. Frank A. 111, 148, 171, 185,
216, 264, 265, 280, 281

Wakefield, Mrs. Robert 178
Walker, Susan B. 86, 133, 168, 199, 334
Wallenstein, Alfred 137
Wallick, First Lieutenant Richard B. 137
Walsh, Joyce 218, 257
War Bonds 109, 173, 231, 234, 236, 263
War Service Committee / Program 228, 231-
238, 240, 241, 252, 263, 273
War Service Fund 109, 208, 263
Ward, Mrs. Jack C. 9, 10, 12, 115, 125, 147,
149, 154, 159, 171, 181-183, 185, 190,
192, 217-219, 261, 262, 266, 280-282,
284, 285, 287, 328-331, 345
Ward, Jack C. 9, 12
Ward, Robert 319
Ward, Samuel A. 268, 270
Wardwell, Linda B. 65
Wardwell, Mrs. Frank S. 41, 73, 334
Waring, Fred 173
Warner, Mrs. Worcester R. 128
Warren, Mrs. William S. 57-60, 64, 68, 71,
74, 92
Warren, Elinor Remick 120
Washington, George 205, 231
Weakley, Mrs. Glen M. 331
Weaver, Mrs. Paul J. 128
Weaver, Paul 254
Weber, Mr. and Mrs. Clayton 190
Webster, Mrs. Curtis 96, 196
Webster, Mrs. John Howard 53, 59, 65, 70,
81-84
Wells, Sumner 283
West, Mrs. Eliot 59
Westminster Choir 137
Wheeler, William 180
Where Men Are Free 170
White Breakfast Candlelighting Ceremony
229
Whitetop Mountain 140
Whitmire, Ross and Alice 139
Whitmore, Mrs. Frank P. 31
Whitney, William L. 175
Wilkinson, Florence 256
Williams, Irena Foreman 98, 123, 124, 204
Williams, Julia E. 97, 98, 104, 108, 128,
130, 205
Wilmerding, Mrs. Charles 31
Wilson, George W. 23
Wolf Trap Farm Park 279

Wolfe, T. F. 273
Woman's Musical Congress 30
Woman's Prison, Raleigh, NC 161
Women's Amateur Musical Clubs 15, 25, 28, 30, 34, 38, 41, 56, 57, 63, 92, 198
Wood, Lucy Uhl 38, 91
Woodbury, Mrs. Herbert E. 280
Woodside, Mrs. Robert I. 89
Works Progress Administration 159
World's Columbian Exposition 15, 17, 22-24, 26, 29, 30, 32, 38, 56, 57, 71, 91-93
World's Fair 15, 22, 26, 33, 40, 43, 64, 92-94, 154, 185, 207, 251, 337

World's Fair Congress of Musicians 25, 53, 197

Yager, Mrs. Louis E. 88, 174
Yang, Honorable You-Chan 318
Yarbrough and Cowan 181, 185
Yarbrough, Joan 181, 185
Young Artists 70, 144, 149, 150, 157, 170-181, 192, 198, 199, 201, 206-213, 219, 220, 250, 268
Young Composers Contest 110
Youse, Glad Robinson 120, 125, 170, 214, 286